PEANUTS

The Food Series

A list of books in the series appears at the back of this book.

PEANUTS

The Illustrious History of the Goober Pea

Andrew F. Smith

University of Illinois Press
Urbana and Chicago

© 2002 by the Board of Trustees
of the University of Illinois
All rights reserved
Manufactured in the United States of America
c 5 4 3 2 1

♾ This book is printed on acid-free paper.

Library of Congress Cataloging-in-Publication Data

Smith, Andrew F., 1946–
Peanuts : the illustrious history of the goober pea / Andrew F. Smith.
p.   cm. — (The food series)
Includes bibliographical references (p.).
ISBN 0-252-02553-9 (cloth : alk. paper)
1. Cookery (Peanuts) 2. Peanuts. I. Title. II. Series.
TX803.P35S65   2001
641.6'56596—dc21   2001003854

To peanut lovers everywhere,
especially Alla Kling,
who has always appreciated the peanut
in all its splendid diversity,
and John Riley FitzSimmons,
the latest addition to our family

Contents

Illustrations follow page 44

Recipes

Preface

In discordant antebellum America, peanuts united the nation's upper classes: the southern aristocracy viewed them as a trash food consumed only by slaves or the poor; the northern elite considered them ungenteel—the very symbol of rowdyism. But on-the-go Americans happily adopted this snack food for it was cheap, tasty, filling, and eminently portable. In rural America, children received gifts of peanuts at holidays and young boys sold their fragrantly toasty wares at fruit stands or plied village streets in horse-drawn, peanut-filled wagons. In urban America, city dwellers could smell the aroma and hear the shout of "Fresh roasted peanuts!" even before they saw the vendors stationed at strategic street corners. Train stations echoed with the calls of peanut sellers, who sometimes jumped on trains and hawked their goods to the passengers. Likewise, fair goers and circus patrons were assailed by peanut hucksters. College students crunched peanuts during theater performances, tossing shells on the ground or in the air and infuriating their elders in the process. Unlike other food fads that quickly passed from the culinary scene, peanuts thrived and eventually became enshrined as an American icon.

How peanuts achieved culinary stardom so quickly was a topic of discussion at the time and the dialogue has continued ever since. The first people to eat peanuts in what is today the United States were slaves, but somehow peanuts achieved mainstream snack status among many Americans in the pre–Civil War period. During the war, however, peanuts became something more. Confronted with Northern blockades, Southerners consumed peanuts as never before, and Union soldiers did likewise as they occupied peanut-growing areas of the Confederacy. After the war, peanut production and consumption escalated, and cookery experts explored the nut's culinary potential. By the turn of the twentieth century, peanuts had been adopted by vegetarians, and the medical profession convinced many Americans that in addition to tasting good, peanuts were a health food. This vegetarian-medical nexus increased consumption further and promulgated new products, including peanut butter.

During World War I, peanut oil became an important food product as the war cut off American access to other vegetable oils. The domestic peanut industry thrived during the war and continued its ascent during the roaring 1920s. When the Depression hit, even poor Americans could afford peanuts, and production soared to even greater heights at the end of the 1930s. But it was during the Second World War that peanuts made the transition to a mainstream staple food.

Today, Americans fry food in peanut oil, spread peanut butter on bread and crackers, sip peanut soups, drink peanut cocktails, snack on peanuts at ball games, munch peanut-filled candy bars, sprinkle peanut pieces on ice cream, and consume peanut products unknowingly in hundreds of processed foods. As few other peoples around the globe consume peanuts in such quantities or in so many ways, the peanut is an American culinary emblem known the world over, its status buttressed by the advertising of the Planters Peanuts "Mr. Peanut," the promotion of peanut butter, and the exploits of the African-America scientist George Washington Carver, known as "the peanut man."

Thousands of articles have been written about peanuts, but these mainly focus on their cultivation, processing, and marketing. Despite the importance of the peanut in America's diet today, its culinary history has never before been written. As a result, peanut myths and peanut fakelore have proliferated, often generated by overzealous public-relations consultants promoting peanut products. Journalists have advanced these myths by repeating them in thousands of newspaper and magazine articles. For instance, for years journalists have proclaimed variously that George Washington Carver or John Harvey Kellogg invented peanut butter. In fact, neither did although both individuals made major contributions to the culinary peanut, as we shall see.

While debunking myths is imperative, what's more significant is that real peanut history is inherently more intriguing than oft-regurgitated stories. How the peanut metamorphosed from a slave food to a mainstream staple is a nutty tale filled with unexpected twists and turns. The story is action-packed, peopled with Amerindians and African Americans, Italian Americans and Greek Americans, entrepreneurial vendors and captains of industry, grocers and scientists, efficiency-conscious processors and managers, commercial artists and hard-hitting advertisers, health-food nuts and anti-nut food allergists, and kids of all ages.

This book on peanut history falls into a larger domain of culinary history, an emerging field of study composed of a diverse group of people throughout the world who are concerned with aspects of the question, Who consumed what, how, when, where, and why? Some culinary historians focus on a particular historical period, such as that of ancient Greece or Rome; others focus on the culinary progress over time among particular geographical regions or specific groups such as a history of food in France, in China, or among African Americans; and still others examine the effects of food consumption patterns for the individual, group, nation, or world. My approach has been to examine popular, ubiquitous, frequently overlooked American food products, such as ketchup, popcorn, tomato soup, and now peanuts, to find out how they came to be part of our culinary landscape, how their history reflects and influences broader historical trends, and what these products can tell us about ourselves as Americans.

I have extensively documented this work for several reasons. First, many books and articles purporting to offer culinary histories are really collections of myths and twice-told stories that have captured the fancy of writers and readers. Frequent repetition of myths does not enhance their accuracy or truthfulness. As many food stories are inaccurate, their reiteration does not improve our understanding of culinary matters or of broader historical contexts. Second, some who write about food history make sweeping statements unsupported by factual evidence. Others have specific ideological positions and present their opinions as fact. While insight, generalizations, ideology, and opinion are noteworthy and should play an important role in culinary works, it is imperative that readers be aware of the factual basis for the writer's statements and conclusions. If the field of culinary history is to thrive, it must promote higher evidentiary standards. Failure to do so will result in culinary history's relegation to the arena of fiction, myth, and trivia. Finally, it is likely that future researchers will uncover additional information that may lead in new directions—or contradict the conclusions I present here. Future culinary historians and writers will make better judgments if they can easily check the sources upon which I have relied. I hope this book encourages others to revise, challenge, and improve the peanut story and the social history in which it is embedded.

While I am concerned with what peanuts can tell us about larger social and historical issues, I am also fascinated by peanuts themselves. As a youth, my grandfather farmed peanuts in Arkansas; as an adult, he grew them in his garden and roasted them in the kitchen oven. The aroma of fresh roasting peanuts remains a vivid memory for me today. I also remember watching grocers grind roasted peanuts to make fresh butter. Ground fresh or taken from a commercial jar, peanut butter spread on white bread with raisins or jelly was a mainstay lunch in my youth. Alas, peanut candies I also enjoyed, as well as peanuts in many other forms. I still do.

Faced with a wealth of articles and other works available about peanuts, I chose to focus on the peanut's culinary history and social traditions. When I first began my explorations, I was informed that peanuts did not become part of America's diet until 1900. Indeed, few references to peanuts appear in traditional American culinary histories, such as Richard Osborn Cummings's *The American and His Food: A History of Food Habits in the United States* or Richard Hooker's *Food and Drink in America*. Yet, during the last five years, I have located more than ten thousand culinary references to peanuts, hundreds of which were published or written in America prior to 1900, and I'm sure there are many more.

The culinary history of the peanut is told in the eleven chapters of this book. These are followed by a tantalizing selection of 125 historical peanut recipes. The book concludes with a selected bibliography of books, agricultural bulletins, commercial booklets, and other materials published by peanut growers, processors, and peanut-promoting groups, and with a list of names, addresses, phone numbers, and Web sites of selected organizations devoted to the peanut.

Acknowledgments

I found two writers and their works to be particularly helpful: F. Roy Johnson's *The Peanut Story;* and two articles by Ray O. Hammons: "Origin and Early History of the Peanut," in *Peanut Science and Technology,* edited by Harold K. Pattee and Clyde T. Young, and "The Origin and History of the Groundnut," in *The Groundnut Crop: A Scientific Basis for Improvement,* edited by J. Smartt. These works in turn guided me to primary sources.

In addition, many individuals helped locate sources, served as interviewees, and commented on parts of this book. I owe particular thanks to James Crawford, curator, Canajoharie Library and Art Gallery, Canajoharie, New York, for forwarding information and providing photographs from the Beech-Nut Company's archives; Fred Dahlinger Jr., director, Collections and Research, Circus World Museum, Baraboo, Wisconsin, for sending material on peanuts and the circus; Joe Carlin, proprietor of Food Heritage Press, Ipswich, Massachusetts; Karen Hess, culinary historian, New York, for locating recipes and providing constant encouragement; William Weaver, culinary historian, Paoli, Pennsylvania, for finding early references to peanuts and groundnuts; James R. Sholar, executive officer, American Peanut Research and Education Society, Stillwater, Oklahoma, for sharing materials and information; staff of the Law Library, State of Michigan, Ann Arbor, for supplying material about John Harvey Kellogg; Janice Little, Del E. Webb Memorial Library, Loma Linda University, Loma Linda, California; Jason D. Stratman, Missouri Historical Society, Saint Louis; the Sanatarium Health Food Company, Berkeley Vale, New South Wales, Australia, for sending material about peanut butter in Australia; librarians at Brown University, Providence, Rhode Island; Janet Gray, author of *Historic Keepsake Cookbooks,* who supplied information about peanut pie during the Civil War; Charles Perry, culinary historian and columnist of the *Los Angeles Times,* for forwarding information about the Bambara groundnut and the peanut in Africa; Joyce Spontak, editor of *Peanut Papers for Pals,* Bridgeville, Pennsylvania, for providing information about Planters Peanuts history; Barbara Kuck, curator, Culinary Archives and Museum, Johnson and Wales University, Providence, Rhode Island, for locating a peanut illustration; Mary Butler, librarian, Battle Creek Historical Society, Battle Creek, Michigan, for finding illustrations; Cynthia Wilson, university archives, Tuskegee University, Tuskegee, Alabama; Leslie Wagner, Peanut Advisory Board, Atlanta, Georgia, for providing illustrations; Dennis R. Laurie, librarian, American Antiquarian Society, Worcester, Massachusetts, for turning up an early peanut reference and illustration; Steve Pappas, Robert Costello, and James Krakker of the National Museum of Natural History, Washington, D.C., for helping to find illustrations; Robert L. Hall, chair, Department of African-American Studies, Northeastern University, Boston, Massachusetts, for locating sources on peanuts and the slave trade; Doris Witt, assistant professor of English, University of Iowa, Ames, Iowa, for bringing to the author's attention June Jordan's poem "Notes on the Peanut"; and Pamela C. Whitenack, archivist, Hershey Community Archives, Hershey, Pennsylvania, who shared information about the history of Hershey products. I also thank Bonnie Slotnick for her extensive editorial comments on the manuscript.

PEANUTS

1

ORIGIN AND DISPERSION

Five centuries ago, European civilization was on the brink of disaster. To the east, the Turks had conquered the Byzantine empire and Turkish armies were quickly consolidating gains in the Balkans. Simultaneously, the Turks were raising a navy in the eastern Mediterranean to rival those of the Italian city states, which were frequently at war with one another or with the papacy in Rome. To the north, Germany was a patchwork of principalities aligned in unstable combinations: some were part of the Holy Roman Empire, ruled from Vienna; others were nominally independent; and still others were associated with France. In the heart of Europe, only three united political entities existed: Portugal, Spain, and France. To the south were hostile Moslems, many of whom had recently been pushed out of the Iberian peninsula; the continent south of North Africa, the continent was almost unknown. The British Isles were not united, and further to the west was the Atlantic Ocean, of unknown and unexplored dimensions.

Beneath the political disunity smoldered the religious ferment that a few decades later ignited, dividing Europe against itself in a succession of religious and civil wars. Just as serious a problem was the shortage of food. Following centuries of traditional agricultural practices, European farmers had exhausted large patches of available arable land. Unfortunately, agricultural production was only marginally increasing, while European population was rapidly multiplying.

European exploration in the fifteenth and sixteenth centuries was in part a response to these problems. As transoceanic voyages frequently lasted for years and explorers often failed to return, the only food products that could recompense voyagers for their expenses were spices, most of which at the time came overland from Asia to the eastern Mediterranean, then were loaded onto ships and sent to the Italian city-states before being re-exported to the rest of western Europe. Portuguese explorers sailed south, circumnavigating Africa and then onto Asia. Simultaneously, Spanish explorers traveling west in hopes of reaching Asia instead ended up in the New World. These explorations uncovered thousands of new food plants unknown previously to Europeans. Only a few New World plants, however, were distributed commercially beyond their point of origin. In many cases, centuries were to pass before even these plants were adopted by peoples in the Old World. Yet, this handful of food plants provided the basis of an unprecedented expansion of the world's food supply and altered the course of history.[1] The peanut (*Arachis hypogaea*) was one of these plants.

DUAL ENCOUNTERS

From the first European encounter with the peanut, patterns emerged that have endured for hundreds of years. Although Columbus likely found the peanut on his voyages to the Americas, the peanut's existence was first recorded by Bartolomé de las Casas, who had arrived on the Caribbean island of Hispañola in 1502. After an eight-year career as a planter, he joined a religious order and served as a missionary for thirty-seven years before returning to Spain, where he compiled his recollections and observations in a manuscript titled "Apologética Historia de las Indias." In this work, de las Casas reported that peanuts, called *mani,* were sown by indigenous peoples in the Caribbean. He equated peanuts to filbert nuts without the shell but also noted their similarity to beans, sweet peas, and chickpeas.[2] This dichotomy has persisted ever since. In the botanical world, the peanut is classified as a legume related to beans and peas. Unlike in other common legumes, the peanut's ovary is fertilized above ground, but the stem then pushes the flower underground, where the fruit matures. In the culinary world, however, the peanut is generally considered a nut due to its hard outer husk and nutty taste when roasted; rarely is it prepared or served as are other legumes.

Although de las Casas may have been the first European to write about the peanut, his manuscript was not published until 1875. The first published notice of the peanut appeared in Gonzalo Fernández de Oviedo y Valdés's *Historia general y natural de las Indias,* in 1535. Oviedo had migrated to Hispañola twelve years after de las Casas. He served as superintendent of gold smelting and later became governor of the island. He claimed that *mani* was a common food consumed raw or roasted by the Indians on Hispañola and other Caribbean islands. The Caribbean Indians considered it a healthy food, but Oviedo noted that true Christians did not use it unless they were unmarried males, children, slaves, or just common people, for it had "a very mediocre taste and little substance."[3] This second dualism—peanuts tasted good but were not a proper food for the elite—has also survived.

French colonists made frequent references to the peanut on other Caribbean islands. Jean Baptiste Dutertre, a French monk who came to Guadalupe in 1625, observed that peanuts were eaten for dessert and that expressed peanut oil was "considered to be equal to sweet almond oil." Jean Baptiste Labat called peanuts "Pistaches des Isles" and noted that when roasted they acquired "the taste and aroma of roasted almonds." He believed that peanuts stimulated "the appetite and thirst; people use them to make sugar peanuts, marzipan, and they are put into hash and stews as a substitute for chestnuts." However, he proclaimed raw peanuts indigestible.[4] There was nothing wrong with eating raw peanuts, but this third dichotomy—that peanuts were fine if cooked but not if eaten raw—has also survived to this day.

PRIMORDIAL PEANUTS

The European explorers of the sixteenth century intentionally sought unusual plants and transported specimens to Europe. Botanists were initially overwhelmed as diverse plants from Africa, Asia, and the Americas flooded the continent. When botanists began to sort out plant origins in the seventeenth century, the peanut presented a puzzle. Not only had Europeans found them growing in the Caribbean, they also discovered them in South America, Africa, Southeast Asia, and on Pacific Islands. Due to this wide dispersal, the peanut's point of origin was disputed until the mid-nineteenth century. That it was a South American species was concluded when archaeological remains of peanuts turned up in pre-Columbian tombs in Peru. But it was not until the mid-twentieth century that researchers narrowed the point of origin to the heart of tropical South America. Although no archeological evidence of peanuts has been uncovered in this area due to its tropical climate, it is in the Guarani region of Paraguay, eastern Bolivia, and central Brazil that the greatest diversity exists within wild varieties of the *Arachis* species. During the 1960s, the point of origin for the cultivated peanut was finally identified as eastern Bolivia.[5]

By the time of European exploration, peanuts had been widely disseminated throughout eastern South America. Ulrich Schmidt, a German adventurer who spent twenty years in the Rio de la Plata basin, came upon them in 1542, when his expedition up the Rio Paraguay encountered the Cheriguanos Indians, who had a flourishing agricultural system with maize, manioc, potatoes, sweet potatoes, and peanuts as main crops. In 1555 Jean de Léry, a French Calvinist missionary living on an island in Rio de Janeiro Bay, wrote that "the savages also have fruits called *manobi*. They grow in the soil like truffles connected one to the other by fine filaments. The pod has a seed the size of a hazelnut and a similar taste; it is grey-brown and the hull has the hardness of the pea." He ate peanuts many times, but due to his isolation on the island, he never saw them cultivated.[6]

Portuguese settlers in Brazil readily adopted the peanut. The naturalist Gabriel Soares de Souza, who arrived in Brazil in 1570, was the first to describe in depth the peanut plant, its cultivation, and the Indian custom of using smoke to cure it. He also reported extensively on the peanut's culinary uses. According to Soares, raw peanuts "have the same taste as raw chick-peas, but they are usually eaten roasted and cooked in the shell, like chestnuts and are very tasty, and toasted outside of the shell they are better." He also noted that Portuguese women living in Brazil prepared peanuts in a manner similar to that of traditional almond confectionery. Hence, peanuts were "cut and covered with a sugar mixture as confections" and were candied and "cured in long, thin pieces."[7] The peanut would regularly be recommended hereafter as a replacement for the almond in traditional European recipes.

After the Dutch gained control of the northeastern coast of Brazil in 1630, Governor-General J. Maurice von Nassau-Siegen commissioned a scientific expedition to the area to be directed by his personal physician, Willem Piso, and his friend George Marcgrave, a naturalist, astronomer, and geographer. After arriving in South America, Marcgrave collected plants and compiled extensive notes on them for ten years, but he died before publishing his findings. Jan de Laet became his literary executor and published the Marcgrave-Piso notes in eight volumes in 1648 under the title *Natural History of Brazil*. The peanut, called *mandubi*, was here described in some detail with an illustration of two-seeded pods, but the drawing erroneously placed the fruits on the roots.[8]

That the words used to identify the peanut were similar in Brazil (*mandubi*) and the Caribbean (*mani*) was no coincidence: Arawak territory extended from central Brazil northward into the Caribbean, and these Amerindians disseminated the peanut along with other staples, such as the cassava and the sweet potato, throughout eastern South America and the Caribbean. A connection with the Arawak language has survived for more than five hundred years: *mani* remains the common word for the peanut in Spain and Spanish America, except for Mexico.[9]

AZTEC TLALCACHUATL

When the Spanish conquered Mexico in 1521, they encountered peanuts. In 1529, Bernardino de Sahagún, a Franciscan, came from Spain to Mexico, where he spent the remainder of his life. While teaching in Santa Cruz de Santiago Tlateloco near Mexico City, he learned Nahuatl, the language of the Aztecs. Under his direction, Aztec scholars compiled manuscripts in their native language, and Sahagún translated them into Spanish. Sahagún's "General History of the Things of New Spain" called peanuts *tlalcachuatl,* which translates as "the chocolate bean that grows underground." This linguistic association between chocolate and the peanut suggests that the Aztecs may have been the first to pair these two foods, although that marriage of tastes did not blossom in the United States until the twentieth century. But perhaps not: Sahagún makes only one reference to the peanut, which states that it was used as a poultice for inflamed gums; nowhere did he mention that the Aztecs ate peanuts.[10]

In fact, peanuts were rare in pre-Columbian Mexico, so much so that Francisco Hernandez—the leader of the first scientific expedition to Mexico, in 1570—concluded that the Spanish had introduced peanuts into Mexico from the Caribbean. Aztec codices lack peanut illustrations, and peanuts were not used as tribute by the Aztecs or the Spanish. Neither were peanuts cultivated in northern Mexico, although the soil and climate were suitable. However, as three-seeded peanut pods have been uncovered at pre-Columbian archeological sites in the Coxcatlan cave in the Tehuacán valley, peanuts were clearly present in Mexico before the Spanish Conquest, but the paucity of documentation and archeological remains has led most observers to conclude that they were not an important crop at that time.[11]

INCA INCHIC

Peanuts were an important crop in Peru, where they had arrived at a very early date. Peruvian civilization apparently dawned along the eastern slopes of the Andes near the tropical lowlands, where many wild relatives of domesticated crops grew, including the peanut. Peanuts were disseminated to the west coast of South America, which was hot and dry. Irrigation systems were constructed beginning about 2000 B.C.E., and these laid the foundation for the growth of Andean civilizations. Archeologists have uncovered well-preserved peanuts in terra-cotta jars in prehistoric burial sites at Ancón on the Peruvian coast north of Lima. One account of uncovering a grave site at Ancón reported that among the mummies were earthen pots, one of which was filled with peanuts. By 500 to 100 B.C.E., peanuts were so common on the coast of Peru that archeologists have exclaimed that some sites dating to this period looked like poorly swept baseball stadiums with peanut shells scattered about. This suggests that peanuts were eaten by the ancient South Americans in exactly the way they are eaten today—toasted in the shell as a snack. What's more, the surviving ancient peanuts were still edible, or so said a twentieth-century botanist, A. Hyatt Verrill, who claimed to have consumed some found at a grave site.[12]

Along the northern coast of Peru, archaeologists found funerary vases decorated with replicas of peanut pods sculpted in relief. An earthenware pan recovered from a grave at a fishing village in Chimbote had peanuts painted on the handles. Near the village of Sipán, Walter Alva found peanut pods made of gold, three times their natural size, decorating necklaces. Many well-preserved Moche graves have been excavated and many contained offerings of food, including peanuts. Two gourd vases now in the Smithsonian Institution, excavated from mummy graves, were filled with peanuts. A basket containing a handful of peanuts suggested to Charles W. Mead "the picture of a woman sitting at her loom eating these nuts."[13] The burial of peanuts at the grave site suggests that they played an important role in pre-Columbian Peru.

In addition to the archeological records, several peanut references appear in early European works about Peru. José de Acosta, a Jesuit missionary, was sent to Peru in 1571. He read all of the existing published material on the Americas, then recorded extensive notes based on his own observations and compiled them into his *Historia natural y moral de las Indias*, first published in 1590. In this work Acosta lists *mani* as one of the "divers rootes."[14] A fuller account was recorded by Garcillosa de la Vega, the son of an Inca princess and a Spanish father, born in Cuzco in 1539. He disclosed in his *Royal Commentaries of the Incas* that the Spanish had borrowed the word *mani* from a Caribbean language and introduced it into Peru. The Incas called peanuts *inchic*. De la Vega supported the earlier mentioned dichotomy that peanuts were "bad for the head if eaten raw, but tasty and wholesome if toasted." He noted that when honey was added to the peanuts, an excellent marzipan-like confection resulted, which was a luxury "of epicures rather than staple foods of the common people." He hastened to add that poor people did collect peanuts and "present them to the rich and powerful."[15] This retains one of the earlier mentioned peanut dualisms but reverses the relationship between the common people and the elite, perhaps because honey was a commodity only for the well-to-do at that time.

Bernabé Cobo, a Jesuit missionary in Peru during the early seventeenth century, also compiled a natural history. Like de la Vega, Cobo remarked that peanuts had a very good taste cooked or roasted, but he claimed that they produced dizziness and headaches when eaten raw. Cobo also stated that peanuts made good nougat for confections, and that peanut milk—which he saw the Incas making—could be used just like almond milk. When peanut milk was mixed with juice obtained from melon or gourd seeds, Cobo reported that it served as a soporific.[16] Cobo's mention of peanut milk is the first located reference to this product, which would again emerge in the twentieth century.

Those peanuts found at archeological sites in Peru differed from those peanuts that Europeans had encountered in the Caribbean or in eastern Brazil. The Peruvian variety, *Arachis hypogaea hirsuta,* has a morphology identical to those of peanuts grown today in coastal Peru. These are also similar to those located by archeologists in Mexico, suggesting a pre-Columbian connection between Andean civilizations and the Mayan and Aztec empires.[17]

EUROPEAN GROUNDNUTS

Shortly after the first European voyages to the New World, peanuts traveled east to Europe. The Seville physician Nicolas Monardes mentioned them in a 1569 work that was translated by John Frampton into English with the title *Joyfull Newes Out of the Newe Founde Worlde.* According to Frampton's translation, Monardes believed that peanuts possessed a "good savour and taste" and were eaten just like other nuts. Peanuts could be eaten raw if dried, but the best way was toasted. Monardes was the first European to complain about eating too many peanuts, which, he claimed, "giveth heavinesse to the hedde."[18]

Peanuts did not reach England and France until long after Spanish and Portuguese explorers had first encountered them. The first known reference to their actual cultivation in England appeared in John Parkinson's 1640 *Theatrum Botanicum: The Theater of Plants.* Parkinson acquired peanuts from Lisbon and declared that they tasted "like a sweet Nut, but more oily." While English botanists may have grown peanuts in their gardens, commercial hothouse cultivation did not commence until 1712. At about the same time in France, peanuts were "raised on hot-beds, and transplanted into the open garden" near Paris. The French consumed peanuts as they did other legumes. Presumably, this meant that the French boiled peanuts like chickpeas and beans.[19]

FOREIGN PEANUTS IN ASIA AND AFRICA

Peanuts migrated west from the New World with early Spanish galleons, first to the Pacific Islands, then to the Philippines and Indonesia. They arrived in Malaysia, Vietnam, and China before 1608 and were widely distributed in Vietnam and South China by the eighteenth century. In China, peanuts were called, among other terms, "foreign beans." From China, peanuts spread to Japan, where they were called "Chinese beans." Peanuts arrived in India most likely from Africa, as one of the plant's earliest Indian names was "Mozambique bean."[20]

That peanuts would have arrived in India from the west comes as no surprise. Peanuts had been introduced into Africa by the Portuguese shortly after their first contact with Brazil in 1500. The Portuguese established enclaves along Africa's coast to resupply their fleets headed for the lucrative spice lands of Asia. Peanuts were an ideal food for mariners. They were easily grown with little effort. As peanuts are protected by a hard outer shell, they could be readily stored and could survive for months with minimum spoilage. In addition, they could be eaten directly from the shell without any preparation. Finally, peanuts were filled with nutrients and oil.

Due to the Portuguese propagation of the legumes in their African enclaves, peanuts quickly spread throughout Africa to such an extent that early botanists assumed that peanuts had in fact originated there. The probable reason for the peanut's broad dissemination outside of the Portuguese colonies related to the existence of an indigenous African groundnut, generally known today as the Bambara groundnut (*Voandzeia subterranea*). These nuts were described by the Arab traveler Ibn Battuta in 1352. On his journey to Mali, he observed natives harvesting "from the ground a grain which looks like [fava] beans (*ful* in Arabic); they roast it and eat it, the taste being like that of roasted chickpeas (*himmas* in Arabic). Sometimes they grind this grain to make a kind of round spongy dough which they fry in gharti," which is shea butter, the oil of *Butyrospermum parkii*.[21]

Prior to the European contact in the fifteenth and sixteenth centuries, the Bambara groundnut had been widely cultivated in Africa. Its range extended from Bambara in West Africa to Natal in South Africa, and its cultivation extended inland as far as Mali and the Congo River basin. In 1682, Father Jerom Merolla de Sorrento, a Capuchin missionary, described it under the name *incumbei*, which, he said, was "like a cultivated musquet-ball and very wholesome and well tasted." In Africa, the Bambara groundnut was eaten raw or boiled. By the late nineteenth century, however, it was "sparingly cultivated" and was chiefly employed "to wash clothes instead of soap." But it made a comeback during the late twentieth century when ground into meal, mixed with oil and condiments, fried in palm oil, and made into cakes or balls, known as *bakuru* in Nigeria. Ground roasted Bambara groundnuts were also employed as a coffee substitute.[22]

The earliest unmistakable reference to peanuts growing in Africa appeared in an account by the Portuguese explorer André Alvares de Almada, who wrote about his travels to Senegal in the 1560s. He reported that a great quantity of peanuts was grown in the Bijagos Archipelago off the coast of what is today Guinea-Bissau. Peanuts rapidly spread throughout tropical Africa. As peanuts became more important in the culinary affairs of West Africans, peanuts borrowed names from the Bambara groundnut. According to the culinary historian and *Los Angeles Times* columnist Charles Perry, the Hausas still use the same name (*gujiya*) for both peanuts and groundnuts. In the Congo, peanuts were called *nguba* and Bambara groundnuts were *nguba si Kongo*. Since groundnuts were less oily, a number of African languages distinguished the two plants by calling the Bambara groundnut the "hard groundnut."[23]

This African linguistic confusion was perpetuated in the New World when the slave trade served to introduce the Bambara groundnut into Brazil, where it was called *Mandubu d'Angola*. The groundnut also immigrated into the United States, where it was variously called the *pindar*, a term derived from the Angolan word *mpinda*, and the *goober*, which derived from *ginguba* and many other similar terms. What becomes even more confusing is that these terms also referred to the peanut.[24] Hence, it is difficult to determine the plant to which early American writers refer unaccompanied by a description.

The similarities between the two plants greatly augmented the African adoption of peanuts, which quickly became dominant because they were much more prolific, possessed a much higher oil content, and were easier to grow. Eclipsed, Bambara groundnuts all but disappeared in Africa and in the New World. Peanuts became an important part of the African diet, particularly from Ambriz to the River Congo, where they were consumed in "considerable quantities." They were seldom eaten raw but were "delicious simply roasted, or better still afterwards covered with a little sugar dried on them in the pan." Peanuts were ground on stones and reduced to paste, which was used to thicken soups, stews, and similar dishes, and the oil was used for culinary purposes. The Africans also ate peanuts "with Bananas, and either the raw Mandiocca root, or some preparation of it, experience showing them

the necessity of the admixture of a farinaceous substance with an excessively oily food."[25]

Peanuts were widely distributed in Africa, Asia, and the Mediterranean
and were readily adopted by diverse peoples. The reasons for this amazing
success were several. Peanuts were generally comparable with other plants
in Asia and Africa. They were cultivated and consumed much like other legumes but could be grown in marginal soil that would not support other
crops. Peanuts required little effort to cultivate and were easily harvested. The
peanut plants were more prolific and produced more fruit than did the alternatives. The peanut seeds were particularly rich in oil—a characteristic that
proved crucial for its adoption outside of the Americas. Perhaps the most
important characteristic was the peanut's versatility. Peanuts could be consumed in thousands of ways—ways that would easily fit in with the culinary
traditions of many different cultures.

SLAVE FOOD TO SNACK FOOD

How peanuts arrived in the British North American colonies has been a topic of conjecture for the past century. Reports of "groundnuts" appear throughout the early exploration and European colonization of the territory that would become the United States. In 1602, Captain Bartholomew Gosnold, for instance, encountered "groundnuts" during his exploration of Virginia. John Brereton mentioned a "great store of Ground nuts, fortie together on a string, some of them as bigge as hennes eggs; they grow not two inches under ground." In 1613, a French leader and his followers "scattered about the woods and shores digging ground-nuts" at Port Royal. During the winter of 1622–23, the Pilgrims "were enforced to live on ground-nuts."[1]

As descriptions of these groundnuts were lacking, some secondary accounts have concluded that these reports refer to peanuts. However, they most likely refer to *Apios tuberosa,* a plant with a tuber that grows underground and is widely dispersed throughout eastern America, but which is botanically unrelated to the peanut. When the Swedish scientist Peter Kalm visited America in 1749, he found Native Americans, Swedes, and English colonists eating them in various ways. When Edwin James explored Missouri in 1819, he reported that in times of hunger, Native Americans were often required to dig up the "ground-pea." In the 1820s Joseph Correa de Serra, the Portuguese ambassador to the United States, recounted that Native Americans and others ate them "greedily when they find them," but that they were not cultivated. Among the more prominent aficionados of this tuber was Henry Thoreau, who ate them as a child and was delighted when he found them by the side of the road. In *Walden,* he sadly reported that "this humble root" was "quite altogether almost exterminated." But *Apios* was occasionally mentioned well into the twentieth century.[2]

THE EARLY AMERICAN PEANUT

Despite the pre-Columbian cultivation of peanuts in the Caribbean and Mexico, no evidence has surfaced indicating that peanuts were grown in what is today the United States prior to European colonization. The first unequivocal reference to the peanut in America was made in 1769 by a Dr. Brownrigg, who pressed oil from peanuts in Edenton, North Carolina. His brother, George Brownrigg, sent an account of this experiment to Sir William Watson in England along with samples of peanuts and their oil. Watson converted Brownrigg's account into a paper, which he delivered before the Royal Society of London. This was published in the society's *Philosophical Transactions.* According to Watson's introduction, peanuts were "well known, and much cultivated, in the Southern colonies" and in the Caribbean, where they were "called ground nuts, or ground pease."[3]

Other accounts suggest that the peanut was grown in southern colonies before 1800.[4] That this was so does not come as a surprise. Many settlers in the southern colonies had lived formerly in the Caribbean, where peanuts grew in abundance. Trade between the southern colonies and islands in the Caribbean was sustained throughout the colonial period. An important part of that trade was the exchange of slaves, who were familiar with peanuts. Watson believed that peanuts had been brought from Africa by slaves, who were very fond of them and ate them "both raw and roasted." In the Caribbean and in the British colonies in North America slaves grew peanuts on small garden plots given them by plantation masters. At the time, the white colonists do not appear to have consumed peanuts directly, but they did eat swine and poultry fattened on unlimited access to "ground pease."[5]

SLAVE FOOD

Peanuts were used to feed slaves almost from the earliest days of the European slave trade, and regular reports of this appeared thereafter. Gonzalo

Fernández de Oviedo y Valdés observed in 1535 that peanuts were eaten by slaves in the Caribbean. The botanist Carolus Clusius reported in the 1601 edition of *Rariorum plantarum historia* that the Portuguese fed peanuts to slaves transported to Lisbon from the island of Sao Thomé, off the African coast. In 1707, the British botanist Hans Sloane collected peanuts in the Caribbean. In the harbor of Port Royal, Jamaica, Sloane found a ship "from *Guinea,* loaded with Blacks to sell. The Ship was very nasty with so many People on Board. I was assured that the Negroes feed on Pindals or Indian Earth-Nuts, a sort of Pea or Bean producing its Pods under ground. Coming from *Guinea* they are fed these Nuts or *Indian* corn boil'd whole twice a day." Sloane acquired part of his information from Henry Barham, who proclaimed in his own book, *Hortus Jamaica,* that he first saw peanuts "in a negro's plantation, who affirmed, that they grew in great plenty in their country." Likewise, Patrick Browne in his *Civil and Natural History of Jamaica* reported that peanuts were "frequently imported to Jamaica in the ships from *Africa*" and were cultivated in very small quantities in Jamaica. So frequently were peanuts brought from Africa that Edward Long, in his 1774 *History of Jamaica,* expressed the belief that peanuts were actually introduced into Jamaica from Africa. Long stated that peanuts were "nourishing, and often given as food to Negroes on voyages from Guiney, where they pass under the name of *gubagubs.*" He noted that the peanuts could "be eaten raw, roasted, or boiled." Yet another report emanated from Fusée Aublet, whose *Histoire des plantes de la Guiane Françoise* recorded that crews fed peanuts to the slaves on their passage from Africa, and that slaves grew peanuts in their gardens in French Guinea.[6]

Slave ships coming to America were provisioned with peanuts, and it was through the slave trade that peanuts were introduced into what is today the United States.[7] In 1804, James Mease, a Philadelphian, reported that peanuts were "called *pinda* by the negroes, by whom they are chiefly cultivated." According to David Ramsay, peanuts were "*sui generis*" about forty miles southwest of Charleston, South Carolina, where they were "planted in small patches chiefly by negroes for market."[8] An ex-slave from Louisiana, Mary Reynolds, fondly remembered her garden where she grew potatoes and peanuts: "Sometimes Massa let niggers have a little patch. They'd raise 'taters or goobers." These gardens had to be worked at night after the normal plantation work was finished.[9]

That peanuts played an important part in African Americans' lives is reflected in their folklore. Peanut superstitions thrived among Africans and African Americans. For instance, Denmark Vesey masterminded an insurrection in South Carolina in 1822. His co-conspirator, Gullah Jack, advised his followers: "Eat only dry food" such as "parched corn and ground nuts, and when you join us, put this crab claw in your mouth and you can't be wounded." The conspirators were apprehended before the insurrection began and many were executed. While peanuts were not again put to this use, they did remain an important part of African-American folklore well into the twentieth century.[10]

EARLY PEANUT CONSUMPTION

While there is no question that slaves ate peanuts, little evidence has been uncovered indicating how they consumed them. All that is known for sure is that African Americans ate them raw, roasted, and boiled. Peanuts were probably eaten as a snack or were added to traditional African dishes, such as stews and soups. Peanuts were likely ground, mixed with water, and consumed as a beverage, a recipe that was common in the Caribbean and later emerged in the American South. As African Americans did the cooking on southern plantations as well as in many urban homes, they introduced peanuts into local cookery. In addition to growing, consuming and introducing peanuts into southern cookery, African Americans were the first peanut vendors. In Wilmington, North Carolina, African Americans sold peanuts on Market Street well before the Civil War. According to an 1855 article in *Ballou's Pictorial Drawing-Room Companion,* African-American freedmen and slaves sold the produce raised in their garden patches from homemade mule carts. When they arrived in town, the mule team was unhitched, the cart was tipped up, and the produce was ready for sale: "On certain days of the week, twenty or more of these market-wagons may be counted from the steps of the hotel."[11] With this cash, African Americans were able to purchase items otherwise unavailable to them.

During the last few decades of the eighteenth century, peanut cultivation migrated northward from the Carolinas. In his *Notes on the State of Virginia,* Thomas Jefferson wrote that peanuts grew in Virginia in 1781. Subsequently, Jefferson planted sixty-five hills of "peendars," which yielded "16 ½ lb weighted green out of the ground which is ¼ lb each." While president, he reported that peanuts were very sweet.[12] By 1787, a small trade in peanuts was carried on between Charleston and New York. The unshelled peanuts were sold by a few vendors, who roasted them at their stalls and sold them to passersby. The Englishman Henry Wansey enjoyed roasted peanuts on his tour of the United States in 1794. He found them unusual enough to acquire a supply and store them in his luggage. When he served them at his home in England, he was somewhat surprised to learn from an acquaintance that peanuts were grown extensively in China. Another interesting point about Wansey's account was that he used the term *pea-nut,* which is the first located use of the term. It is ironic that *peanut* was first published in England, where *groundnut* was then, and continues to be, the preferred word for the *Arachis hypogaea.* Even in the United States, the term *groundnut* was commonly used until the Civil War as a synonym for peanut.[13]

On the eve of the nineteenth century, peanuts were grown in gardens in Philadelphia. These were most likely introduced by French Creole refugees, who had settled there after escaping the 1791 slave insurrection in Haiti. One Philadelphian recalled that these families "brought slaves with them as nurses or attendants," who prepared peanuts in a variety of ways. These slaves also introduced peanut cookery to Philadelphia. Wearing bright madras turbans, they sat on low stools on Philadelphia market corners and sold peanut cakes.[14] As recipes for these later appeared in cookbooks in the North, it is extremely likely that Haitian slaves were also responsible for the use of peanuts in American cookery.

But the main early culinary use of peanuts in northern cities was as a snack food. Throughout the nineteenth century, peanuts were mainly sold roasted in their shells. On January 23, 1803, a letter written by "Jonathan Oldstyle" appeared in New York's *Morning Chronicle* complaining about the "crackling of nuts" at the Theater on Park Row, then New York City's only theater. Another correspondent, "Philo Dramaticus," lauded Oldstyle for his grievance against gentlemen who were accustomed to stand "on the seats with dirty boots, and to the parings of apples and oranges, and the shells of peanuts, which they distribute plentifully around them." Jonathan Oldstyle was the pen name of Washington Irving. He also made reports of peanut eating in his other works. For instance, Irving later reported, presumably humorously, that college students enjoyed "pea-nuts and beer, after the fatiguing morning studies."[15]

Peanut shells continued to be a nuisance throughout the nineteenth century. In 1834, the New York *Sun* announced that the pit at the theater on the Bowery "was usually filled with a set of pea-nut-eating-geniuses." The following year, William Dunlap complained about those "peanut fellows" who stood on theater seats, cracked peanuts, and tossed the debris on the floor. By 1845, New York finally had more than one theater, but eating peanuts at the Cheltanham and Bowery theaters was still the "rage" of the theatergoers. Twenty-five years later, observers still complained about the peanut shells.[16]

By the 1830s, peanuts were sold by merchants as well as by snack food vendors. For instance, a merchant in Pottsville, Pennsylvania, proudly announced in 1836 that his peanut shipment had just arrived and urged customers to buy them. Sale by merchants increased the demand for peanuts. To meet this expanding need, peanuts were regularly shipped from North Carolina. As this became a lucrative trade, other southern farmers were interested to know how to get in on it. The editor of the *New England Farmer* published a request for more information about peanuts from a Mr. E. W. Haring of Cayuga, Mississippi, who wanted "information related to the article of Pindars, by some called groundnuts, by some *Goober Peas,* &c." Specifically, he wished to know the quantity of them sold in Boston, as the soil and climate in Cayuga were "well adapted to the growth of the article, and I am wishing to learn if it will do to ship." Whether peanuts were actually grown for export in Mississippi at that time is unknown, but they were exported from South Carolina at a profit during the 1840s. One account stated, however, that they were "troublesome to prepare."[17]

In addition to acquiring peanuts from southern states, northern states imported them from West Africa. The first recorded imports from Gambia occurred in 1835. At this time, the total annual value of peanuts imported into the United States was estimated at a measly £26, but two years later, this annual trade jumped to £5,642. By 1841, the value of this trade reached £8,127. In addition, peanuts were imported from other West African areas. The firm of Robert Brookhouse and William Hunt of Salem, Massachusetts, dispatched vessels on round-trip voyages expressly for the purpose of acquiring well-dried, "bright new nuts" with no mold. The captains of the ships were given precise instructions on how to pack the peanuts to avoid spoilage on the return trip. In 1838, a Philadelphia merchant realized $12,000 by importing peanuts from Liberia. Southern peanut growers complained about this foreign competition, and the U.S. Congress levied a one-cent-per-pound tariff on imported peanuts in 1842. This did not stop the peanut trade with West Africa, however, which thrived throughout the 1850s and 1860s.[18]

Before the creation of the U.S. Department of Agriculture (USDA) in 1862, the federal government's agricultural office fell under the control of the Commissioner of Patents. Beginning in 1847, the commissioner issued agricultural reports. Peanuts were mentioned in the first report and were frequently discussed in subsequent reports. Farm journals, farming manuals, and newspapers published articles on peanuts beginning in the late 1840s. The *Tallahassee Floridian,* for instance, proclaimed "goubers" to be "one of the surest crops, not withholding a generous yield even on poor land, and amply acknowledging the superiority of rich land if light and friable." Based on this article, the 1847 agricultural *Report* of the Commissioner of Patents concluded that peanuts were "well worth a thorough experiment." In 1848, the *Southern Cultivator* published its first article on peanuts, written by J. C.

Paulette, who offered advice on how to cultivate them. In 1849, R. L. Anderson's *American Farm Book* was the first major agricultural work to publish a discussion of the peanut.[19] These reports, however, were just the beginning. During the next two decades, hundreds of peanut accounts appeared in reports, books, journals, and newspapers.

These references point to a wide geographical dispersion of peanut culture throughout the United States and a fast-growing consumption pattern. Emily P. Burke, who had lived on a slave plantation in Georgia during the 1840s, recounted that "Great quantities of peanuts" were raised there both as an article of export and as a fodder for fattening pigs. In 1849, John Dent described the peanut's progress in Barbour County, Alabama. Two years later, W. B. Easby of Vernon, Tennessee, related that peanuts had first been raised in Nashville for market in the fall of 1845. During the next few years, the peanut crop around Nashville reached 25,000 bushels. During the late 1840s and early 1850s, George Noble Jones cultivated peanuts at El Destino and Chemonie plantations in Florida. According to his records, he harvested from 20 to 80 bushels per year. In 1852 M. W. Philips reported from Edwards, Mississippi, that he fed "bacon hogs" in "pindar patches." The following year, John B. C. Gazzo of La Fourche Parish, Louisiana, divulged that his peanuts produced 60 to 75 bushels per acre. The prominent agricultural journal *Country Gentleman* "discovered" peanuts in May 1857, when an article disclosed that great quantities of these nuts were "brought every year to the Baltimore market, from the counties in Virginia bordering the southern portion of the Chesapeake." One month later, a farmer reported that in Surry County, Virginia, peanuts were extensively "cultivated in this and adjoining counties." Even in far-off California, peanuts were grown in abundance, according to a report from Yolo County that appeared in the *Sacramento Times*. Farmers even tried to grow peanuts in northern states, but the crop did not prove profitable. As Fearing Burr concluded in 1863, the peanut was "rather tropical in its character, and cannot be cultivated with success in either the Northern or Middle States."[20]

EARLY CULINARY USE

An unusual early culinary use of peanuts was as a beverage. The eighteenth-century botanist William Bartram of Philadelphia proclaimed that peanuts combined with pulverized sassafras bark produced an excellent substitute for chocolate. David Ramsay's 1809 *History of South Carolina* reported a similar use and, thirty years later, the British *Gardener's Chronicle* still noted that South Carolinians roasted and ground peanuts, then added hot water, and consumed the concoction as a beverage. This practice was not limited to the United States. John Lunan's *Hortus Jamaicensis,* published in Jamaica in 1814, stated that peanuts, when roasted, ground, and boiled, made "a good substitute for chocolate." French sources recommended that ground peanuts be substituted for coffee, which was precisely what was done in South Carolina before 1849. A medical botanist, Francis Porcher, claimed that he even had difficulty distinguishing peanut coffee from the real thing.[21]

The first published reference to peanuts in an American cookbook appeared in 1837. The author, Eliza Leslie, was born in Philadelphia and educated at home. When her father died in 1803, her mother opened a boardinghouse. Eliza later attended Elizabeth Goodfellow's cooking school in Philadelphia. Leslie's *Directions for Cookery,* a seminal work in American cookery, included several peanut recipes, perhaps inspired by the dishes prepared by the Haitian Creoles and their slaves who had migrated to Philadelphia forty years before. In her recipe for "Cocoa-nut Maccaroons," she told the reader that they could also be made "in a similar manner of pounded cream-nuts, ground-nuts, filberts, or English walnuts." Likewise, her recipe for "Molasses Candy" suggested substituting "ground-nuts" for almonds, producing an early version of peanut brittle. Similar recipes were published by Mrs. A. L. Webster in 1844, Catharine Beecher in the following year, and many others subsequently.[22]

Although southern cookbooks had been published since 1824, the first one to print peanut recipes was Sarah Rutledge's *Carolina Housewife,* first published in 1847. Her "Ground-Nut Soup" is the first known reference to peanut soup. As we have seen previously, ground peanuts had been used in soups in Africa and it is likely that this dish had been made for years by African Americans but simply had not been previously recorded. Rutledge's recipes for "Ground-nut Cheese Cake" and "Ground-nut Cake" produced small cakes or cookies, using peanuts ground into a paste with a mortar and pestle. This recipe may have originated with the Haitian refugees, who also migrated to Charleston after the 1791 slave uprising. The second edition of her work included a recipe for "Ekbaladoolas," which Rutledge identifies as a "Hindoo" recipe, presumably from India. The recipe featured almonds, but the cookbook editor noted that peanuts were also "very nice prepared in this way."[23] Francis Porcher noted in 1849 that peanuts were used extensively on plantations "as an article of food, and for various domestic purposes." For instance, parched peanuts could be "beaten with sugar, and served as a condiment or dessert." Porcher was the first American physician to proclaim that peanuts were "rich and nutritious" and could be substituted for meat dishes.[24]

During the 1850s, the only other significant peanut recipe published was for "Ground-Nut Macaroons" developed by Eliza Leslie. This was a major expansion of Sarah Rutledge's recipe for "Ground-Nut Cakes." In Leslie's recipe the peanuts were roasted and blanched, and then "pounded to a smooth, light paste." Egg whites were beaten to a froth, and powdered loaf-sugar, mace, and nutmeg were added. This combination was then added to the peanut paste, and the resulting dough was rolled into little balls that were placed onto baking tins and flattened into a cookie shape. Powdered sugar was sifted over them and they were baked in a brisk oven for about ten minutes.[25]

Before the Civil War, the most important peanut-growing region was around Cape Fear, North Carolina. Commercial peanuts had been raised in this area at least since 1818. Beginning in the 1830s, peanut prices were listed in Wilmington newspapers, and by the mid-1850s, African Americans sold peanuts on the streets. By 1856, this area produced over 100,000 bushels annually, valued at $125,000. Four years later, peanuts were the principal crop, which was more profitable than cotton. One Wilmington-area planter generated an annual income of $6,000 from his peanut crop alone. In addition, enough peanuts had been left in the ground to fatten pigs, which generated even more income through the sale of pork. By 1860, the total peanut production in the United States amounted to about 150,000 bushels, of which two-thirds were cultivated in North Carolina.[26]

3 SOLDIERS AND VENDORS

Even before the American Civil War began in 1861, peanut cultivation and consumption were increasing. When the war broke out, the peanut's value was enhanced. As the Northern blockade prevented the importation of goods to the South, peanut oil was used as a substitute for whale oil in Southern industry to lubricate machinery. At least four factories were established in the South to convert peanuts into oil. This was "used quite extensively as a lubricant for railroad locomotives, wood and cotton spindles." Peanut oil was even considered to be superior to whale oil "for the reason that it does not gum at all." Peanut oil was also extensively employed in medicines. When burned in lamps, it did not smoke. In general, Southern housewives substituted peanut oil for lard as shortening in bread and pastry, and for olive oil in salad dressings.[1] Despite the success of peanut oil during the Civil War, when the war ended so did its manufacture.

Peanuts were used more extensively in cooking as malnutrition and hunger stalked parts of the Confederacy. One enterprising army cook in the Civil War tried to make a pie out of peanuts. A soldier reported, "Our cook couldn't find any walnuts so he made a pie with peanuts. It didn't taste very good and two of our men got sick." Southerners also used peanuts as a beverage, again substituting for unavailable coffee and chocolate. A recipe for this concoction was offered by an Alabaman, Virginia Clay-Clopton, who roasted peanuts, pounded them in a mortar, and blended the resulting paste with boiled milk and a little sugar. It was then ready for serving, and Clay-Clopton family and friends "found it delightful to our palates." This appreciation was real, as southerners continued to drink peanut beverages decades after the war ended. The author of the first American book on peanuts, Brian W. Jones, confirmed in 1885 that peanut "chocolate" was "made in some Southern families by beating the properly roasted nuts in a mortar with sugar, and flavoring with cinnamon or vanilla as may be desired." Recipes for peanut beverages continued to be published for decades.[2]

Perhaps due to their increased stature in the South, peanuts turned up in Civil War–era songs. "Eating Goober Peas," for instance, included the chorus: "Peas! Peas! Peas! Peas! Eating goober peas! / Goodness, how delicious, eating goober peas!" And the following stanzas:

> Sitting by the roadside on a summer day,
> Chatting with my messmates, passing time away,
> Lying in the shadow underneath the trees,
> Goodness, how delicious, eating goober peas!
> When a horseman passes, the soldiers have a rule,
> To cry out at their loudest, "Mister, here's your mule,"
> But another pleasure enchantinger than these,
> Is wearing out your grinders, eating goobers peas!
>
> Just before the battle the General hears a row,
> He says, "The Yanks are coming, I hear their rifles now,"
> He turns around in wonder, and what do you think he sees?
> The Georgia militia eating goober peas!
> I think my song has lasted almost long enough,
> The subject's interesting, but the rhymes are mighty rough,
> I wish this war was over, when free from rags and fleas,
> We'd kiss our wives and sweethearts and gobble goober peas![3]

In addition to lack of oil and food, the South was also confronted with a manpower shortage. To meet the increased demand for peanuts and the lack of skilled labor in the South during the Civil War, Thomas L. Colville, a mechanic living in Wilmington, North Carolina, built two machines—one for separating the nuts from the vines and the other for removing the shells. Neither machine was patented nor particularly successful. But the inventions

did stimulate further experimentation over the next few decades, which resulted in the development of successful mechanized peanut processing.[4]

The Civil War influenced peanut consumption in Northern states as well.
When Southern peanuts were cut off during the early years of the war, Northern importation of peanuts increased fivefold from 1860 to 1864. When
Northern armies occupied nut-growing areas in the South, Union soldiers
were exposed to the peanut's culinary influence. When these soldiers returned
home, they wanted peanuts. By 1867 Thomas Devoe's report on conditions
in the grocery trade notes that peanuts were "found for sale in all our principal cities, and in all seasons of the year." They were sold "chiefly in fruit
stores, and after having been roasted, everywhere, in the markets, on the street
corners, apple-stands, basket pedlers." To meet this demand for peanuts,
Northerners vastly expanded their imports from the Caribbean and Africa
after the war. Peanut imports increased from 4.8 million pounds in 1865 to
11.5 million pounds in 1868.[5]

THE RECONSTRUCTED PEANUT

Economic dislocation in the South caused by the Civil War created opportunities for those bold enough to experiment commercially with this potentially lucrative agricultural product. In 1867, the total southern peanut crop
did not amount to more than 200,000 bushels, most of which were grown
in the Wilmington area of North Carolina. In war-ravaged Norfolk, Virginia, Thomas Rowland bought peanuts from farmers and shipped a small batch
to commission merchants in New York. He had attempted to export peanuts
before the war but had been unsuccessful. His 1867 venture did not succeed
either. But Rowland believed in the potential for peanut sales in northern
states and the following year encouraged Norfolk planters to cultivate more
peanuts, which he again sent northward. These ended up with an Italian
commission man, who sent out Italian peddlers to sell the consignment. This
venture was so successful that Rowland sent even more peanuts the following year. The Italian commission man recruited more peddlers and this time
equipped each one with a pushcart and a bag of peanuts on credit. The peddlers were required to sell a certain quantity of peanuts within a given period of time or their carts were taken away and they were refused further supplies. Successful vendors returned 25 percent of their sales to the commission
agents and pocketed the remaining 75 percent.[6]

By 1870, several hundred vendors sold peanuts in the streets of New York
alone. Some vendors moved from New York, settling in other cities, and became wholesale peanut dealers, hiring other immigrants themselves. Italians

placed peanut-vending operations in Boston and Cincinnati, the latter becoming the great peanut mart of the Midwest during that epoch. Other Italians were recruited to come to America with the specific intent of selling peanuts for a living, as one contemporary observer noted, "for the business was much magnified in the visions of far-off Italy. It was popularly supposed, over there, that Americans were voracious for peanuts."[7]

African Americans filled a position in southern cities similar to that of the Italian vendors in northern cities. One observer remarked that the Savannah, Georgia, docks were filled with African-American women "sheltered by the tattered umbrella, and surrounded by heaping baskets of roasted peanuts." African Americans also sold peanuts at circuses and other public events in southern states after the Civil War.[8]

Likewise, peanuts were sold in the West. A San Francisco visitor exclaimed that "the olfactories of street pedestrians" were "treated to the fragrances of roasting peanuts from the stands of the peanut salesmen who are to be found about every other block with a small cart-load of peanuts, really the finest ever found in the market of any city; and the heating ovens sending out an odorous testimonial of the roasting process." Californians agreed that their peanuts were the "very best in the world."[9]

Increased sales by vendors, however, did not immediately imply acceptance of the peanut by all segments of American society. An article in *Harper's Weekly* in 1870 divulged that eating peanuts was considered "ungenteel" by polite society. Boys loved peanuts, but otherwise these snacks were chiefly confined to people who frequented such places of amusement as the Bower Theatre: "Such people, indeed, munch them every where—as they walk the street, on the cars, in the stages, and aboard the ferryboats, scattering the shells abroad with the utmost indifference, and littering the dress of every person in their neighborhood." Even worse, according to the author, peanuts imparted "a pungent odor to the breath, which makes the eater almost as great a nuisance in a crowd as one who indulges in the luxury of Limburger cheese."[10]

The *Harper's* article also claimed that vendors generated only "a few shillings worth of pea-nuts, with perhaps a dozen or two apples." However, the author greatly underestimated the income of peanut vendors, some of whom made small fortunes. In 1887, a house on Mulberry Street in New York City was sold at auction to a man who bid more than $24,000. Much to the surprise of those at the auction and other members of New York's elite, the buyer "was a dingy, dwarfish specimen of Italian immigration, who began his mercantile course as a proprietor of a pea-nut stand in the classic region of Park Street." When the peanut stand operator won the bid, "the unwashed swarm of polylingual fellow-citizens" applauded "wildly as he coolly drew out a dirty red pocket handkerchief, and began to count out from it the purchase money, which he supposed must be paid on the spot."[11]

The 1870 article in *Harper's* predicted that peanuts would not likely "ever rise above their present position here." This prognostication was wrong. Peanut sales escalated every year during the 1870s. During this decade, Virginia replaced North Carolina as the major peanut-producing state, and both were followed by Tennessee, Georgia, and South Carolina. In addition, about 100,000 bushels of peanuts were imported annually from Africa. In an article in *Scientific American,* H. E. Colton noted this vast increase in peanut production and asked, "But who eats them?" A vendor, whose sales were over a thousand bushels a year, responded that everybody ate them, "from the wealthy banker to the homeless newsboy."[12]

To help peanut growers improve their yields, agricultural journals and farming manuals offered advice on how to cultivate peanuts. Widespread attempts were made to grow them beyond the traditional peanut-growing area extending from Virginia to northern Florida. Production began in many parts of the United States, including New Hampshire, Illinois, Alabama, Texas, West Virginia, Kentucky, and New Jersey. By the 1880s, peanut production had reached two million bushels, of which one-fourth were sold in New York. The peanut had become so successful with growers that it acquired new monikers, such as "currency," "cash," and "credit."[13]

PEANUT MIDDLEMEN

In addition to Thomas Rowland, many others served as middlemen buying from the farmers and selling to concession men in northern cities. L. Franklin Bain, who had operated a country store in Wakefield, Virginia, bought peanuts from farmers in surrounding Surry, Sussex, and Southampton counties. At the time, peanuts were shipped in the condition they arrived from the farm. Bain cleaned the peanuts by hand and quickly gained a reputation for shipping quality nuts. His business prospered, and in 1890 the Bain Peanut Company constructed its first plant in an abandoned cotton mill. The company was incorporated fourteen years later and its first president was P. D. Bain, the grandson of L. Franklin Bain.[14]

P. D. Gwaltney returned to Virginia after the Civil War and turned to peanut cultivation. In 1870, he moved to Smithfield—where Smithfield hams had been sold commercially since the eighteenth century—and began cleaning peanuts. Some of these peanuts were used to feed hogs. A. Bunkley bought into the business and the Gwaltney-Bunkley Peanut Company was incorporated in 1891. In 1904 the company exhibited its wares at the Louisiana Purchase Exposition in Saint Louis and issued a booklet announcing that it was "largest peanut concern in the world." The booklet included a section titled "Whence High-Priced Hams Come," with an advertisement for Gwaltney Hams. The company became even larger when P. D. Gwaltney and P. D. Bain consolidated their efforts and bought the Norfolk Storage Company for cleaning and storing peanuts. The new company was renamed the American Peanut Corporation. Several other companies were launched in Smithfield, specializing in selling peanuts and peanut-fed hogs. In 1926 the General Assembly of Virginia enacted into law a definition of a Smithfield ham as one from hogs that had been peanut-fed.[15]

After the Civil War, John Pretlow began raising peanuts on a commercial scale in Franklin, Virginia. He had contacts in the northern states who were willing to broker his peanuts. At the time, the peanuts on his thousand-acre plantation were picked by hand, cleaned by hand, and sorted into bags according to quality. The bags were hauled from the fields by mule and cart. Horses furnished the power to operate primitive cleaning equipment. Pretlow built a peanut-cleaning plant in Suffolk, Virginia, which soon became the major center for the peanut processing industry. His major buyers were Lummis, Devine and Company of Philadelphia, and Ehlen and Company of Baltimore.[16]

Spikes Beale grew peanuts on Virginia's Isle of Wright in the late 1860s. By 1870 the Beale family was growing peanuts in Franklin and selling them in their hulls for twenty cents a bushel. In 1904, Spikes Beale's grandson J. I. Beale founded the Franklin Peanut Company. As one of its advertising cards boasted, "Peanuts! Peanuts! We raise them down our way. We clean them, we grade them, we shell them every day, and if YOU FOLKS WANT PEANUTS, just send your orders down, for we have *The Best That Can Be Gotten.*"[17]

THE CIRCUS PEANUT

When peanuts first entered into the circus is unclear, but they were present by the 1840s, when George Odell reported, "Too much circus is perhaps bad for the peanut-crop; there is a limit to all joys." According to Stuart Thayer, the first located contract for circus vendors, who presumably sold peanuts, was dated 1841. After the Civil War, peanuts became a staple at circuses. Secondary sources attribute the popularity of the circus peanut to the legendary P. T. Barnum, who introduced "Jumbo the Elephant" to America. The notion that elephants liked peanuts dates to about this time. According to legend, an Italian peanut commission-house owner named Petroni attended a performance of the Barnum and Bailey circus in Connecticut. Afterwards, he approached Barnum seeking a contract to sell peanuts at the circus, and Barnum signed a multiyear contract with him. Petroni purportedly made a fortune out of the deal and Barnum is said to have regretted agreeing to it.[18]

When the circus came to town, local people would line the path to the entrance, selling snack foods. In the South, Gil Robinson recalled that the corridors leading to the circus grounds were always lined with snack stands operated by African Americans, who also circulated among the crowds, selling baskets of peanuts and other commodities. An article in the *Syracuse Courier* reported that when the circus was in town "scattered along the streets were stands where the unsophisticated could buy colored water for lemonade, peanuts, ginger cakes, lager beer and other refreshments." While performing in Waco, Texas, in 1898 Ernie Millette observed that the Big Top entrance was "fronted ten-deep with snack stands selling beer, peanuts, chili con carne and every kind of edibles from candies to luncheons." These vendors were not affiliated with the circus and generated considerable hostility from circus-goers. Some peanut vendors engaged in fraud. Peanut bags were packed fifty to sixty per bag. Dishonest vendors picked up used bags and filled them with fewer peanuts until concessionaires caught on and responded by stapling the bags shut to prevent reuse. An article in the *Lansing Republican* commented on the "nuisance which threatens to diminish the patronage of such shows, namely the boisterous and continuous peddling of peanuts."[19]

Not only were concession sales a problem outside the circus, but vendors constantly solicited attendees inside the tents. During the show, incessant shouts of "Fresh roasted peanuts!" filled the air. Some circuses refused to sanction vendors and proudly announced this policy in their advertisements. For instance, Cooper and Bailey avowed that "Objectionable features such as candy, lemonade and peanut vendors have been eliminated." The *Pantagraph* of Bloomington, Illinois, advertised a circus with the statement that there were "no candy, lemonade or peanut swindlers with us." In York, Pennsylvania, the *Evening Dispatch* reported that a circus confined all refreshments to a single tent, with the result that the "audience sat in peace during the entire performance, not once being bothered with vendors of peanuts or bad lemonade." A member of the Montgomery Queens Company cited a performance in Jackson, Mississippi, where the circus manager had been extremely "successful in abolishing all sideshows, candy and peanut stands, peddlers and mountebanks." In Rochester, Minnesota, the *Post* reported in 1880 that the "peanut vendors were unexpectedly courteous."[20] Despite these successes, vendors continued to be nuisances inside and outside the circus well into the twentieth century.

THE LITERARY PEANUT

Even before the Civil War, peanut references appeared in literary works. Charles Fenno Hoffman introduced peanuts into his *Winter in the West*. Harriet Beecher Stowe's *Dred: A Tale of the Great Dismal Swamp* mentioned a "shower of peanut-shells" and peanut candy. After the war, Samuel L. Clemens, writing under his pen name of Mark Twain, referred in *The Gilded Age* to "peanut-boys" on trains. Mary Akins's *The Little Pea-nut Merchant*, published in 1869, revolved around Harvard, a young boy who decided to sell peanuts near schools to generate money for his destitute family. He was wise enough to purchase the peanuts on the wharves, where they were cheaper than at the stores. At first, his business was a success, but it soon became less lucrative, for "Other boys, seeing how well he was doing, engaged in it. To his surprise, they sold larger quantities for the same money than he was able to." When Harvard caught two other boys filling their pockets with peanuts from a grocer's display, while the shopkeeper waited on other customers, he was confronted with a moral dilemma—should he tell the grocer?[21]

At Yale University, students seemed less interested in moral dilemmas and more interested in eating peanuts. They held a "peanut bum" whenever a member of a society won an honor in some college contest. This event involved emptying a sack containing one or two bushels of peanuts onto the floor, followed by an indiscriminate scramble "by the upper-class guests and their freshmen entertainers." And it was a Harvard undergraduate who was among the first to use the term "peanut gallery," which by the 1890s denoted the uppermost gallery in a theater. As this section was farthest from the stage, the tickets were cheapest, and this was where rowdyism often erupted, sullying the reputation of the gallery and the peanut.[22]

The year 1885 saw the publication of the first English-language monograph on the peanut. Brian Jones's *The Peanut Plant: Its Cultivation and Uses* went through several additional printings. Of roasted peanuts, Jones wrote, "Almost every person residing in the eastern section of our country, must necessarily know something of the value of roasted peanuts. One cannot pass along the streets of any of our larger cities and towns, without encountering, at every turn, the little peanut stands, where roasted peanuts are sold by the pint. They are kept for sale in numerous shops, they are peddled on the railroad cars, and sold to the loungers at every depot. Roasted peanuts are more common then roasted chestnuts once were, and almost everybody eats them. Even the ladies are fond of them, and frequently have them at their parties."[23]

At first, wholesale grocers across America considered peanuts beneath their dignity and retail grocers laughed at the street vendors. As vendors increased their sales, the possibility of a lucrative profit finally dawned on the grocery world and peanut sales entered into stores. Grocers initially sold peanuts from large glass jars. Each held about a dozen individual bags, and these were replenished as the peanuts were sold. By the 1880s, peanuts and peanut oils were regularly sold by grocers who advertised them in magazines.[24]

Peanuts were sold in vending machines even before the twentieth century. These coin-operated machines were first placed on the platforms of New York train stations in 1897. The first patent for a peanut vending machine was issued in 1898. Vending machines did not catch on nationally until 1901, when F. W. and H. S. Mills brought out the penny-in-the-slot peanut machine in Chicago. These machines gave great impetus to the popularity of the little round Spanish peanuts chiefly grown in North Carolina. During its first year of operation, the Mills Company bought 4 million pounds of Spanish peanuts. Within a few years, 15,000 machines selling peanuts were placed across America. Twelve years later, the number of machines had tripled. By 1926, there was a vending machine for every 100 people in America, generating a total of a million dollars per day. While vending machines offered other snacks, salted peanuts or peanut products, such as peanut butter and cracker sandwiches or peanut candies, accounted for fourteen of the twenty leading items sold in the machines.[25]

The man who ignited the peanut revolution, Thomas Rowland, continued in the trade almost until his death in 1918. But during the 1890s he had been overshadowed by other entrepreneurs with larger aggregations of capital. This new breed built plants for cleaning, shelling, and grading peanuts, introduced new machinery, and developed networks of traveling salesmen to sell their products. The field was highly competitive. By 1895, eight million bushels of peanuts were produced in the United States. That year, the wholesale buyers and dealers of Virginia and North Carolina formed a peanut trust called the Virginia Peanut Association. The trust sent out a total of only two salesmen. The intent was to decrease supply in hopes of increasing the price for peanuts, but the plan backfired. Within months, wholesale peanuts had dropped to their lowest price in ten years, and sales fell off 60 percent. Panic overtook the Virginia Peanut Association, and the trust split. The episode proved that Americans could live without peanuts, and that peanuts had to be marketed.[26]

Shortly after the beginning of the twentieth century, the *Richmond Dispatch* proclaimed that the "persistent effort [that] has been made to stamp the peanut with the smack of vulgarity" was a total failure. While peanuts had been "synonyms of circus rowdyism, gallery gods' obstreperousness, and festive occasions of the proletariat," the goober had become so popular that it had crowded "its haughty kinsman, the salted almond, off the festal board, and it is rapidly receiving wide recognition as a delicacy." *Good Housekeeping* magazine trumpeted the peanut's new status in an article titled "Social Rise of the Peanut." The peanut had finally been accepted by genteel society. Three months later, Etta Morse Hudders promulgated the rise of the peanut in an article in *Table Talk*. She outlined only a "few of the culinary possibilities of the peanut in the newly-found relation to the daily menu." She concluded that not only was the peanut "destined to be a staple addition to our food resources, but a commercial factor in our prosperity." By 1914, the peanut had become America's national nut. As one observer noted, "Go where you will—through cities, towns and villages, to circuses, baseball games, camp meetings, political assemblies, fair grounds, picnics—you will find peanut vendors hustling to supply the demand."[27]

4 DOCTORS AND VEGETARIANS

Peanut butter first surfaced as a health food on the American culinary scene a little over a century ago. Within a decade, it was produced by dozens of manufacturers and appeared on shelves of almost every grocery store in the United States. Recipes for making homemade peanut butter or employing it in other dishes were featured in magazines and cookbooks. Dainty tearooms and high-class restaurants proudly announced that their salads, sandwiches, and soups were made with peanut butter. Confectioners added peanut butter fillings to their candy. That this culinary revolution could have occurred in such a short period astounded observers at the time.

Beginning in 1918, observers tried to identify the individual who had invented this wonder product. In the ensuing years, dozens of stories circulated. According to the local historian Eleanor Rosakranse, for instance, peanut butter was invented by Rose Davis, who during the 1840s resided an Alligerville, New York. Rose Davis's son, Ross, traveled to Cuba, where he saw women grind peanuts and smear the paste on bread. Ross told his mother about the practice, and she employed the peanut paste for making sandwiches. Another peanut butter story was told by the manufacturer G. W. Nash, who claimed that the first peanut butter "was made in a New York City hospital by a physician and given to patients having digestive troubles. This was in 1870, and the butter was made by grinding the nuts in a mortar with a pestle." Others claim that an unknown medical professional in Saint Louis invented peanut butter in 1890. This unnamed physician reportedly gave the recipe to George A. Bayles, who, it was claimed, was the first to manufacture peanut butter. Still others proclaimed that Joseph Lambert of Battle Creek, Michigan, was peanut butter's originator and that it was he who was the father of the peanut butter industry.[1]

JOHN HARVEY KELLOGG

The one person who claimed to have invented peanut butter himself was Dr. John Harvey Kellogg.[2] One of sixteen children, Kellogg was born in 1852 in Tyrone, Michigan. When he was four years old, his family moved to Battle Creek, where his father was one of the founders of the Western Reform Institute, a Seventh-Day Adventist health clinic specializing in hydrotherapy ("the water cure") and vegetarianism. The Seventh-Day Adventists were the largest American religious denomination to endorse vegetarianism, but they did not require it.

Advocates for vegetarianism had been present in America before the Revolution. Two early nineteenth-century vegetarians were Sylvester Graham, who especially recommended the consumption of unsifted whole wheat flour and bread products made from it, and Dr. William Alcott, father of Louisa May Alcott, who argued for vegetarianism on medical grounds.[3] Graham and Alcott formed the first vegetarian society in America in 1850. Their foundation established a health food tradition that reverberates in American vegetarian circles today.

As a teenager, John Harvey Kellogg read a book that claimed that the natural diet for humans was fruits, nuts, grains, tender shoots, and succulent roots. Kellogg was also impressed with the writings of Sylvester Graham. At the age of twenty he enrolled at Bellevue Hospital College in New York to study medicine. While there, he wrote articles for the *Health Reformer*, the publication of the Western Reform Institute. The institute was headed for financial collapse when its board asked Kellogg to take over its administration in 1876. At the time, the institute had no trained staff and only one treatment room: male and female patients had to be treated on alternate days. With vigor, Kellogg assumed the institute's leadership. He subsequently changed the enterprise's name to the Sanitarium and renamed its publication *Good Health*.[4]

In addition to his strong support of vegetarianism, Kellogg was a strong believer in the importance of thorough mastication of food. He had interviewed and written an article about Horace Fletcher, the major advocate of the science of chewing. Kellogg referred to the process of mastication as *Fletcherism*, a term that survives to this day. Needless to say, patients with sore teeth, some missing teeth, or no teeth had difficulty chewing hard substances such as zwieback, then a common food in hospitals and a food advocated by Kellogg. To make it easier for patients to chew hard substances, Kellogg ground it into small pieces or granules. He named the resulting product *Granola*. He subsequently experimented with rolling food. Among the early successes were wheat and maize kernels flattened between rollers and then baked in the oven. The resulting flakes were a culinary success at the Sanatarium and Kellogg decided to mass produce his new product. Machinery was invented and large ovens were constructed to manufacture breakfast cereals on a commercial basis. To develop this further, Kellogg formed the Toasted Corn Flake Company. After it was launched, he sold out his interest to his brother Will Kellogg. The company was such a success that imitators soon sprang up and churned out hundreds of similar products. Kellogg's creation had launched the cold cereal industry.[5]

Not one to rest on his success, John Harvey Kellogg also flattened other seeds, including peanuts. This resulted in two products: one was a "fine and comparatively dry and nearly white nutmeal," while the other was "moist, pasty, adhesive, and brown, which for distinction is termed 'butter' or 'paste.'" As Kellogg used the term *butter* in his patent application for the substance, later writers concluded that he had invented peanut butter. In fact, the two resulting products have no identifiable relationship with peanut butter, which was made from ground, whole peanuts. Neither did Kellogg patent the process for making peanut butter, and he proudly proclaimed in 1899 that he intentionally had not done so. He thought about patenting peanut butter but "did not think it was a good thing to do." Instead, he "thought that it was a thing that the world ought to have; let everybody that wants it have it, and make the best use of it."[6]

When Kellogg got around to writing about peanut butter, he announced that it should be manufactured from raw—not roasted—peanuts. He removed their skins and placed the peanuts and an equal quantity of water in a covered dish, which was heated in the oven for several hours until the water evaporated. He then rubbed the cooked peanuts through a colander and added a little salt. Kellogg claimed that this was "the most delicious nut butter you ever tasted in your life," and more important to him, it was "perfectly digestible."[7]

Kellogg was an excellent promoter. He lectured to hundreds of thousands of Americans throughout the nation in over five thousand public presentations. In many of them he extolled the virtues of peanut butter. The most prophetic presentation was at Tuskegee Institute in Alabama, where he met George Washington Carver and influenced the course of peanut history, a topic covered in chapter 8.[8] In addition, America's elite visited the Battle Creek sanitarium and spread Kellogg's wisdom across the United States and around the world. As he had done with cold cereal, Kellogg energetically promoted peanut butter. He created the Sanitas Nut Food Company and again placed Will Kellogg in charge. The company sold "Nut Butters" by 1897.[9] While nut butters could be made from any nuts, peanuts were the least expensive, and nut butters became exclusively made with peanuts. Due in large part to the efforts of the Kellogg brothers, peanut butter quickly became an American fad food. Its culinary use was limitless: it was employed as a substitute for cream and regular butter; it was used in soups, cereals, sandwiches, and drinks; and it was served as a dressing on vegetables.[10] And this was only the beginning.

The first located advertisement specifically for peanut butter was published by the Vegetarian Supply Company in Providence, Rhode Island. Its promotional piece, *I've Come Out of My Burrow to Borrow,* was die-cut in the shape of a peanut; its message was in verse:

In the butter I shall bring you
There is nothing, I can tell
(Save the salt) that was not taken
from a little peanut shell.[11]

Vegetarians adopted peanut butter almost immediately, and recipes for making and using it appeared in almost all vegetarian cookbooks published from 1899. E. G. Fulton's *Vegetarian Cook Book: Substitutes for Flesh Foods,* for instance, featured three recipes for peanut butter and one for peanut meal. In 1904, the vegetarian Ella E. Kellogg published a revision of her *Science in the Kitchen* with extensive recipes for nut butters.[12]

Nut butters were employed to make many dishes, but particularly mock foods. The first located recipe was for "Chicken Legs," published by Ella Kellogg's protégé Almeda Lambert in her *Guide for Nut Cookery,* a cookbook published in 1899 by her husband, Joseph Lambert. The faux chicken legs were shaped from a mixture of pecan meal, nut butter, hickory cream, zwieola (a kind of zwieback meal), gluten, and water. Lambert also offered recipes for mock turkey and mock trout employing peanuts. Many vegetarians pointed out that peanut butter was ideally suited for making mock meats or meat substitutes. Recipes utilizing peanut butter were published for mock veal cutlets, tenderloin steak, oysters, and meat loaf.[13] The intent behind mock foods was manifold. In part, a mock preparation was intended as a surprise: one food appearing as if it were another. Also, the availability of peanuts throughout the year as substitutes for scarce or expensive ingredients was an influencing factor. However, the major attraction was for vegetarians who wanted to prepare and consume foods that resembled meat dishes but did not contain meat.

Since peanut butter started out as a vegetarian health food, many vegetarians extolled its virtues and introduced others to it. In January 1903, a writer in *Table Talk* magazine reported that she had been introduced to peanut butter by vegetarian friends. Peanut butter "has taken favorably with the public in general, and first-class grocers now sell it in bulk for about twenty cents a pound or put up in glass jars at a slightly advanced price."[14]

The first major application of peanut butter among nonvegetarians was to make sandwiches. In antebellum America, sandwiches filled with thin slices of beef, ham, boned fish, or tongue were popular. The bread was spread with mustard and ketchup, and sandwiches were served for tea, supper, picnics, or the convenience of travelers. After the Civil War, an innovative cookbook author listed cheese, cold boiled eggs, stewed fruit, jelly, and preserves as sandwich fillings.[15] However, the sandwich did not become an important mode of eating food until the last decades of the nineteenth century, precisely the time when ground peanuts became popular.

Kellogg himself made no recommendation that peanut butter be spread on bread, but it was his use of the word "butter" in "nut butter" that led to this now classic combination. Dairy butter had been spread on bread at least since the Middle Ages. As "peanut butter" could just as easily be spread on bread, it was a logical application. Peanut butter sandwich recipes burst onto the culinary scene in 1896. In May, an article in *Good Housekeeping* magazine, written by Anna Churchill Carey, urged homemakers to use a meat grinder to make peanut butter and spread the result on bread. In June, the culinary magazine *Table Talk* published a peanut butter sandwich recipe, recommending adding mayonnaise to the peanut butter. In the same year, peanut butter sandwich recipes appeared for the first time in cookbooks. Mary Virginia Terhune, writing under the pseudonym Marion Harlan, and her daughter Christine Terhune Herrick spiced peanut butter with cayenne pepper and paprika. The Women's Guild of Saint Mark's Church of Seattle recommended adding Worcestershire sauce to the peanut butter. The author of that recipe, Mrs. Nathaniel Waldo Emerson of Boston, believed that these peanut butter sandwiches were good appetizers and were "nice to serve at '5 o'clock tea.'" The following year, a recipe in the *Philadelphia Press* combined peanut butter with cream cheese. Before the end of the nineteenth century, recipes appeared in cookbooks all over the nation, including one catering to German Americans.[16]

The first located reference to the now immortal peanut butter and jelly sandwich was published by Julia Davis Chandler in 1901. This immediately became a hit with America's youth, who loved the double-sweet combination, and it has remained a favorite ever since. But diverse recipes for peanut butter sandwiches proliferated throughout the twentieth century. During the early 1900s peanut butter was considered a delicacy and as such it was served at upscale affairs and in New York's finest tearooms. Ye Olde English Coffee House made a "Peanut Butter and Pimento Sandwich." The Cosey Tea Shop sold a "Peanut Butter and Nasturtium Sandwich." The Thistle featured a "Peanut Butter and Cheese Sandwich." The Vanity Fair Tea-Room served its peanut butter with watercress. A shop called At the Sign of the Green Tea Pot prepared peanut butter and celery sandwiches. The Dainty Maid Tea-Room created club sandwiches with layers of meat, lettuce, and peanut butter. The Colonia Tea-Room served peanut butter on toast triangles and soda crackers.[17] That peanut butter could be combined with so many diverse products demonstrated that it was a relatively neutral platform providing a nutty taste and a sticky texture that bound together various ingredients.

Peanut butter sandwiches moved down the class structure as the price of peanut butter declined due to the commercialization of the industry. Peanut butter's use also moved down the age structure of the nation as manufacturers added sugar to the peanut butter, which appealed to children. The relationship between children and peanut butter was cemented in the late 1920s, when Gustav Papendick invented a process for slicing and wrapping bread. Sliced bread meant that children could make sandwiches themselves without slicing the bread with a potentially dangerous knife. As a consequence of low cost, high nutrition, and ease of assembling, peanut butter sandwiches became one of the top children's meals during the Depression.

In addition to its use in sandwiches, peanut butter was also regularly recommended as an ingredient in other recipes. According to Almeda Lambert, peanut butter could be substituted for butter in many recipes. She preferred it for "making soups and puddings, in cooking grains, and in seasoning vegetables." She also highlighted peanut butter in recipes for meatless mock "Peanut Sausages" and mock "Turkey Legs." Sarah Tyson Rorer used peanut butter to make "Cream of Peanut Soup" and "Peanut Wafers." Others featured peanut butter in recipes for salad dressings, timbales, soups, fruit rolls, custard pie, rolls, hash, and mayonnaise.[18]

In New York, the tearoom at the Happen Inn prepared a salad with apples and celery mixed with peanut butter and mayonnaise. The Garden Tea-Room blended peanut butter and oranges to make a salad. The Colonia Tea-Room presented a pineapple salad with peanut butter, while the Cosey Tea Shop served a banana and peanut butter salad. The Clover Tea Shop developed a peanut butter fudge recipe, and the Martha Washington Tea-Room sold peanut butter balls. The Dainty Maid Tea-Room offered pudding with peanut butter as an ingredient, while the Nova Club Tea-Room made peanut butter marguerites. Other tearooms made peanut butter biscuits, muffins, cookies, and breads.[19]

By the 1920s, peanut butter was a major culinary product in America. While Kellogg did not invent ground peanuts, he spread the good news about peanut butter's healthful qualities and was its greatest popularizer. Following the adoption of nut butters at the Sanitarium in Battle Creek, the popularity of peanut butter quickly spread among American promoters of health food and vegetarianism. Peanut butter also traveled across the Pacific Ocean to Australia and across the Atlantic Ocean to South Africa by 1899.[20] The missionary zeal of vegetarians helped to introduce peanut butter into the American culinary mainstream and was instrumental in establishing the peanut butter industry.

COMMERCE AND INDUSTRY

Although the practice of grinding peanuts to a paste did not originate in the United States, there is something quintessentially American about peanut butter. Today, 85 percent of all American homes have jars of peanut butter in their cupboards. And it's not just for sandwiches: peanut butter appears as an ingredient in hundreds of recipes in modern American cookbooks. The earliest published recipes called for cooks to roast and hand-grind the peanuts. Although homemade meat grinders had been constructed since at least the 1840s and commercial grinders had been sold since the 1850s, they were not common in American households until the eve of the twentieth century.[21] This meant that if a homemaker was interested in producing peanut butter, only a few nuts could be ground at one time in a mortar and pestle or with a rolling pin on a flat surface. As this was a slow and tedious process, it was unlikely that peanut butter would ever have become a major culinary product. It was at this point that technological innovation intervened and converted a health food fad into an industry.

The earliest commercial peanut butter was ground in meat grinders, which did not produce a smooth butter. Only about one hundred pounds of peanut butter could be hand ground in an hour. Joseph Lambert was an employee at Kellogg's sanitarium when peanut butter was first made: reportedly, he was the first to make it, in 1894. Lambert experimented with the design of the meat grinder to render it more suitable for making peanut butter. Lambert left the sanitarium and launched a business selling nut products in 1896. He invented small appliances and acquired the rights to others, which were intended to simplify making nuts in the home. These were a peanut roaster with a hand crank to be operated on a stove top; a small blancher; and a hand grinder for making nut butter.[22]

Lambert mailed offers to households throughout the United States. Some recipients purchased these machines and developed small businesses selling peanut products. As peanut butter became more popular, these machines proved inadequate, so Lambert developed larger machines in 1898. Lambert also published leaflets and booklets extolling the high food value of nuts and peanut butter. It was during the following year that Lambert published the *Guide for Nut Cookery*, written by his wife, as a means of educating the public about the healthfulness of nuts—and advertising his company, Joseph Lambert and Company of Battle Creek, Michigan, "maker of Nut Grinders, Blanchers and Peanut Roasters." It sold "all kinds of nuts, shelled and unshelled" and had "a fine variety of 'Pure and Wholesome NUT FOODS.'"[23]

Lambert perfected the machinery for manufacturing peanut butter and organized a new enterprise, the Lambert Food Company, in 1901, with headquarters in Marshall, Michigan. Although the company continued to sell nut butters, it increasingly focused on making machinery. In 1908, the company changed its name to the Lambert Machine Company, discontinued peanut butter production, and concentrated on making equipment.[24]

As Lambert's efforts proved successful, others entered the market. Dr. Ambrose W. Straub also had experimented with making peanut butter and he patented the second peanut butter mill in 1903. He established the A. W. Straub Company to manufacture peanut butter grinding machinery in Philadelphia and Chicago. Using one of Straub's grinders, C. H. Sumner, a concessionaire at the 1904 Louisiana Purchase Exposition, sold peanut butter as a health food. He grossed a total of $705 and generated a slim profit of $200. Still, Sumner introduced thousands of fair-goers to this new product.[25]

THE EARLY YEARS

During the early years peanut butter was manufactured in a small quantities by individuals and sold from house to house; then small factories sprang up and peanut butter became a familiar article on grocers' shelves. The first recorded peanut butter trademark was granted to the Atlantic Peanut Refinery in Philadelphia in December 1898. As Kellogg and the Sanitas Food Company used the term "nut butter," the Atlantic Peanut Refinery was the first company to place the name "peanut butter" on its labels. The term was quickly adopted by other commercial manufacturers. Shortly thereafter, Peanolia Peanut-Butter made its debut, a product of the Peanolia Food Company of New Haven, Connecticut. An analysis of these two peanut butters reported that they consisted only of ground peanuts with some salt added. They were "rich in protein or 'flesh-forming' material, and in fat."[26]

By 1899, an estimated two million pounds of peanut butter was manufactured in the United States. The following year, ten peanut-butter manufacturers dotted the culinary landscape. In addition to the Sanitas Food Company, the main manufacturers were the Purity Nut Fruit Company, Van Pragg and Company, and the Fulton Mills Company in New York, and the Battle Creek Company, Battle Creek, Michigan. Peanut butter was promoted as a "hygienic and nourishing compound" with "more nutriment than veal, beef, flour, milk, and many other articles of daily consumption." In an interview with New York's *Journal of Commerce,* an agent for a peanut butter maker reported in 1900 that peanut butter was "rapidly coming to the front as an article of common use." The largest producers were located in the South and West. As demand steadily increased, some manufacturers used inferior peanuts and cheap ingredients, which rapidly turned rancid. Grocers who bought this inferior product threw it out or sold it for use as wagon grease. They became leery of selling peanut butter, but observers noted that there was "a good demand for a first-class article, and the withdrawal of the cheap product from the market has stimulated sales to a great extent."[27]

In March 1903, *Table Talk* writer Etta Morse Hudders proclaimed peanut butter to be both digestible and highly nutritious. She had visited a commercial peanut butter plant and was the first to describe its workings. Although peanut butter was sold under several brand names, the method of preparation was the same. She recommended that the consumer add cold water when removing the peanut butter from the can and rubbing it smooth with a spoon until the mixture was the consistency of very thick cream. She cautioned that "only as much as can be eaten should be prepared at a time and just before it is needed."[28]

As the total cost for equipment needed for making peanut butter commercially was about a thousand dollars, almost anyone could become a manufacturer. A good example of an early peanut butter manufacturer was A. A. Forester, who made a modest living in 1899 by peddling butter and eggs from a wagon to the citizens of Natick, Massachusetts. Vegetarian friends introduced him to homemade peanut butter and Forester added peanut butter to his list of products. At the time, his customers liked peanuts but snubbed peanut butter. Forester handed out free samples of his fresh peanut butter and sales picked up. By 1912, he incorporated his business and began manufacturing "Forester's Peanut Butter." He started selling to surrounding cities, and his horse and wagon gave way to a truck. His business continued to thrive, and Forester became a major distributor of peanut butter in New England. Another pioneer was F. M. Hoyt of Amesbury, Massachusetts, who purchased his first bag of peanuts and ground them into peanut butter in a hand mill in 1902. During a visit to the World's Fair in Buffalo, he decided to name his brand "Buffalo." His first year's sales amounted to a thousand dollars. He then moved into the wholesale business and branched out into salted peanuts. By 1923, his peanut butter was sold throughout the United States, Canada, and eight other foreign countries.[29]

Other early peanut butter manufacturers included C. M. Taylor and Company in Philadelphia, which began making Old Dominion Peanut Butter in 1902, and George A. Bayles, who manufactured peanut butter in Saint Louis at about the same time. Beech-Nut Packing Company of Canajoharie, New York, started making the product by 1905.[30]

By 1908, one observer reported, "Peanut butter daily grows more popular as the consumer learns of its delicious flavor and its nourishing quality." By 1911, a single manufacturer used over 130 railroad cars filled with shelled peanuts to produce six million small jars of peanut butter. Other peanut butter manufacturers also used large quantities of peanuts, and the total consumption amounted to approximately one thousand carloads of shelled goods, or one million bushels. A year later, several large factories and a large number of smaller ones were solely "devoted to the manufacture of this product with which to supply the rapidly increasing demand." The H. J. Heinz Company of Pittsburgh began manufacturing peanut butter by 1913. The Bosman and Lohman Company of Norfolk, Virginia, entered the market the next year. By this date, there were twenty-one brands of peanut butter available in Kansas alone.[31]

By 1916, three manufacturers produced six million pounds of peanut butter from four million bushels of peanuts.[32] Three years later, a single manufacturer produced six million pounds, and dozens of other large factories and hundreds of smaller ones churned out large quantities of peanut butter. Peanut butter had become "the most important peanut product manufactured in the United States. The peanuts used in making the butter in 1919 probably totaled six or eight million bushels, being at least five times the quantity used for this purpose in 1907." In 1929, one observer wrote that there was hardly a city that did not have one or more peanut butter factories, and that its consumption during the past five or six years equaled that of all preceding years combined. In addition, thousands of grocery stores installed peanut grinders and churned out fresh peanut butter daily.[33]

BEECH-NUT AND HEINZ PEANUT BUTTER

The two most important early peanut butter manufacturers were the Beech-Nut Packing Company and the H. J. Heinz Company. Beech-Nut was founded through the efforts of Ephraim Lipe, a farmer near Canajoharie, New York, famous for his delicious smoked hams. His son Raymond and a friend, John D. Zieley, decided to form a company to sell Lipe's ham to a wider market. John's father was willing to stake them provided that Bartlett Arkell, the son of a local manufacturer, became president. They assented, and in 1891, the Imperial Packing Company was launched. The Lipes and the Zieleys left the company, and Arkell incorporated it in 1899 under the name Beech-Nut Packing Company. Under Arkell's direction, the company expanded its line of products. Peanut butter was first retailed in 1905. In making peanut butter, only hand-sorted No. 1 Virginia and No. 1 Spanish peanuts were used. When peanuts were ground and lost their identity, splits, seconds, or inferior grades could have been used or mixed with the best and most consumers would be none the wiser. Still, Beech-Nut's makers believed that "there would be a perceptible difference in the quality and the taste of the product."[34]

An editor of the *American Grocer* was given a tour of the Beech-Nut plant in Canajoharie. According to the editor, extreme care was taken to produce the best peanut butter possible. The shelled nuts were roasted under the watchful eye of skilled operators to ensure that the proper heat was applied and the nuts were roasted "just long enough to develop a rich, delicious flavor." The roasted nuts were then set on racks where forced air cooled them, "thus avoiding altogether the chance of their having a burned flavor." When cool, the nuts were taken to the blancher. It scraped off the outer brown skins and removed the hearts, "which, if left in, would have the tendency to produce a strong and bitter flavor." The nuts were then blended to obtain the desired flavor. After blending, the nuts were ground and combined with salt. Beech-Nut's machines produced "a very soft butter, resembling creamery butter in its consistency." The peanut butter was then packed in three sizes of vacuum jars, small, medium, and large. According to the editor, Beech-Nut's vacuum jar was "the most practical jar and the best jar for peanut butter on the market." Beech-Nut Peanut Butter neither separated nor became rancid in the jar.[35]

By 1912, Beech-Nut believed it had a major product that should be advertised. As the company considered its peanut butter a top-of-the-line delicacy, its first advertisement was a letter to upperclass New York residents announcing that Beech-Nut had express-shipped a "dainty glass" of Beech-Nut Peanut Butter to a local distributor for each of them. All the recipient had to do was return an enclosed prestamped card, permitting the distributor to send the sample jar to his home.[36]

Two years later, Beech-Nut published its first peanut butter cookbooklet. Many recipes in this booklet had been contributed by the owners of New York tearooms and by clever hostesses in all parts of the country, which suggests that Beech-Nut peanut butter was considered an upscale item. Beech-Nut published additional recipe booklets featuring peanuts and peanut butter during the following years. These advertising schemes worked. By 1915, Beech-Nut was the largest peanut butter manufacturer in the country.[37]

Another early peanut butter manufacturer was the H. J. Heinz Company, which had started in Sharpsburg, Pennsylvania. Its first factory was a six-by-eight-foot room surrounded by a three-quarter-acre garden patch. The workforce consisted of two women. E. J. Noble joined the firm in 1872, and the name was changed to the Heinz, Noble Company.[38] Due in part to its rapid expansion and a major national downturn in business, that company went into bankruptcy in December 1875. Two months later, the F. and J. Heinz Company emerged from the ashes with Henry Heinz as the leader. The business thrived and by 1888, Heinz had paid off his debts and renamed the company the H. J. Heinz Company. It rapidly expanded operations and distribution facilities throughout the United States and other countries.

Heinz first manufactured peanut butter during the early 1900s. In 1913, an advertisement for Heinz's peanut butter proclaimed "Do You Know that Heinz Peanut Butter Is Good for Children? Children like it because it tastes so good. And wise Parents *encourage* them to eat it. Food Scientists will tell you that Heinz Peanut Butter peculiarly supplies the solid nutriment that makes thin legs grow plump—that builds firm flesh—gives rosy color. Use it, not as an occasional treat, but as an every day diet. Everyone likes it. Selected fresh peanuts ground and prepared with care." In 1922, a visitor to the Heinz Peanut Butter factory proclaimed that the aroma of the roasted nuts took "visitors back to childhood visits to circuses, ball games and picnics." Conveyor belts carried the nuts "down between two rows of sharp-eyed girls who remove any pieces of hulls or husk, blackened or imperfect nuts." The only additive that Heinz used was salt. In 1925, another advertisement divulged that Heinz Peanut Butter was "particularly high in food value." It was "a smooth, moist mixture of choice roasted ground peanuts, of varieties blended to secure a distinctive and uniform quality." Heinz removed "the bitter little heart-shaped point from every peanut to improve the flavor!"[39]

Both Heinz and Beech-Nut peanut butters were premium products. Many competitors turned to inferior raw materials. Others failed to keep their machinery clean and frequently added mineral oil to cover up defects or lower the cost. These lower-cost goods flooded the market and gave peanut butter manufacturers a bad name. At the time, there were no standards on peanut butter contents and no uniform standard for packaging. In June 1922, the major producers banded together and created the National Peanut Butter Manufacturers Association to help set standards and improve the quality of peanut butter in America.[40]

SKIPPY AND PETER PAN

Early peanut butters had several problems. The first was that peanut oil has a melting point below room temperature. Gravity separated the oil, which then oxidized and turned rancid. Likewise, salt added to the peanut butter separated and crystallized. Grocers received peanut butter in tubs or pails and were advised to use a wooden paddle to stir it frequently. Another problem was that peanut butter stuck to the roof of the consumer's mouth. This became a more serious problem as the peanut butter was more finely ground.[41]

During the early years of the twentieth century, William Norman, an English chemist, invented a method of saturating unsaturated and polyunsaturated fatty acids, thus preventing them from turning rancid. In 1922, Joseph L. Rosefield of the Rosefield Packing Company of Alameda, California, applied these principles to peanut butter. He developed a process to prevent oil separation and spoilage in peanut butter. He removed 18 percent of the liquid oil and replaced it with an equal amount of hydrogenated oil, which was solid at room temperature. The result was a semisolid peanut butter; no oil rose to the surface. The peanut butter was thick and creamy and did not stick to the roof of the mouth as much as previous products. Hydrogenated oil permitted a finer grinding of peanuts, which prevented the salt from separating from the peanut butter. Rosefield continued his experiments and found several different ways of making peanut butter. He patented a process for a "Malted Peanut Butter," in which the peanut was allowed to germinate and then roasted, blanched, and ground into peanut butter. Rosefield asserted that this yielded a product with a higher content of vitamins and a richer, nutty flavor.[42]

Rosefield selected the name "Skippy" for his new peanut butter. Most likely, the name was derived from a children's comic strip also called "Skippy," launched by Percy L. Crosby in 1923. The use of the name "Skippy" generated several lawsuits, which were eventually settled out of court. Undeterred, Rosefield introduced creamy and chunky-style peanut butter in 1932. Three years later, the company inaugurated its first wide-mouth peanut-butter jar, which became the industry standard.[43]

Yet another peanut butter company was launched by Henry Clay Derby, who was born in Canton, Massachusetts. He was apprenticed to a butcher who operated a tripe and pigs' feet shop. Derby took over the business, which became known as the Boston Fresh Tripe Company. In 1888, he opened a branch in Chicago called the E. K. Pond Packing Company and put his cousin, E. K. Pond, in charge of it. In 1904, he sold the business to Swift and Company. The E. K. Pond Company manufactured peanut butter beginning in 1920, but its sales were limited. The lackluster sales encouraged the company to change the name to Peter Pan after the popular fantasy character popularized in the 1903 James M. Barrie play. *Peter Pan* had been a children's classic ever since and in the 1920s had been made into a silent movie. As soon as the E. K. Pond Company adopted the name, sales took off. According to the company, its peanut butter was "smooth, does not stick to the roof of the mouth or have that puckery taste in some brands made out of cheap material; requires no mixing; bright, snappy, clean and appetizing appearance, free of oil on top." Like Beech-Nut and Heinz, Pond issued a cookbooklet chock full of recipes using Peter Pan Peanut Butter. In addition to sandwiches, there were recipes for cream soup, ham scallop, brown betty, dates, dressing for poultry or roast pork, muffins, cakes, hot ham dainties, marguerites, fudge, popcorn balls, caramel nut pie, sauces, dressings, salads, and oyster stew.[44]

Peter Pan was separated from the other Derby products in 1940, and a major marketing campaign was inaugurated. It was advertised nationally in the mid-1940s. The radio program *Sky King* was sponsored by Peter Pan. The *Sky King* radio serial began on October 28, 1946, and ran daily in fifteen-minute installments. In 1947, it ran on Tuesdays and Thursdays, each show lasting thirty minutes. When the program moved to television in September 1951, Peter Pan continued to sponsor it until October 1952. Peter Pan was initially packaged in a tin can similar to a coffee can with a turnkey and re-sealable lid. A metal shortage during World War II forced the company to switch to glass jars. The first was a tumbler type with a friction cap. It was replaced in 1955 by the jar with a screw-off cap still used today.[45]

IN SUCH A SHORT TIME

Peanut butter was born at the end of the nineteenth century as a health and vegetarian food, but by the 1920s it was a major national product. Its success story is in part embedded within the peanut's broader history. In less than twenty-five years, peanut butter evolved from a hand-ground delicacy to a mass-produced commercial commodity sold in almost every grocery store in America. It was employed in virtually every type of food from soups, salads, sauces, and main courses to desserts and snacks of every description.

Peanut butter was versatile, inexpensive, available, and ready to use. Its makers appealed to children, who could make their own sandwiches and other peanut butter treats. Peanut butter was regularly touted as a healthy food by the medical establishment, and the peanut butter industry amplified these reports in their advertisements and promotional cookbooklets. Few other products in American culinary history have achieved such influence in so many ways in such a short period of time.

The first known illustration of an African American peanut vendor, Savannah, Georgia. From "Pea-Nuts," *Harper's Weekly* 14 (July 16, 1870): 449. Photo courtesy of Barbara Kuck, Curator, Culinary Archives and Museum, Johnson and Wales University, Providence, Rhode Island.

— A Centennial Pea Nut Merchant —

"A Centennial Pea Nut Merchant," illustration of a peanut vendor in 1876 at Philadelphia's Centennial Exposition. Centennial Scrapbook, Print and Picture Collection, Free Library of Philadelphia. Photo by Will Brown.

The Origin of Mr. Peanut?
This peanut figure with monocle, top hat, and cane looks
suspiciously like Mr. Peanut
but predates the Planters
figure by fourteen years.
From "The Social Rise of the
Peanut," *Good Housekeeping*,
December 1902, 468. Photo,
author's collection.

Social Rise of the Peanut

"A persistent effort long has been made to
stamp the peanut with the mark of vulgarity,
but this nefarious
scheme has been a total
failure," says the *Dis-
patch,* of Richmond, Va.
"Never was the peanut
so popular as it is to-
day. It is crowding its
haughty kinsman, the
salted almond, off the
festal board, and it is
rapidly receiving wide
recognition as a deli-
cacy. Time was when
goobers were synonyms
of circus rowdyism, gal-
lery gods' obstreperousness, and festive occasions of the proletariat. Now the peanut—
especially the Virginia product—travels on its
merits and comes in contact with the best
people of our land."

A peanut poem directed at
young children with a peanut
figure caricature. From Elizabeth Gordon, *Mother Earth's
Children: The Frolics of Fruits
and Vegetables* (Chicago: P. F.
Volland, 1913), 74. Photo, author's collection.

MOTHER EARTH'S CHILDREN

SAID Mrs. Peanut, in a flutter,
  "I quite forgot to salt the butter;"
The little Peanut children said:
  "Why then, Mama, we'll salt the bread."

In the 1920s, most peanut butter was sold in tin pails. From "Black Diamond Trade Mark. Peanut and Peanut Butter Containers" (Wilkes-Barre, Pa.: Wilkes-Barre Can Co., n.d.). Photo, author's collection.

Peanut planting, circa 1900. Photo courtesy of the Peanut Advisory Board, Atlanta, Georgia.

Peanut harvesting, circa 1900. Photo courtesy of the Peanut Advisory Board, Atlanta, Georgia.

Peanut picking, circa 1900. Photo courtesy of the Peanut Advisory Board, Atlanta, Georgia.

George Washington Carver surrounded by peanut products, circa 1925. Photo courtesy of Tuskegee University Archives, Tuskegee, Alabama; photo copied by Hawkins Studio, Tuskegee, Alabama.

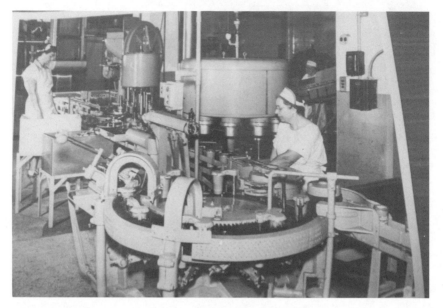

The peanut butter assembly line at the Beech-Nut Packing Company, circa 1930. Photo courtesy of James Crawford, Curator, Canajoharie Library and Art Gallery, Canajoharie, New York.

Filling peanut butter bottles at the Beech-Nut Packing Company, circa 1930. Photo courtesy of James Crawford, Curator, Canajoharie Library and Art Gallery, Canajoharie, New York.

The sheet music for "The Peanut Vendor," a song that swept the Americas and Europe in the 1930s and has become a golden oldie. From Don Azpiazu, *The Peanut Vendor (El Manisero)* (New York: Edward B. Marks, 1930). Photo, author's collection.

Pre-Columbian pot from a grave of the Moche (200–800 C.E.) of northern Peru. Coastal cultivation of the peanut began about 1500–1000 B.C.E. Photo, catalog #32249, courtesy of the Department of Anthropology, Smithsonian Institution, Washington, D.C.

Peanuts were stacked for drying, which usually took a week or two depending upon the weather. Artemas Ward, *The Encyclopedia of Food* (New York: Baker and Taylor, 1929), 383. Photo courtesy of Barbara Kuck, Curator, Culinary Archives and Museum, Johnson and Wales University, Providence, Rhode Island.

After World War II, peanut oil producers such as Planters sought to attract new purchasers. In 1948 Planters produced this cookbook in Hebrew to attract Jewish customers. Photo, author's collection.

Mr. Peanut was trade-marked in 1917 and Planters has regularly employed the image ever since. This advertisement published during the 1920s was intended to attract children. Photo, author's collection.

Early peanut butter advertising focused on adults. This 1920s Beech-Nut brand advertisement targets children, who remain the largest consumers of peanut butter today. Photo, author's collection.

Beech-Nut was one of the largest peanut butter producers during the first half of the twentieth century. In 1912 it commenced a major promotional campaign that included a cookbooklet using its peanut butter in every recipe. This third edition was published in 1920. Photo, author's collection.

Peanuts were wholesaled in sacks by hundreds of different processing companies. The Franklin Peanut Company in Franklin, Virginia, sold four grades and types of peanuts. The most expensive were the "Extra Large Virginia Shelled Peanuts"; its second grade was the "Extra Large Jumbo Whale Brand Hand Picked Peanuts"); and its lowest grade was the "Extra Hand Picked Goat-Brand Peanuts." Photos, author's collection.

5   UNSHELLED AND SHELLED

Peanut vendors were active in New York City by the dawn of the nineteenth century. By the 1840s, they appeared at circuses and fairs. At first children were their main customers, but as these children grew up, they continued to buy peanuts. Perhaps the continuing attraction was the appetizing odor of peanuts and the associated recollections of the good times of childhood. At the time, few other foods could be so easily produced, transported, distributed, and prepared for sale. Street vendors cultivated sales in New York, Boston, Philadelphia, and other port cities. Then they began selling their wares at train stations, which served to spread the roasted peanut trade to other cities. After the Civil War, peanuts became America's favorite snack food.[1]

From the vendors' standpoint, peanuts were an obvious choice. Little experience or preparation was needed to sell them. Equipment could be purchased at low cost or even devised at home. Inexpensive unshelled peanuts could be purchased easily, and the fragrance of roasting peanuts attracted customers—so there was little need to advertise. Bags of peanuts sold for five or ten cents, depending on size, and the profit was close to 80 percent. With a good location, a vendor could recover the cost of the peanut roaster in a matter of weeks. From then on, sales generated solid profits. Many peanut vendors were immigrants, and Italian vendors were the first immigrants to sell peanuts on the streets of New York. After the Civil War, Italians dominated the retail peanut trade. Louis Onetto arrived from Italy in 1866, settling in Buffalo, New York. At the time, only nine other Italian families lived in the city. Onetto first opened an ice cream parlor, but in 1872 he became a jobber for peanuts, a trade he stuck with for the next sixty-six years.[2]

The Italians were challenged by other immigrant groups, particularly Greeks, such as John Courtsounis, who came to the United States in 1901. He sold roasted peanuts on the street outside Columbia University in New York. After selling peanuts for three years, he had saved enough money to send for his unmarried sister. After she arrived, he saved an additional seven hundred dollars for her dowry. Courtsounis then saved more money to bring his second sister, then his two brothers, whom he sent to night school. After that, Courtsounis bought a restaurant. He finally married in 1919 and then he began saving money in hopes of sending his children to Columbia University. In Washington, D.C., another Greek immigrant, Steve Vasilakops, began selling peanuts in 1905 in front of the White House, where tourists and presidents bought peanuts from him for thirty-eight years. When he died in 1943, his peanut wagon was given to the Smithsonian. In Chicago, the competition between the Italian and the Greek peanut vendors turned into ethnic rivalry in which blood flowed. By 1920 the Greek vendors had prevailed in this war. In Baltimore, Greek immigrants also gained control of peanut sales on the streets. During the 1920s, when many Americans were opposed to further immigration, a law was passed in Baltimore requiring peanut vendors to have applied for American citizenship.[3]

Peanut vendors were assisted by the invention of mobile peanut wagons. Charles Cretors purchased a peanut roaster from a manufacturer in Iowa. After examining it, he concluded that he could make a better one and he launched C. Cretors and Company in Chicago in 1885. Cretors's initial inventions focused on steam-powered roasters. His "No. 1 Roaster" was 22 inches wide, 30 inches long, 46 inches high, and weighed 175 pounds. The machine could roast peanuts, coffee beans, and chestnuts. A steam condenser warmed the peanuts in the storage compartment. Attracting passersby was a little mechanical, red-suited "Tosty Rosty" clown, who cranked a tumbler full of peanuts and appeared to be running the machine. Initially, sales of roasters were limited. Two years after its launch, C. Cretors and Company had turned out only thirty machines, but the company demonstrated steady growth.[4]

At the 1893 World's Columbian Exposition in Chicago, Cretors introduced two new models. One, later dubbed the "Earn More," was targeted at grocery store owners. It was compact—20 inches square and 65 inches high—an important factor for shopkeepers with limited floor space. Its large rear wheels enabled the owner to roll it outside during the day and inside at night or during inclement weather. It promised to be one of the most economical investments a storekeeper could make. The other new machine offered for sale by Cretors was the first enclosed horse-drawn wagon with both a peanut warmer and a popcorn popper.[5] It was a major hit at the Columbian Exposition. The clown perched atop the wagon cranked furiously. As the enticing aroma of warm peanuts and hot popcorn drifted down the Midway, the crowds grew larger, attracted as much by the novelty of the show put on by the steam engine and the little clown as by the promise of freshly prepared snacks.

One purchaser of the Cretors wagon was H. Hummels of Jersey City, New Jersey. According to an article in *Scientific American,* Hummels's vehicle was "light and strong, and weighing but 400 or 500 pounds, can be drawn readily by a boy or by a small pony to any picnic ground, fair, political rally, etc., and to many other places where a good business could be done for a day or two." The peanut roaster and a corn popper were run by steam power. Hummels bought raw peanuts at about five cents a pound, but after roasting, he sold them for two to three times that price. The wagon's advantage was that it was a completely self-contained unit: Hummels transported it wherever he thought he could find customers. If sales were slow in one location, he simply moved the wagon to a place with better prospects. While previous vendors had maintained stationary stands, the wagon created a new class of mobile vendors who traversed America's streets for almost a half-century, selling popcorn and peanuts. By 1916, street vendors were annually roasting twenty-six million pounds of peanuts.[6]

Some vendors had been extremely successful. George Grice, for instance, began roasting peanuts in 1871 in Atchison, Kansas. He was a humble man who quietly sold his peanuts on a stand mounted on a wheelbarrow. He established a reputation for selling quality products. His business thrived and he hired his brother to work with him. Rain or shine, Grice sold peanuts until he died in 1922, leaving an estate of $100,000.[7]

Many successful Americans started their careers in the peanut-roasting business. In 1874, at the age of fourteen, Charles Curtis sold peanuts at the train station in Topeka, Kansas. He earned enough money to pay his way through law school and was admitted to the bar in 1881. He was elected to the House of Representatives, where he served for twelve years. He was then elected to the Senate in 1907 and served with the exception of two years until 1929, when Herbert Hoover selected him as his vice-presidential running mate. Curtis served as vice president until 1933.[8]

To maintain high profits, many vendors dealt in cheap, inferior peanuts. Beginning in 1923, newspapers commented upon the poor quality of peanuts being sold to the public by vendors, specifically those at baseball stadiums. Peanuts had been associated with baseball almost from the beginning. This relationship had been immortalized by the lyricist Jack Norworth and the composer Albert von Tilzer in their 1908 song "Take Me Out to the Ball Game." However, the peanuts sold at baseball games were not freshly roasted and were frequently stale. Some attempts were made to correct this. The Brooklyn Dodgers, for instance, recognized the problem and announced that all peanuts sold at the ballpark would be roasted that same day. Vendors proudly announced, "Jumbo peanuts, roasted on premises daily, sold at Ebbets Field, 10 cents."[9] Unshelled roasted peanuts continued to be sold at baseball stadiums until the owners concluded that the cost of cleaning up the shells was far greater than the revenue generated by their sale.

As automobiles began to clog America's streets and roads, many cities passed laws licensing and restricting street vendors to prevent congestion. Likewise, peanut shells littered public places until "finally a revulsion came and the nuisance began to be restricted." The heyday of the unshelled peanut was soon over. By 1928, an observer noted that street peanut carts were only a novelty.[10]

When the heyday of the street vendor ended, vendors purchased their own fruit stands, grocery stores, or restaurants, or drifted into other lines of work. Some continued in peanuts but shifted to selling shelled, salted peanuts indoors. The sale of shelled salted peanuts dated to at least the 1860s, when children tended peanut roasters in front of almost every fruit or candy shop. When the peanuts were roasted, the young vendors shelled them and sprinkled salt on them. As the salt did not stay on the peanuts, they were less than popular. Around 1885, vendors observed that if peanuts were fried in oil, the salt would stick better. Salting peanuts soon became an art as temperature, time, and the oil used influenced the taste of the finished product. One early experimenter was John C. Wampler of Crawfordsville, Indiana, who called himself the "King of Confectioners." He sold his first order of salted peanuts to an Indianapolis druggist in 1885. Wampler was still selling salted peanuts thirty-five years later. Salted peanuts were sold in vending machines at the turn of the century. By 1903 the salted peanut was "fast displacing the almond, and when prepared at home is an inexpensive luxury."[11]

Some salted, shelled peanut vendors were extremely successful. R. L. Hatch saved up $5,000 and decided to enter the shelled and salted peanut business in 1904. He plunked down $2,500 for nine months' rent on a four-foot-wide shop at a busy intersection on Broadway in New York's Times

Square. Hatch started off with the assumption that he needed to develop a repeat trade by selling only the best quality goods. Because much of his trade was with tourists, he also realized that he ought to encourage mail orders for his products. He solicited orders from visiting tourists, and money orders, checks, and cash flowed in. By 1921, he owned four stores and counted four thousand accounts—some as far away as Cuba, the Philippines, South America, and Europe.[12]

PLANTERS

A few entrepreneurs converted their salted peanut sales into major enterprises. A successful vendor was one Amedeo Obici, who had been born in Oderzo, Italy, on July 15, 1877, the son of Pietro and Luigia Obici. At the age of eleven, Amedeo was sent by his parents to live with his uncle in Scranton, Pennsylvania. Obici traveled unaccompanied in steerage and ate in shifts with the other steerage passengers from tin plates and cups. He landed in New York on Saint Patrick's Day in 1889, but his uncle was unaware of Amedeo's landing date and did not meet the ship. Amedeo did not speak English, but someone read the tag around his neck, put him on a train, and instructed the conductor to tell Obici to get off at Scranton. A policeman found him when he exited the train and took him to an Italian grocer, who happened to know Obici's uncle. At the time, Scranton was a fairly small town with thirty thousand inhabitants. Obici attended school for three months, then was hired by a cigar factory. Friends offered him a job in the fruit-stand business at a salary of six dollars per month plus board. Later he worked in a bar owned by Andrew Lynch, who asked Obici to engage in "missionary" work among the Italians on behalf of political candidates during elections.[13]

Obici bought a peanut roaster for $4.50 and in 1896 went into business selling peanuts to shopkeepers from a horse-drawn cart in Wilkes-Barre, Pennsylvania. He mounted a whistle on the wagon to gain attention. Obici first specialized in roasted unshelled peanuts. When this business was flourishing, he turned his attention to shelled peanuts. After considerable experimentation, Obici developed a way of blanching the red skin from shelled Virginia peanuts without splitting the kernel. Then he moved into the cooking and salting process. Finally, Obici noted that the roasted peanuts he supplied to grocers went stale before they were sold to customers. He bought back the peanuts at a reduced price and often used them in peanut products, such as peanut bars. To support this endeavor, in 1902 Obici developed and trademarked a brand name, "The Specialist."[14]

While working in Scranton, Obici met another immigrant, Mario Peruzzi, who hailed from Treviso, Italy—fifteen miles from Obici's birthplace. The nineteen-year-old Peruzzi immigrated to America with his father in 1894. They settled in New York, then moved to Hazleton, Pennsylvania, where Mario's first job was as a janitor; later on, he moved to Scranton, where he ran the confectionery department of a wholesale grocer, the Wentz and Duffy Company. Obici met Peruzzi while selling peanuts, and the two became close friends.[15]

In the first years of the twentieth century, Obici opened a small peanut and fruit stand at 15 East Market Street in Wilkes-Barre. By 1906, he was ready for a new venture. In May he and Peruzzi formed the Planters Peanut Company. They chose the name "Planters" because they thought it sounded important. Obici and Peruzzi began their operation in a small two-story factory in Wilkes-Barre with a monthly rent of twenty-five dollars. With eight employees, they began packaging and marketing their blanched and salted Virginia peanuts. In eastern Pennsylvania shelled peanuts were still a novelty. Small, unshelled Spanish peanuts were sold in bulk at ten cents a pound; retailers kept nuts in glass jars and measured out the amount that each customer wanted into a paper envelope. Obici and Peruzzi roasted and salted the larger Virginia peanuts and sold them in two-ounce bags for five cents each. They constantly improved their products and packaging. One concern was keeping the peanuts fresh. At first, they packaged the peanuts in glassine paper, but switched to cellophane, then glass jars, and finally to vacuum-sealed tins.[16]

Business was slow for the Planters Peanut Company, but it increased as shelled, salted peanuts caught on. Obici and Peruzzi trademarked the name "Pennant" brand and incorporated the business two years later with a new name, Planters Nut and Chocolate Company, which was capitalized at $50,000, only a portion of which was cash. In a most unusual arrangement, they purchased the building for $39,000 with a mortgage of the same amount. They invested their initial capital in acquiring new equipment. Profits were slow in coming and Obici and Peruzzi were stretched thin financially. In 1909 losses amounted to $4,000 and the bank gave them a second mortgage on their factory, which had appreciated in value. Still, by 1911 they showed a profit of only $4,000. When they projected that their factory would soon need to expand, Obici and Peruzzi again approached the bank in Wilkes-Barre to help underwrite the proposed expansion, but the bank refused.[17]

Obici and Peruzzi searched for alternative locations to build a new facility. As one reason for the low profit was the cost of transporting the peanuts to Wilkes-Barre, the partners concluded that they needed to establish a factory closer to where the peanuts were grown. If they could shell the peanuts close to the fields, transportation expenses would be reduced. Moreover, shelled peanuts took up less space. Obici and Peruzzi settled on Suffolk, Virginia, in the heart of the peanut-growing district. This area produced the larger types of peanuts better adapted to the salting process. Suffolk was not far from the North Carolina border, and five railroad lines ran through the town—a great asset for distribution.[18]

With little cash, Obici approached bankers in Suffolk with a proposal for a loan to build a two-story factory for shelling and cleaning peanuts. Based on Obici's letters of reference, Suffolk bankers lent him the money. The small factory was opened in 1914. At the time, the total annual income of the company was $400,000. Later, Obici rented another factory on the other side of town. It was subsequently disassembled and moved next to the first factory. These operations simply supplied the Wilkes-Barre plant with raw peanuts. As business expanded, additional factories were constructed, but the production of roasted, salted peanuts in Suffolk did not begin until 1917.[19]

The Planters company continued to grow. To meet increased demand, the firm's employees designed and invented most of the labor-saving equipment used in its manufacturing processes. It acquired an eight-acre site in Suffolk and this later expanded to nineteen. When a problem with containers for the peanuts developed, Planters opened a box-making factory and a sawmill in Suffolk and then set up a tin-can factory, which produced thirteen thousand cans per day. Planters operated a kiln for jar making and printed its own bags. By 1922, the operation consisted of ten buildings that filled a city block and employed thirteen hundred people. It was an integrated industrial unit that cleaned, shelled, graded, roasted, and converted peanuts into saleable products. Planters established distribution centers in New York, Chicago, and Boston to ensure fast, direct deliveries and opened another manufacturing plant in San Francisco. While Planters closed the Wilkes-Barre factory, it maintained its headquarters in that city. As expansion became more rapid, the Planters management found it easier to purchase other peanut companies rather than build new facilities. In 1926 Planters purchased the John King Peanut Company and the following year acquired the Old Dominion Peanut Company. In 1929, Planters launched a chain of retail outlets through a subsidiary, the National Peanut Corporation.[20]

Mario Peruzzi married Obici's sister Elizabeth. Obici married Louise Musante in 1916. Louise, born in Genoa in 1864, moved with her father to the United States, settling in Pennsylvania in 1868. As an adult, she operated a small peanut stand in Wilkes-Barre, which was where Obici met and married her. After their marriage, the Obicis lived modestly in Suffolk, Virginia, for thirteen years until 1925, when Amedeo Obici bought a 260-acre farm on the Nanesmond River in Virginia. There they indulged their passion for flowers, flowering shrubs, and ornamental trees. Obici became a board member of William and Mary College, where he endowed a chair of Italian language. As naturalized American citizens, the couple made frequent trips to Italy. On one trip, Obici was honored by the king of Italy, who bestowed on him the Commendatore of the Crown.[21]

MR. PEANUT

One problem faced by all peanut processors was that peanuts spoiled when exposed to air. Obici had tried to sell his peanuts packaged in glassine bags, but they were difficult to fill and transportation expenses increased appreciably. The cost of a small glassine bag brought the price to ten cents, which the market would not bear. So Planters, like most other peanut shellers and cleaners, sold peanuts in large tins from which the shopkeepers scooped out the peanuts for the customer. When the Planters tin was empty, some unscrupulous retailers refilled it with less expensive peanuts, and customers assumed that they were buying Planters products, which imperiled the company's reputation for high quality. To prevent substitution, Obici devised an ingenious solution. Peanuts were sold to jobbers in ten-pound tin cans with ninety Pennant brand glassine bags packed in the top. Retailers were supposed to fill the bags with the Planters peanuts and sell them for a nickel. The only problem in this plan was that the public was unaware that Planters peanuts were to be sold only in these bags. Obici realized that he needed to communicate directly with the public. It was time to advertise.[22]

At the time, no other peanut product manufacturer had advertised nationwide. Obici had previously approached other peanut sellers and processors in an attempt to promote the importance of peanuts as a food, but he was told that national advertising was a waste of money. However, Obici had a gift for advertising and promotion. While in Wilkes-Barre, he had written one letter of his full name on small pieces of paper and placed one in each peanut package. Anyone who collected all the letters received a package of peanuts, and later a dollar watch. As Planters expanded, Obici depended on confectionery jobbers with the assistance of "missionary men," who worked directly with grocers and other retail outlets. The key was a loyal sales force that went out and sold Planters products to the jobbers. At the time, other peanut merchants had "order takers," who simply asked jobbers if they wanted to buy their product. With a national sales force in place, Planters issued its first advertising booklet in 1917, titled *Peanuts: A Little Journey through the Virginia Peanut Plantations and the Factories of the Planters Nut & Chocolate*

Co. But the booklet was nothing more than a dry, factual description of how the peanut was grown and cultivated in Virginia.[23]

Obici wanted something more effective, so in 1916 Planters conducted a contest to develop a trademark, offering a prize worth five dollars for the best-designed symbol. The winner was a fourteen-year-old boy named Anthony Gentile, who submitted a drawing of "a little peanut person." With this image as a starting point, Planters hired a Chicago art firm, which commissioned a commercial artist named Andrew Wallach to draw several different caricatures. Obici selected the peanut person with a top hat, monocle, cane, and the look of a raffish gentleman. At least, this was the story that Planters circulated. In fact, peanut figures had been published for years. Specifically, fourteen years before the purported invention of Mr. Peanut, "a little peanut person," complete with top hat, monocle, cane, and gloves, had illustrated an article in *Good Housekeeping* magazine, which may well have been seen by Obici. In the same year, Obici had trademarked a human figure with a top hat and cane flanked by two peanuts, which he used to market his "Specialist" brand.[24]

Whatever the truth behind Mr. Peanut's origin, it was a solid advertising gimmick aimed at the major market for peanuts—America's youth. Planters applied for a trademark on March 12, 1917. During that year, Mr. Peanut made his debut in New England newspapers and on advertising posters in the New York subway trains that went to Coney Island, the home of several amusement parks. In these advertisements, Mr. Peanut was the mouthpiece for the text, which explained the origin of the shelled peanut and highlighted the nut's nutritive value. The text included quotes from Dr. H. W. Wiley, the former chief chemist for the U.S. Department of Agriculture who had led the charge for the reform and regulation of the food industry. He encouraged the increased consumption of peanuts because they were a good alternative to meat. Peanuts were also abundant, readily secured, and inexpensive.[25] Planters built Wiley into the dialogue in one advertisement, which ran:

Mr. Peanut: "Doctor, are peanuts good for kids?"
Dr. H. W. Wiley: "The peanut is a very valuable food. It is highly nutritious."

Mr. Peanut then led the reader through the Virginia plantations where the peanuts grew and into the store, where he pointed out with his cane the glassine bags with their trademarked name and the glass counter jar. Other Planters advertisements promoted peanuts as the perfect food at picnics and baseball games, and as an ingredient in main dishes served for lunch and dinner. Planters spent eighty thousand dollars on this regional campaign.[26]

The Planters campaign in New England and New York succeeded "beyond expectations." Obici and Peruzzi quickly followed up with a national campaign. The first national Planters advertisement featuring Mr. Peanut appeared in the *Saturday Evening Post* in February 1918. These were so successful that Planters increased its advertising budget for each succeeding year, spending hundreds of thousands of dollars on ads in the best newspapers and magazines in the country. The company used other media as well: they published a *Mr. Peanut's Paint Book,* and a game, "Planters Peanut Party," which at one point was distributed at the rate of twenty-five thousand copies per month. The company's print promotions moved from commonplace advertising to novel schemes that drew in readers. Advertising paid off. Sales rose from $1 million in 1917 to $7 million five years later.[27]

Obici had commenced his advertising campaign just before the United States entered World War I; as the nation joined the war effort, the federal government launched a concerted attempt to encourage Americans to eat more peanuts and thus less wheat, since grain was needed by European allies and the American armed forces. In addition, the availability of sugar for civilian use dropped 50 percent because of the war, making it difficult for candy makers to operate at full capacity. Candy bars sold out almost as soon as they appeared on shelves at kiosks and grocery stores. Peanuts were the alternative, and peanut sales skyrocketed. Unfortunately, even with the vast increase in peanut cultivation during the war years, supply could not keep up with demand. Planters still could not acquire enough peanuts to meet the demand for its products. However, Obici wanted to build goodwill and national recognition so that after the war the company could survive the anticipated cutthroat price competition. He also wanted to diversify the products sold by Planters. During this time, Planters introduced its Peanut Bar, which required little sugar and sold well during and after the war.[28]

Within these few years, salted peanuts and confections bearing Mr. Peanut's picture became known "everywhere in this broad land of America." Planters opened a store along the Boardwalk in Atlantic City, New Jersey. A man dressed up in a Mr. Peanut outfit greeted visitors outside the store and became one of the most memorable figures along the Boardwalk. In New York City, Mr. Peanut, complete with silk hat and cane, appeared on a dazzling sign at Forty-sixth Street and Broadway in Times Square. This sign was later moved to Forty-seventh Street and refurbished at a cost of $96,000 into a "dazzling electrical display" 55 feet high and 49 feet wide: 2,600 square feet of "brilliant, colorful, scintillating advertising message." The illustration of the bag of peanuts was 9 feet high and 22 feet long. The display employed 6,700 lamps, which flashed out various messages.[29]

During the 1920s, Planters unveiled the "Peanut Car," the body of which was the exact shape, contour, and color of a mammoth peanut, mounted on a Dodge chassis. The trunk was filled with salesmen's samples and baggage. A Mr. Peanut effigy was mounted on the back of the car. These peanut cars roamed around America, selling Planters products and promoting the company through appearances at parades and fairs. In the 1930s, one car appeared in the National Tobacco Festival. Planters also sponsored a float covered with 250,000 peanuts in the festival held in South Boston, Virginia, which was viewed by seventy-five thousand people who lined the parade route.[30]

Planters was also the first peanut company to advertise regularly on radio programs. At first, its advertising was limited to Norfolk, Virginia, but in 1929 the company launched a coordinated national advertising campaign through radio, newspapers, and magazines. The radio advertising focused on musical programs "selected because of their fitness in connection with the peanut industry, and peanuts were sung into the heart of the country through the inevitable southern melodies and Negro spirituals redolent with the green fields of Dixie, enabling hearers to visualize what they had never seen." This advertising campaign elicited thousands of letters from across the country and Planters sales continued to escalate.[31]

The following year, the Depression struck. Planters lost $67,000 in 1932 alone. The company faced its greatest challenge with the greatest advertising campaign in its history. A national radio hook-up reached every section of the country. The electronic messages tied in with national print promotions: the advertisement in the *Saturday Evening Post* cost $38,000 for each insertion. Planters launched an orchestra called "Planters Peanut Pickers" along with a "Negro" quartet, which sang spirituals. This campaign was heard by some thirty million people week after week. Most other companies cut back expenses by reducing employees and cutting salaries. Planters increased the salaries of its workers during the Depression and paid its workers 20 percent more than other companies.[32]

As the Depression worsened, Planters redoubled its advertising. It discontinued the ads in major magazines and shifted to a campaign aimed at school-age children in such periodicals as *Boy's Life* and *Scholastic*. By 1935 Planters was spending an average of $500,000 per year on advertising and publicity alone, of which $75,000 went for poster cards for the New York City subways. By the mid-1930s, Mr. Peanut had become the symbol for the entire peanut industry.[33]

Even during the Depression, Planters operations sprawled all over the United States, and branches were established in Canada and Great Britain. By 1937 Planters did $10.8 million worth of business. The company had grown from a tiny firm paying $25 rent with 7 employees in 1906 to a $60 million operation, employing approximately 5,000 people, when Obici died in 1947.[34]

6   *SOUP TO OIL NUTS*

During the quarter century from 1895 to 1920, peanuts were transformed from a snack food to an important component of the American diet. Clearly, the most influential forces in this transition were vegetarians such as John Harvey Kellogg. Almeda Lambert's *Guide for Nut Cookery* reflected the progress made in nut cookery by vegetarians during the late 1890s. It included numerous peanut recipes, most of which had never before been published, and eased peanut cookery into the American mainstream. Lambert's creative recipes soon inspired others—including nonvegetarians—through cookbooks and cookery magazines.[1]

Peanut cookery was publicized in recipe booklets published by commercial peanut processors, peanut butter manufacturers, and equipment makers. These recipes were often developed by professional cooks and represented the pinnacle of peanut cookery. Peanut journals appeared in 1917 and helped to consolidate the geographically diverse and heterogeneous peanut industry. One function of the publications was to encourage peanut cookery; thousands of peanut recipes appeared in these journals over the years. Recipes from commercial cookbooklets and peanut journals were regularly reprinted in popular magazines and mainstream cookbooks.

Another influence on peanut cookery was the U.S. Department of Agriculture, the federal and state agricultural experiment stations, and county extension services, which published many peanut recipes and booklets devoted to encouraging Americans to consume more peanuts. One outstanding example—which will be discussed further in chapter 8—was George Washington Carver's *How to Grow the Peanut and 105 Ways of Preparing It for Human Consumption,* first published as a bulletin by the Tuskegee Agricultural Experiment Station in March 1916. Carver had gathered recipes from magazines and cookbooks for inclusion in the bulletin.[2] This publication received extremely wide circulation, going through eight editions during the next thirty years. During both world wars, government publications particularly encouraged the consumption of peanuts, as an American-grown crop. Peanuts were a rich source of nutrients and could be converted into vegetable oil. Peanut flour was substituted for wheat, thereby sparing grain for the war effort.

The final source of peanut recipes was mainstream cookery magazines and cookbooks. Cookery magazines published peanut recipes and articles beginning in the 1880s. Etta Morse Hudders's "The Rise of the Peanut," appearing in the March 1903 issue of *Table Talk* magazine, noted that "the patrician palate has generally tabooed the peanut" probably "because this little plebeian has shown a marked preference for the sawdust of the circus, and those upper regions in amusement circles where the gallery gods do congregate." However, Hudders pointed out that "men and children have long yielded to the wiles of the toothsome peanut taffy; neither have they passed by the vendor of 'fresh-roasted peanuts, only five cents a glass.'" She specifically proclaimed that "in spite of social ostracism, scientific investigation combined with the commercial instinct, has finally placed the products of the American peanut on the home table."[3]

Mainstream cookbooks published peanut recipes starting in the mid-nineteenth century. By the early twentieth century these recipes became more sophisticated and more diverse. While many cookbooks featured peanut recipes, Bessie R. Murphy's *Peanuts for Breakfast, Dinner, Supper,* published in 1920, was the first dedicated solely to peanut cookery. It was a collection of recipes mainly developed during World War I.[4]

Taken together these sources evidence thousands of diverse recipes with peanuts as an ingredient. Peanuts appeared in almost every conceivable form from peanut butter, peanut beverages, and mock peanut foods, as previously discussed, to peanut confections, which are examined in the next chapter. But the major culinary consumption of peanuts is in everyday meals.

PEANUT SOUP

Most likely, peanuts had been made into soup by the enslaved and the "really poor" for generations before a recipe for peanut soup ever turned up in a cookbook. Sarah Rutledge's *Carolina Housewife* published the first located recipe for "Ground-Nut Soup" in 1847. Her recipe used peanuts "well beaten up," with flour, blended with a pint of oysters to accent the mixture. The *National Cookery Book,* published in 1876, offered another recipe, which told the reader to make a smooth paste of peanuts combined with boiling water. Black pepper and cayenne pepper were added as seasoning, but oysters were optional ingredients. Ella Kellogg suggested that peanuts be used to make a soup stock to replace meat broth in other soups. Peanut soup recipes began appearing in food magazines during the 1890s. *Table Talk*'s 1894 recipe created the standard for such recipes. It combined peanut purée, using one quart of milk for each pint of peanuts. No mention was made of oysters. As the peanuts were mashed by hand, some recipes recommended straining out the larger pieces of peanuts before serving.[5]

Peanut soup could be also based on peanut flour. The *Philadelphia Press* suggested that the soup be made just like split-pea soup. Peanut flour was mixed with water and seasoned with bay leaf, celery, mace, and onion. After boiling for four or five hours, it was rubbed through a sieve, enriched with cream, and served with croutons. Almeda Lambert preferred to make peanut soup with raw, unroasted peanut butter supplied by one of the companies owned by John Harvey Kellogg. Her *Guide for Nut Cookery* presented a recipe for oyster soup with peanuts, two recipes for peanut soup, one for raw peanut milk soup, and two for peanut tomato soup. She also was the first to recommend that mills be used to grind peanuts, which is no coincidence since her husband sold peanuts and manufactured peanut mills.[6]

As peanut butter became more available, home cooks discovered that commercial peanut butter could be used for making peanut soup. This avoided the messy and time-consuming task of grinding peanuts. Peanut soup recipes continued to be published throughout the twentieth century, and the variations included such ingredients as corn starch, celery, dried mint, oatmeal water, rice, rice water, butter, barley, sardines, and red and green peppers. The largest collection of peanut soup recipes was in the bulletin compiled by George Washington Carver. He included three recipes for peanut soup, one for peanut bisque, one for peanut consommé, and two for peanut purée in addition to other soup recipes with peanuts as an ingredient. The National Peanut Council came close to Carver's record when it published six soup recipes in 1941, the year the council was founded.[7]

Published recipes for other kinds of soup—including pea soup, corn soup, tomato soup, bean soup, fish soup, lettuce soup, and celery soup—called for peanuts or peanut butter as minor ingredients. In North Dakota, the Grand Forks YMCA published an unusual recipe in 1924 for "Peanut and Cheese Chowder" with rice, potatoes, and a can of tomato soup. Two years later, the Ebell Society of the Santa Ana Valley in California offered another unusual one for "Peanut Noodle Soup."[8]

Interest in peanut soup was not unique to Americans. In the late nineteenth century, Dr. P. Furbringer reported in the *Berliner Klinische Wochenschrift* that the peanut was "rich in albumen, of which it contains forty-seven per cent, together with nineteen per cent of fat and non-nitrogenous extractive matters." He recommended the use of roasted peanuts in the form of soup or mush. Due to peanuts' low cost compared with other foods, Furbringer recommended also that peanut soups be used in poorhouses and "as an article of food for the corpulent, for diabetics, and for subjects of kidney disease."[9]

"Groundnut Soup" recipes originated in the Caribbean and Africa. In central Africa, peanut soup was made with tomatoes, onions, and a soup bone. Another popular Sudanese soup, *shorba,* was made with lamb bones, garlic, rice, and peanut butter. According to Theodore Garrett, editor of the 1890 *Encyclopaedia of Practical Cookery,* Africans made a soup called *munduli* from peanuts and ate it "with much relish."[10]

PEANUT SALAD

Prior to the Civil War, American salads were largely composed of poultry and cooked vegetables usually bound with a thick sauce. The upper class enjoyed European-style salads in the new restaurants opening in cities during the early nineteenth century. In New York, for instance, Delmonico's specialized in novel green salads and salad dressings. Salads were also popular fare at formal balls, evening parties, and afternoon teas. There were lobster, oyster, crab, and turkey salads and that particular favorite, chicken salad. An English visitor to Newport in 1869 found peanut salad was always served at suppers. A writer who claimed expertise on salad said peanut salad was "justly regarded as an American dainty" and never found in perfection elsewhere—and often not even in America.[11]

During the 1880s, salads burst into the culinary mainstream. "Molded" or "congealed" salads, made with gelatin or aspic and sugar or fruits, were created. As a light dish, salad was suited to a population that was becoming urban and sedentary. Salads were in harmony with the new emphasis on healthful eating. Cookbooks expanded their salad sections to offer recipes using hard-cooked eggs, cabbage, celery, salmon, beef, tomatoes, onions, apples, apricots, bananas, beans, walnuts, cauliflower, or oranges. By the end of the century, salads were commonplace in many middle-class homes and restaurants. It was during this expansion that salads with peanuts began to appear. In the first located recipe, "Peanut Cream Salad," published in *Good Housekeeping* in 1900, the peanuts were combined with mustard, sugar, chopped olives, and cream to form a dressing to pour over fresh greens in the summer or "over celery, thinly sliced, in winter." A few months later, *Good Housekeeping* suggested that peanuts could be substituted for walnuts in other salad recipes.[12]

Following this advice, Mary Virginia Terhune offered a recipe for "Peanut and Tomato Salad" in her *Complete Cook Book*. In a 1912 issue of *Good Housekeeping*, Gertrude R. Lombard provided a recipe for "Cabbage and Peanut Salad," in which she sprinkled "one cupful of salted peanuts freed from their skins" on shredded cabbage. She also recommended that peanut butter and mayonnaise be combined to make a dressing for salads. Just before World War I, *Good Housekeeping*'s recipes showed that peanuts could be added to a variety of traditional salads, including "Crab-meat and Peanut Salad," "Cherry and Peanut Salad," and "Cream Cheese and Peanut Salad." George Washington Carver's 1916 bulletin offered six peanut salad and salad dressing recipes, including ones using cabbage, bananas, apples, and celery. In 1918 Frances Lowe Smith's *More Recipes for Fifty* featured recipes for "Potato and Peanut Salad" and one for "Beechcroft Salad" with Neufchâtel cheese and apples. The soft cheese and peanut combination appeared for several years.[13]

When commercial manufacturers began issuing recipe booklets, Americans discovered many more ways to use peanuts in salads. Beech-Nut Peanut Butter was said to blend "delightfully with fresh fruit" and was recommended for use in fruit salads. A Beech-Nut booklet from 1914 offered recipes for combining peanut butter with celery, apples, oranges, grapes, peas, walnuts, pineapples, and bananas. Its recipe for "Beech-Nut Peanut Butter Salad Dressing" combined the peanut butter with egg yolks, flour, vinegar, mustard, red pepper, and milk. According to the author, this gave a "German effect for potato salad." A subsequent Beech-Nut advertising booklet, published in 1920, incorporated peanut butter into salads with peaches, grapes, cherries, peas, cucumbers, tomatoes, pears, and pineapples. It recommended recipes for "Peanut Butter Garden Salad," "Peanut Butter Shamrock Salad," and "Peanut Butter Salad Nouveau." Salads were also prepared by stuffing peanuts into vegetable cases, such as hollowed-out tomatoes, figs, olives, and green peppers.[14]

The makers of Nut-Let Peanut Butter issued a recipe booklet that used peanuts in a chicken salad recipe. Nut-Let's salad dressing recipe was almost exactly the same as Beech-Nut's—basically a seasoned white sauce. According to the authors, their recipe was "suitable for most any salad." The manufacturers of Yacht Club Salad Dressing recommended combining their product with ground peanuts to make yet another dressing for salads.[15] The producers of Larkin Salad Dressing suggested a similar use for their product.[16]

Recipes published in peanut journals and advertising cookbooklets frequently reappeared in community cookbooks. Shortly after the 1914 Beech-Nut booklet was issued, a "Peanut Salad" recipe using bananas found its way into a cookbook compiled by the Ladies of the Parish Aid Society of Saint John's Church in Brooklyn. Most peanut salad recipes subsequently published were similar to existing recipes, although some did add new ingredients to the traditional salads, including pimentos, raisins, curry powder, and carrots. One with extreme novelty was the "Three P's Salad," composed of chopped sweet pickles, peanuts, and peas, published in a Seattle cookbook in 1924. The same book included another salad made of peanuts, canned pimentos, hard-boiled eggs, and sweet pickles—all chopped and stuffed into scooped-out tomatoes.[17]

PEANUT FLOUR, BREAD, AND BISCUITS

Ground peanuts replaced lard in bread recipes in the South during the Civil War.[18] After the war, an article in the *Cultivator and Country Gentleman* noted that a paste made from peanuts could be mixed with flour or corn meal to make excellent bread and tea cakes. In 1885, the first American peanut bread recipe called for ground peanuts kneaded into a flour-based dough. By 1892, Ella Kellogg reported that "an immense peanut crop in the Southern States was utilized for bread-making purposes," although she offered no recipe herself. Other writers noted that peanut flour was "quite extensively used in Europe and made into bread, cakes, biscuits." According to consular reports, peanut flour was one of the favorite articles of food served in hospitals in Germany.[19]

Several recipes for peanut bread appeared in magazines and bulletins of agricultural experiment stations. In his 1916 essay, George Washington Carver compiled seven such recipes, including ones based on oats and Graham flour.[20] It was World War I, however, that gave peanut bread real importance.

To conserve flour, the Department of Agriculture and several patriotic cook-book authors promoted peanut flour and its use as a substitute for wheat flour and other essential grains. As H. S. Bailey and J. A. LeClerc asserted in the *USDA Yearbook for 1917*, the use of peanut flour "in bread making will save an equivalent quantity of wheat for the allies."[21] A USDA circular titled *Use Peanut Flour to Save Wheat* included numerous recipes using peanut flour in bread, biscuits, muffins, cakes, waffles, cereal mush, gingerbread, cookies, puddings, soups, and sauces. Peanut flour was also used to stuff peppers and tomatoes and to make cottage cheese rolls.[22]

Peanut bread was touted as the "Perfect Food" during World War I, but recipes for it barely survived the war. Bessie R. Murphy's *Peanuts for Breakfast, Dinner, Supper* listed four recipes for peanut breads and incorporated peanut flour into many others. Likewise, Homer Columbus Thompson published more peanut flour recipes in his 1920 booklet on manufacturing peanut butter. But with the war over and grain once again plentiful, the use of peanut flour declined. By 1929, the *Peanut Journal* reported that peanut flour was unobtainable in the United States and R. C. Moseley of Bellingham, Washington, had to order it from Nut-Foods in Sydney, Australia. Moseley used this flour to make muffin and waffle mixes. As imported flour cost nine cents per pound, the products made from it were luxuries. As soon as the Depression hit, they disappeared.[23]

Not until World War II broke out in Europe was peanut flour revived. In January 1941, the National Bakers Service of Chicago launched the first commercial peanut bread, which they named "Brer Rabbit Peanut Bread," inspired by Joel Chandler Harris's Brer Rabbit and Uncle Remus stories. The baking of peanut bread was further encouraged by the fact that American peanut farms had just yielded the largest peanut harvest in history.[24] Peanut bread was consumed during the war, but again once the war and its attendant shortages were over, peanut flour and peanut bread were once again forgotten.

PEANUT COOKIES, DOUGHNUTS, AND CAKES

Eliza Leslie offered the first published recipe for peanut macaroons in 1837. Her recipe, titled "Cocoa-nut Maccaroons," offered several potential replacements for coconut, one of which was ground peanuts. Leslie published a second recipe in 1854 titled "Ground-nut Maccaroons," which used roasted peanuts "pounded to a smooth, light paste." Others published similar recipes through the early twentieth century. Oatmeal macaroons, for instance, were suggested by Bessie R. Murphy in 1920. After peanut butter became popular, it was frequently suggested as an ingredient to make macaroons.[25]

Macaroons were overshadowed by peanut cookies, which became a sensation in 1896, when recipes were simultaneously published in *Table Talk*, *The Boston Cooking-School Magazine*, and Fannie Farmer's *Boston Cooking-School Cook Book*. The recipe in *Table Talk* used ground roasted peanuts while the other two used finely chopped peanuts. Numerous recipes for peanut cookies were subsequently published. Peanut butter manufacturers pushed peanut cookies made from their products beginning about 1914. These recipes were regularly reprinted in cooking magazines and cookbooks, which contributed to making peanut butter cookies a national favorite. During World War I, the government encouraged consumption of cookies in which peanut flour replaced some wheat flour. Other peanut cookie recipes promulgated during the war replaced the flour with other grains, such as oats. Peanut cookies made with oatmeal survived for a few years after the war. But in the main, between the two world wars, recipes for peanut cookies went back to the original ingredients. Some creative variations arose with a variety of added spices such as cinnamon, cloves, nutmeg, and ginger. Another recipe topped the cookies with banana icing. The first located recipe to describe using a fork to make a crisscross pattern on the top of the unbaked cookie appeared in 1939, and most homemade peanut butter cookies are still made this way.[26]

Doughnuts, originally termed *oly-cakes* in America, most likely originated in the Netherlands. Doughnuts were made in New Amsterdam before the British conquest but did not become popular in the United States until the beginning of the nineteenth century. At first, doughnuts were simply deep-fried balls of dough sprinkled with sugar. The doughnut with the hole was a later American invention. Doughnut recipes with peanuts as ingredients appeared early in the twentieth century. Doughnuts were also made with peanut butter. These recipes occasionally reappeared throughout the rest of the twentieth century, but the use of peanuts in doughnuts was usually limited to sprinkling them with chopped peanuts.[27]

Among the earliest uses of peanuts in baking was in cakes. As noted earlier, Sarah Rutledge offered a recipe for "Ground-Nut Cake" and one for peanut cheesecake in the mid-nineteenth century. These recipes were frequently reprinted. Peanuts also appeared as an ingredient in tea cakes. During the later nineteenth century, peanuts were added to other cake recipes. Almeda Lambert offered several in her *Guide for Nut Cookery*, including one for "Raw Peanut Cream Cake," and Ella Kellogg published a recipe for "Peanut Pound Cake." Peanut cake recipes proliferated throughout the twentieth century. These included layer cakes, cupcakes, griddle cakes, pancakes, peanut roll cakes, metropolitan cakes, breakfast cakes, coffee cakes, shortcakes, waffles, biscuits, and muffins. Peanuts were also used to make fillings and frostings for cakes and rolls.[28]

SOME LIKE THEM RAW OR BOILED

As a true legume, the peanut can be eaten in much the same way that beans and peas are consumed. Raw and boiled peanuts have been eaten for centuries in South America and Africa. It is likely that enslaved people brought the custom of eating raw and boiled peanuts from Africa to the Caribbean and North America. Yet, it was not until 1899 that the first formal recipe for boiled peanuts was published by Almeda Lambert. She also offered recipes for "Raw Peanut Butter" and "Raw Peanut Milk." Other people offered recipes for "Raw Peanut Soup," "Peanut Beans," and "Stewed Peanuts." Boiled peanuts were said to taste like lima beans, kidney beans, or baked beans.[29]

While it is likely that many Americans prepared freshly dug, unripe peanuts by boiling them in a weak brine, boiled peanuts as a commodity did not emerge in the southern mainstream until the early twentieth century. This tradition of preparation may have started in Orangeburg, South Carolina. A 1925 account stated that during July and August, the city streets were crowded with boys hawking "boiled peanuts—five cents a bag!" The nuts were considered a "choice viand and folks all over this section of the state have so accustomed themselves to this delicacy that they miss them when away from home." Peanut "boilings," where bushels of peanuts were cooked in big pots, became a social event that vied "in popularity with watermelon cuttings and the old time candy pullings." After August, peanuts became "too ripe and hard to make real good boiled peanuts and the munching of this tidbit will have to cease until another year rolls around and pindars are again in the mutton." Boiled peanuts were also canned for out-of-season consumption. However, boiled peanuts have remained a southern delicacy.[30]

Attempts were made to commercialize raw peanuts. In 1920, the S. S. Kresge Company sponsored a demonstration featuring raw peanuts at its store in Norfolk. According to an observer, many people tried the raw peanuts simply because of their novelty, but others expressed a preference for raw peanuts and many volunteered "testimonials to the medicinal value of raw peanuts as an aid to digestion or a cure for insomnia." A medical professional reported that raw peanuts had solved her stomach problems. In the late 1930s, H. G. Ray created Uncle Remus Brand raw peanuts. For a while during World War II, the British packed fourteen pounds of raw peanuts in each lifeboat as emergency rations.[31] As soon as alternative foods were available, however, this practice was discontinued.

PEANUT-FED PORK

In addition to the direct consumption of peanuts and peanut products, Americans have long consumed peanuts indirectly in many other ways, such as through peanut oil or eating pork that has been peanut-fed. Peanut oil was one of the first culinary uses of the peanut in Europe and America. Hans Sloan reported in 1707 that peanut oil was "as good as that of Almonds," but Dr. Brownrigg of Edenton, North Carolina, was unaware of previous attempts to produce peanut oil when he carried out his own experiments in 1768. Brownrigg bruised the peanuts, placed them in canvas bags, and then expressed "a pure, clear, well tasted oil, useful for the same purposes as the oils of olives or almonds." Even after an eight-month voyage from North Carolina to England, the peanut oil did not turn rancid. Although the samples had not been subjected to "extraordinary care, and had undergone the heats of the summer," the oil had remained "perfectly sweet and good." A bushel of peanuts yielded one gallon of oil. When heat was applied, a much larger quantity resulted but of inferior quality. Brownrigg projected that the British colonies could supply all their own oil needs replacing imported olive oil and "even make a considerable article of their export." Brownrigg's comments were subsequently cited by other observers and may have encouraged Europeans to begin efforts at the commercial manufacture of peanut oil.[32] In America, however, no one paid much attention.

The major reason for the lack of interest in peanut oil was that lard was America's preferred frying medium. Of all the stock animals introduced into America in colonial times, the pig was the most successful. Spanish explorers such as Hernando de Soto brought a herd of pigs as a fresh meat supply for his men. Likewise, Spanish colonists introduced domestic pigs into their settlements in Florida and the Southwest. Pigs were also brought to New England and New Amsterdam, and they flourished there as well. In the southern colonies, with their mild winters, pigs lived off the land and multiplied. English settlers imported three swine to Jamestown in 1608; within eighteen months the original trio had multiplied to sixty. By the end of the century, Virginia and Maryland exported pork and were famous for their hams. Along with maize, pork became the great staple of the American diet. Pork was easy to preserve and provided both meat and lard.[33]

Peanuts were used to feed the pigs. In 1768, Dr. Brownrigg declared that the "cake" that remained after the peanut oil was expressed was an "excellent food for swine." He reported that some planters raise a considerable quantity of peanuts "for feeding of swine and poultry, which are very fond of the ground pease; and when they are permitted to eat freely of them, soon become fat." The editor of the *Floridian* proclaimed that peanut cake was "admirable for hogs" and that the peanut vine could be saved, cured, mixed "with rye, barley oats and rice," and fed to stock. He predicted that the peanut oil manufactured in the United States could become "a successful rival of the best table oil of Europe." By 1849, the main use of peanuts was to fatten swine, which were allowed to run in the fields and dig them up. One Georgia plantation mistress, Emily P. Burke, reported that planters usually fed peanuts to their swine "in the fall previous to slaughter."[34]

Peanut-flavored pork was considered a delicacy and was sold at a premium. The cured hams from peanut-fed hogs were, and still are, associated with Smithfield, Virginia. As peanuts were low in minerals, peanut-fed hogs suffered from weak bone structure, which resulted in broken bones and a large economic loss. Later, when farmers fed mineral supplements to hogs, this problem was eliminated. But a peanut diet also created soft pork, which had a flabby appearance and lacked eye appeal. This was resolved by taking hogs off the peanut feed about three weeks before slaughter. Today, although peanuts are still used in some brands of hog feed to produce a particular flavor, corn has largely replaced peanuts.[35]

FOREIGN OIL

While peanut oil made no headway in the United States, it eventually flowed freely in Europe. By 1787, a great quantity of peanuts was imported into Portugal and Spain, and experiments in growing peanuts were conducted in Italy, where a small peanut industry had developed by 1807. Peanut oil often took the place of almond oil in soap making, and powdered peanuts served as a substitute for cocoa or were added to flour to make bread. France became particularly interested in the peanut. Lucien Bonaparte, then the French ambassador to Spain, sent peanut seeds to Bordeaux in 1801. During the time that England enforced a blockade on France during the Napoleonic wars, peanuts were widely grown in southern France, where they were crushed to make oil, which was used to adulterate olive oil and chocolate. Due to political upheavals in France, however, peanut cultivation was discontinued by 1815. Five years later France's olive crop was destroyed by frosts, and peanut cultivation boomed, as it did again in 1830. But by 1840 it had finally become clear that France just did not have the right climate and soil conditions to cultivate peanuts efficiently. As neither animal fats nor olives provided enough oil to meet the increasing demands of the soap industry, another source for oil was needed. In 1840, France revised its tariffs and eliminated a high import duty on vegetable oil, and manufacturers began to explore alternative oil sources in Africa.[36]

Peanuts had been grown commercially in West Africa since 1823 by the Wesleyan Mission on MacCarthy Island in the Gambia River. After the British ended slavery throughout their empire, some freed slaves returned to Africa. The British government resettled some of them in Gambia and gave them land to grow peanuts. A few baskets of peanuts were exported in 1830, but no more were exported until 1834, when 213 baskets were dispatched. This jumped to 47 tons the following year, and a oil mill was constructed in London to crush the peanuts. In 1837, the total production equaled 671 tons, and the following year, it reached 2,304 tons, finally hitting 11,095 tons in 1851. Simultaneously, peanuts were commercially cultivated in Senegal and Cape Verde. During the 1840s, a Marseilles firm invested $40,000 to acquire 671 tons of peanuts from West Africa; this venture was successful, and the French imported about 11,000 tons of peanuts from West Africa annually until 1871, when the total jumped to 17,000 tons. Peanuts were also grown in Portuguese Guinea, Sierra Leone, and Angola, and peanut oil mills soon emerged in Genoa, London, Rotterdam, and Hamburg. Forty years after the commencement of the peanut trade, France alone imported 55,000 tons of peanuts from Africa.[37]

By the 1890s, seventeen factories in Marseilles were engaged in the peanut oil industry, processing 69 million pounds of peanuts annually for oil valued at $5 million. The American counsel in Marseilles, R. B. Skinner, visited these factories in 1894 and described the process of making oil. When the peanuts arrived at the factory, they were placed in a machine that removed all dirt and other foreign substances. The nuts were then conveyed to the shelling machine, consisting of a pair of cast-iron rollers, which smashed the peanuts into pieces. After the shells were removed, the peanut chunks were ground finely. The resulting meal was sieved and the coarse pieces returned to the rollers to be re-crushed. The fine meal was then subjected to a pressure of 2,850 pounds per square inch for one hour. The meal was removed and ground a second time, then heated and pressed a second time. If a high-quality oil was required, the peanuts were crushed only once: this oil was largely devoted to the manufacture of white soap. Quality peanut oil was also used as salad oil and in the manufacture of margarine. The residue left after pressing was employed in making bread, cakes, and biscuits. As it was rich in nitrogen, it was also converted into cattle food.[38]

A thriving peanut oil industry developed in Germany following its acquisition of peanut-growing colonies in Africa. After the oil had been expressed from the peanuts, the leftover cake was employed in making several different types of food. The German military was particularly interested in peanuts and the troops were served peanut mush and biscuits during the 1890s, but this proved unsuccessful. When World War I cut off access to the peanut-producing colonies in Africa, the German oil industry withered. When these colonies were removed from German control after World War I, some Germans migrated to Tsingtao and Shantung in China, where they developed a peanut trade that continued until it was destroyed by World War II.[39]

Shortly after the completion of the Suez Canal in 1869, peanut cultivation dramatically increased in India, where peanut oil had long served as a substitute for olive oil in medicinal preparations. Peanuts were mainly used in Asia for their oil, and today China and India are among the largest peanut oil producers in the world.[40]

AMERICAN OIL

After lard, olive oil was the most important oil in America prior to the twentieth century. Olives had been gathered since prehistoric times and olive presses have been located in archaeological sites. Olives and olive oil were of great importance to the ancient Greeks and Romans. In the ancient world, olive oil was likely used for frying, baking, and preserving, as well as for dressing salads. Like almonds, olives were introduced into the New World by the Spanish. However, due to climatic conditions, neither almonds nor olives thrived in eastern North America, and those who wanted vegetable oil had to import it at great expense. Peanut oil was relatively inexpensive, so in addition to serving as a substitute for olive oil, peanut oil was often used as an adulterant. As one grocer later put it, a great quantity of peanut oil was "sold as olive oil without the admixture of any of the genuine article."[41]

Peanut oil had been used for domestic purposes during the nineteenth century, at least in the American South. As previously mentioned, Dr. Brownrigg of North Carolina had developed a process for extracting "a well tasted" oil from peanuts, which was "useful for the same purposes as the oils of olives or almonds." By the 1840s, peanut oil was employed in the United States as a cooking oil in its own right. As one observer noted, the peanut was "easily gathered and with less labor than any of the seeds or beans." When pressed, it became "liquid and pure, and when immediately bottled and sealed appears to remain in a state of freshness and retains the fine odor so highly agreeable to the amateurs of vegetable oils in the preparation of food." Peanut oil was "unequaled, as an accompaniment to the table: in its natural state this oil has no rival, clear and mild, with a peculiar taste extremely gratifying to the palate, rich and buttery; it is of that consistency so much admired in the preparation of salads, anchovies, &c., for table use." If the "oil was fairly introduced into the Northern states, it would take a high rank at the table of the bon-vivants" and after a little use "it would become a successful rival of the best table oil of Europe."[42]

Although peanut oil was important in the South during the Civil War, the large-scale production of peanut oil in America disappeared as soon as the war was over. In the 1880s, American grocers began to stock imported peanut oil as an article in its own right. In the United States, it was largely used for domestic and culinary purposes: "for mixture with olive-oil, and for cloth-dressing, though its chief use in Europe is for the manufacture of soap and lubricating machinery." As a lamp oil it burned longer than olive oil, but its illuminating power was inferior. Peanut oil's advantage over other oils was that it could be "kept for a much longer time without becoming rancid." However, as a lamp fuel, its days were numbered once kerosene came into general use.[43]

During the late nineteenth and early twentieth centuries, many observers urged the development of an American peanut oil business to "obviate our dependence upon foreign oil." Numerous reports on the French peanut oil industry appeared in American magazines and newspapers. Following on the success of the peanut oil business in France, a peanut oil factory was planned for Norfolk, Virginia. The company was capitalized at $60,000. The prospectus issued by the company projected that five tons of peanuts would produce 225 gallons of refined oil, 3,680 pounds of flour and meal, and 3,680 pounds of stock feed, generating total gross receipts of $415.90 per day.[44] Despite a valiant effort, the operation failed and the United States continued to import peanut and olive oil.

Some peanut oil was manufactured in the United States before World War I. The Dawson Cotton Oil Company, for instance, was organized in 1904 in Georgia. Led by Ed Stevens, the firm changed its name to Stevens Industries and expanded its operations, becoming one of the largest peanut cleaning, shelling, and crushing companies in the industry. Stevens Industries eventually operated the largest peanut butter factory in the world.[45]

Although small amounts of peanut oil were manufactured in the United States, one and one half million pounds of it were imported, much of it from Germany. When World War I broke out in Europe, all such trade ceased as the British blockaded German ports. Because peanut oil was needed to manufacture glycerin, a compound used in making explosives, the U.S. military ordered peanut oil from domestic manufacturers. When the United States entered the war in 1917, the demand for peanut oil skyrocketed. To meet this increased demand, peanut oil mills sprang up everywhere, and farmers greatly increased their cultivation of peanuts. The quality of peanut oil improved tre-

mendously, and during the war the oil was used for cooking, as well as manufacturing cosmetics, soap, miner's lamps, medicinal emulsions, kid gloves,
putty, "washing powder, black grease, roofing linoleums, insulating material,
oilcloth, paint base, cotton rubber, and artificial leather."[46] One major use of
peanut oil during World War I was the manufacture of margarine.

PEANUT MARGARINE

In his day, Napoleon III took great interest in the production and improvement of the French food supply. He was particularly interested in finding a
cheap butter substitute to conform as closely as possible to butter's physical
and chemical characteristics. A chemist named Hyppolyte Mouriès was commissioned by the French government to develop this product. Mouriès pressed
beef suet into milk, creating a product with enough fat that it could be churned
into butter. His experiments came to fruition in 1869, when he patented a
product that he called "Margarine Mouriès." It was called margarine because
at the time it was illegal to associate the term *butter* with anything other than
the real dairy product, and it was believed that margaric acid was a common
component of all fats and oils. The importance of Mouriès's discovery became
evident immediately. When the Franco-Prussian War broke out in 1870, the
Prussian army besieged Paris and prevented food from entering the city, causing a food shortage. As underfed dairy cows could not produce rich butter,
butter almost completely disappeared. After the war, margarine factories were
built in France in 1872 and in Austria the following year.[47]

The first margarine factory in the United States began production in 1874.
In its natural state, margarine is almost white, so manufacturers added yellow food coloring to make it appear more like butter. This was so successful
that within six years the dairy industry launched an anti-margarine crusade
at the state and national levels. States passed anti-margarine laws, and in 1886
Congress stepped in and passed legislation regulating and taxing the manufacture of margarine. This law was amended in 1902 to lower the tax on margarine, but it still levied a tax of ten cent per pound on any margarine that
used artificial food coloring as an ingredient. Margarine manufacturers responded by selling their product with an envelope of yellow food coloring that
the seller could mix with the margarine to make it appear more like butter.[48]

In principle, any fat could be used to make margarine, and experimentation commenced using different vegetable oils. Peanut oil was used as early as 1896 but was not particularly successful. During World War I, a shortage of animal fats again struck. Experimentation began anew with oil-bearing
seeds and nuts. In 1916, a new type of margarine came into existence, made

of milk, butter, and a mixture of peanut and coconut oil. The ingredients tended to separate, but in 1920 a process was discovered for completely emulsifying nut oils so that they would not separate even when melted. The great advantage of peanuts was that they imparted a natural yellow color to margarine, which was legally permitted. Margarine made from peanuts was taxed at a much lower rate, and manufacturers scrambled for peanuts. In 1923, 4 million pounds of peanuts were used in the production of margarine. By 1925, 100 million pounds of margarine were manufactured in the United States.[49]

As soon as trade returned to normal after the war, and the shortage of animal fats abated, the anti-margarine crusade cranked up again. The Dairyman's League Co-operative Association and National Association of Creamery Butter Makers passed resolutions encouraging the enactment of laws prohibiting the manufacture and importation of margarine. Creameries in dairy districts launched boycotts of merchants who sold margarine. In Tillamook County, Oregon, dairy farmers signed agreements with newspapers and retail stores not to handle, sell, or advertise margarine. The dairy farmers boycotted any store or newspaper refusing to sign the agreement.[50]

The Institute of Margarine Manufacturers claimed that all its products were produced by American farmers too. Margarine, made under government supervision, was purer, safer, and more wholesome than dairy butter, or so the institute claimed. The Southwest Association of Consumers called the anti-margarine laws "Unconstitutional and Un-American." During the Depression, claimed the association, the higher butter prices supported by these laws deprived "50 million American poor of a lower cost table spread." The Federal Trade Commission found that anti-margarine boycotts, some organized by county agricultural agents, constituted unfair trading practices. During World War II, animal and vegetable oil again became scarce, and even margarine was rationed. But the anti-margarine crusade did not subside until well after the war ended.[51]

By the mid-twentieth century, a vast array of peanut recipes had been developed for use from breakfast to dinner, and in every course from soup to dessert. Few other food or food products demonstrated such a wide diversity of uses. In addition, peanuts remained perennially popular as a snack food between meals.

7   *SWEET AND NUTTY*

Molasses was the most common sweetener in America prior to the twentieth century. Molasses was an inexpensive byproduct of the sugar-refining process. Sugar cane was crushed, and the juice was extracted and heated. When it cooled, some of it crystallized; this was considered raw sugar. Left behind was a sweet residue called treacle or molasses, which could not be further refined by traditional methods.[1] Its advantage was that it mimicked America's first sweetener—honey—and it was much less expensive than white crystallized sugar. Caribbean molasses was poured into kegs and shipped to the British North American colonies and subsequently to the United States, where much of it was used to make rum. But it was also employed as a sweetener in many recipes, particularly for confections, as demonstrated by numerous "Molasses Candy" recipes that appeared in nineteenth-century cookbooks. As manufacturing processes became more efficient and the price of molasses and sugar declined, the amount of sweetening in American cookery ballooned.

Peanuts were connected with molasses early in America. Many nineteenth-century recipes included molasses and peanuts as ingredients. In her

Domestic Receipt Book, published in 1846, Catharine Beecher includes peanuts as an ingredient in her molasses candy recipe. Beecher noted parenthetically that "all children are fond of this article." Her sister, Harriet Beecher Stowe, the author of *Uncle Tom's Cabin,* also was fond of "peanut candy," for she made several references to it in her book *Dred: A Tale of the Great Dismal Swamp.*[2]

Many molasses candy recipes also mentioned popcorn as an ingredient, including Beecher's recipe cited above. Although maize originated in Central America, it is likely that popcorn had been brought to New England by American sailors who encountered it in Chile about 1800. Popcorn and peanuts were both grown in small garden plots, and both were generally eaten as salty snacks. Both products appealed to children and both were connected with children's holidays: one Virginian, J. A. Riddick, recalled around 1800 that peanuts "were cultivated chiefly in gardens in very small patches like popcorn, and distributed at Christmas time by the mothers and grandmothers among the children."[3]

Finally, peanuts and popcorn served similar snack functions. Outside the home, they were both sold to crowds at political rallies, fairs, circuses, and later at sporting events and in theaters. In the home, peanuts and popcorn were usually served apart from meals. Peanuts and popcorn filled the same culinary niche, and many recipes featured popcorn and peanuts as interchangeable ingredients. For instance, *The Web-Foot Cook Book,* the first cookbook printed in Oregon, featured a recipe for "Crystalized Pop-Corn or Nuts," in which popped corn or peanuts were coated with sugar.[4] But it was the combination of molasses, peanuts, and popcorn that became America's most popular confection during the early twentieth century.

THE RUECKHEIMS

When Chicago started to rebuild after the fire that swept the city in 1871, laborers streamed in, searching for work. One person who heeded the call was Frederick W. Rueckheim. He had immigrated to Illinois from Germany in 1869 and worked on a farm outside the city. At the time of the fire, he had saved two hundred dollars from his farm wages. Upon arriving in Chicago, he met William Brinkmeyer, whose popcorn stand had burned down in the fire. Brinkmeyer convinced Rueckheim to become his partner and invest in his "Popcorn Specialties" business.[5]

Catering to those rebuilding fire-ravaged Chicago, Brinkmeyer and Rueckheim operated out of a rented room. Their business prospered, and a year later Brinkmeyer sold his share to Rueckheim, who sent for his brother in Germany to help him with his business. When Louis Rueckheim arrived, the operation was renamed F. W. Rueckheim and Brother. The two ran their company out of a back-room kitchen equipped only with a single molasses kettle and one hand popper.[6] All their confections were made by hand until 1884, when the brothers acquired steam-powered machinery. Like many other vendors, the Rueckheims experimented with sugar-coating different products. They tested various sweeteners with a variety of combinations of marshmallows, nuts, and other ingredients until finally they hit on a confection composed of popcorn, molasses, and various roasted nuts. In 1893, they settled on the least expensive nut—the peanut.[7]

When the Columbian Exposition opened in Chicago in 1893, the Rueckheims offered their confection, as yet unnamed, to the crowds flocking to the exhibits. Frederick Rueckheim later commented that no matter how carefully they tried to plan, orders always exceeded production. When they attempted to increase output, they confronted several stumbling blocks. In large batches, the molasses-covered popcorn and peanuts stuck together, combining into irregular blobs; with low volume, it was possible to spread the sticky confection on large drying pans, then stir it together when it was cool and dry. The old way needed to change and Louis Rueckheim solved the problem in late 1895. He created a quick-drying process for the molasses-coated peanuts and popcorn, permitting swift and continuous packaging. With this solution in place, the Rueckheims invested in new equipment, enabling them to boost dramatically their production capability.[8]

CRACKER JACK ADVERTISING

Before the Rueckheims could advertise their product, they needed to choose a brand name. The most common account of the selection process told of John Berg, a company salesman, who, upon sampling the new confection, reportedly exclaimed, "That's a crackerjack!" Frederick Rueckheim looked at him and said, "Why not call it by that name?" Berg responded, "I see no objection." Rueckheim's decisive reply was, "That settles it then." And so the name Cracker Jack was born—or so goes the story. It was probably apocryphal. The Cracker Jack Company published several different versions of how the name was chosen. The term "cracker jack" was a commonly used slang term that meant first-rate or excellent. The *Historical Dictionary of American Slang* lists its first published appearance as 1895, but references suggest that the term had been used in speech during the 1880s. Whatever its derivation, the Rueckheims began using the name Cracker Jack on January 28,

1896, and they applied for a trademark on February 17, 1896. Thirty-six days later, the U.S. Patent Office issued the trademark.[9]

Shortly thereafter, the Rueckheims launched a major promotional and marketing blitz in Chicago, followed closely by campaigns in New York and Philadelphia. Three different advertisements appeared in the July 13, 1896, issue of Philadelphia's *Grocery World.* These promotions announced that Cracker Jack was a new confection, not yet six months old, that had "made the most instantaneous success of anything ever introduced." It was called the "1896 sensation." Also in the advertisements was the phrase, "the more you eat the more you want." To meet the needs generated by aggressive marketing, the company produced four and one-half tons of Cracker Jack daily. From May 5 through June 1, 1896, fourteen railroad cars of Cracker Jack were sold in New York City. In Philadelphia, four carloads were distributed during the first ten days of the promotional campaign. Cracker Jack was touted as "The Greatest Seller of Its Kind." This campaign was so successful that the company brought out in January 1897 "the little brother to 'Cracker Jack,'" known as Nut Cracker Jack. This contained more peanuts than did the original but was not marketed aggressively. Nonetheless it did lead the way for hundreds of new products manufactured by the company over the next few decades.[10]

At first, Cracker Jack was sold in cardboard boxes, but the Rueckheims discovered that it was hard to maintain the product's crispness even under the best conditions. After the box was opened, humidity turned the snack soggy. Henry G. Eckstein, a former general superintendent of a Chicago confectionery company and a friend of the Rueckheims, proposed a new packaging system to keep out moisture and maintain crispness by packing the Cracker Jack in a wax-sealed box. But even this did not successfully keep out moisture. So Eckstein visited Germany looking for new packaging techniques. He found one that had been invented by a German scientist. Eckstein paid the scientist five hundred dollars to teach him the method of making waxed paper. Eckstein improved the process, finally enclosing the Cracker Jack in three protective layers. The packaging problem was finally solved.[11]

The Rueckheims launched another national advertising campaign in *Billboard* just to promote the new packaging. The advertisement promoted Cracker Jack as "A delicious Pop Corn Confection, packed in moisture proof packages, that keep it fresh for a long time." It was "A QUICK SELLER" and "A MONEY MAKER for the concessionist."[12] Consumer sales soared, thanks mainly to the advertising and the new packaging. In recognition of his role in this phenomenal success, Eckstein was named a partner and the firm was renamed Rueckheim Brothers and Eckstein. Eckstein eventually realized millions of dollars through his improvement of Cracker Jack packaging.

The new and improved Cracker Jack was an instant success. Recipes for homemade versions immediately appeared in cookery books. Faced with the problem of the peanuts and popcorn sticking together, cookbook authors recommended creating Cracker Jack cakes or balls. The Knights of the Globe Home in Freeport, Illinois, published a recipe for "K. of G. Cracker Jack," in which the peanuts, popcorn, and molasses were formed into small balls. Other homemade recipes were made with butter, sorghum, soda, cream of tartar, almond extract, and vanilla flavoring.[13]

CHILDREN'S TOYS

Cracker Jack remained a singularly popular confection mainly because of extensive national advertising. Some advertisements proclaimed Cracker Jack "a healthful, nourishing food-confection." In 1912, an advertisement reported that boxes of Cracker Jack "Don't Stay Long on the Shelf!" Another advertisement claimed that Cracker Jack was the "Standard Popcorn Confection" by which all others were judged. The advertisement also announced that "A Valuable Premium Coupon" was attached to every package. From 1910 to 1913, coupons for premiums were affixed on and placed in Cracker Jack boxes. The coupons could be redeemed for over three hundred "varieties of handsome and useful articles, such as Watches, Jewelry, Silverware, Sporting Goods, Toys, Games, Sewing Machines and many other useful Household articles." In 1912, a children's toy was enclosed in every package. Two years later, Cracker Jack advertisements reported that "over 500 varieties of handsome and useful articles" were to be found in the boxes.[14] The little sailor boy and his dog Bingo were first used in advertisements in 1916, and three years later they first appeared on a Cracker Jack box. The design was based on a picture of Frederick Rueckheim's grandson, Robert, with his dog. Robert died of pneumonia shortly after the package was introduced.

EXPANSION

Throughout the early twentieth century, Rueckheim Brothers and Eckstein expanded. A 1913 advertisement proclaimed Cracker Jack "THE WORLD'S FAMOUS CONFECTION." By 1918, the company was generating three million dollars in sales. In a 1919 advertisement in the *Saturday Evening Post,* the company touted Cracker Jack as "America's Famous Food Confection." To augment its Chicago operations, the company established sales offices in

Brooklyn, New York, and sales continued to rise. In 1922, Rueckheim Brothers and Eckstein celebrated its fiftieth anniversary and marked the occasion by changing its name to the Cracker Jack Company. That same year, the Rueckheims and Eckstein elected their next generation as vice presidents: Frederick Rueckheim Jr., Henry Eckstein Jr., and Fred Warren, son-in-law of Louis Rueckheim. Within four years, the Cracker Jack Company was selling more than 138 million boxes annually. The company realized its largest pre–World War II profit in 1928—$716,659 before taxes.[15]

During the Depression, many other snack foods floundered. However, on the whole, the Cracker Jack Company weathered the Depression remarkably well. Its premier product was inexpensive; at a nickel a box it was within reach of most Americans. The company even launched new products during the Depression. Cracker Jack Brittle and Cracker Jack Peanuts were introduced, as was chocolate-covered Cracker Jack. Most of the new products were novelties that quickly disappeared, but the original Cracker Jack remained on the market. To boost sales, the company began purchasing sophisticated prizes from Europe and Japan.[16]

Two major reasons for the Cracker Jack Company's profits were steadily improved marketing and increasingly efficient operations. Automation permitted Cracker Jack to undersell its competition while still making a solid profit. The confection cost about 1 cent per box to produce and the packaging about 2 cents more. Grocers and vendors paid 3¼ cents per box generating a quarter-cent profit for the company. This may seem a tiny profit, but Cracker Jack sold millions of boxes per year. Cracker Jack's competitors charged 3½ cents per box, which meant that grocers and vendors made a greater profit by selling Cracker Jack. This encouraged retailers to stock Cracker Jack rather than competing brands. Sales soared, even during the Depression. By 1937, the Cracker Jack Company declared itself producer of "America's Oldest, Best Known and Most Popular Confection."[17]

CHOCOLATE CONFECTIONS

Cracker Jack was but one confection marketed during the early twentieth century. Many more were based on chocolate, a New World product that had been popular in Europe during the seventeenth century, when it was served only as a drink. French chefs had made one-ounce tablets for use in making hot chocolate, but when the chefs tried to make chocolate bars in the late eighteenth century, the bars were dry and brittle. In 1815, Coenraad Van Houten of Holland developed a process to lower the fat content of chocolate. He then put the product through an alkalizing process. This process created "Dutch Chocolate," which was dark in color and mild in flavor. These processes made possible the manufacture of powdered cocoa, which was achieved in 1828. Eventually, this led to the large-scale manufacture of chocolate in powder and solid form. In 1847 Joseph Storrs Fry, a British Quaker, invented a process of combining cocoa powder, sugar, and melted cocoa butter that produced a thin paste which could be shaped in a mold. Soon, J. S. Fry and Company was the largest manufacturer of chocolate in the world.[18]

In Switzerland, Henri Nestlé developed the process of making milk chocolate in 1867. Another Swiss chocolate manufacturer, Daniel Peter, used Nestlé's chocolate to make a milk chocolate bar in 1879. A third Swiss, Jean Tobler, marketed his Toblerone, a triangular chocolate bar with almond-and-honey nougat.[19]

From the earliest European settlements in North America, sugar was imported. It remained a luxury item for almost two centuries. As the price of sugar dropped during the nineteenth century, candy began to be mass produced with the help of immigrants, who brought candy-making skills from Europe. While chocolate was sold in Massachusetts by 1670, it was served only as a drink until the end of the nineteenth century. But by the 1870s, an English visitor proclaimed candy—including chocolate-covered candy—and caramels to be American institutions.[20]

Peanuts were made into candy well before the molasses candy recipes appeared in the 1830s. Peanuts simply replaced almonds, which had been the nut most used in candy in America and Europe. Most early peanut candy recipes produced confections similar to peanut brittle. After the Civil War, peanut molasses candy became more common. For instance, Tilton's *Art of Confectionery*, published in Boston in 1865, suggested stirring peanuts into "molasses-candy."[21] It was sold commercially by confectioners around this time.

The first recipe titled "Ground Pea Candy" was published in New York in 1867 by Mrs. A. P. Hill, the wife of a former Confederate general. A similar recipe was featured in M. L. Tyson's *Queen of the Kitchen*, subtitled a "Collection of Old Maryland Receipts for Cooking from a Receipt Book Used for Many Years." In this book, the candy was called "Peanut Taffy." The first real recipe for peanut brittle, although still called "Peanut Candy," was published by Mary Virginia Terhune. Unlike previous peanut candy recipes, this one called specifically for using a shallow pan, and baking soda was an ingredient. Soda created tiny bubbles in the candy, making it more brittle and easier to break and chew. Many similar recipes followed.[22]

When the nation celebrated its centennial in 1876, Philadelphia hosted the nation's Centennial Exposition. This fair inspired the development of the *National Cookery Book* by the Women's Centennial Committee. This was a professionally written cookbook, and copies sold briskly as souvenirs. A special feature of the book was that the committee addressed the question asked by foreigners about America's "national dishes" by sending a request for recipes to every "State and territory in the union." The only peanut recipe, "Groundnut Cakes," was from Philadelphia. It produced a confection that resembled small pieces of peanut brittle. According to the anonymous contributor, these "cakes" had been introduced into Philadelphia by refugees from the Haitian revolution in 1791.[23] Whatever the source of the recipe, this "ground nut candy" was preferred to all other sweets by the 1840s, a position it held for at least the next thirty years.[24] The number and diversity of peanut candy recipes expanded during the 1870s.[25] Although peanuts were never a particularly important foodstuff in Europe, peanut candy recipes were published in England, beginning in 1890.[26]

In 1901, peanut confections began to be made on a major scale in New York and Norfolk. Peanut candy was cheap to manufacture: all that was needed were a couple of copper pans, a candy stove, sieves, a thermometer, and a large marble slab. The candy was packed in boxes or pails that held twenty-five to thirty pounds. The product was easily shipped, and it kept fairly well. Peanut candies were "always good sellers" in rural towns, and there was traditionally an especially big demand in winter.[27]

Many commercial peanut confections emerged during the early twentieth century. Peanut brittle had frequently been made in the home. The first known person to commercialize it was L. G. Doup, president of the West Indies Limes Company of Kansas City, Missouri, who developed the idea of making, packing, and promoting the sale of high-quality peanut brittle. He shipped boxes to baseball teams for the publicity. He called his product Kris-P-nut Squares. The packages came in two sizes, one selling for twenty-five cents and the other for a dime. Ernest Wilson of San Francisco manufactured Wilsonettes—chocolate-covered peanuts. He patented a process to make an outer coating that did not mar. In December 1923, Wilson put chocolate-covered peanuts on the market at the popular price of five cents a box with 150 pieces of candy inside. Wilsonettes were an immediate success. Similarly, in 1925 the Blumenthal Chocolate Company of Philadelphia began manufacturing Goobers—chocolate-covered peanuts. They remain a favorite in movie theaters to this day.[28]

THE DEVELOPMENT OF CANDY BARS

Before 1885, peanuts were used in the commercial production of "flat bars" composed of peanut pieces held together by melted sugar or molasses and pressed into the shape of a bar. Recipes for peanut bars appeared in most candy-making books during the first decades of the twentieth century, and advertisements for commercial peanut bars appeared shortly thereafter. They sold for a penny apiece but made up for their low price with high volume. "Grandmother's Original Peanut Bar" was promoted as "The Most Delicious Peanut Confection Ever Offered to the Consumer."[29]

Prior to 1893, candy bars were made by hand in the United States. Walter M. Lowney, a candymaker from Boston specializing in handmade chocolate bars, exhibited his wares at Chicago's Columbian Exposition in 1893. Milton S. Hershey, a caramel maker from Lancaster, Pennsylvania, visited Lowney's exhibit, and he also viewed the chocolate-making machinery at the fair manufactured by Lehmann and Company of Dresden, Germany. He ordered the machinery and, early in 1894, created the Hershey Chocolate Company as a subsidiary of his caramel business. In addition to chocolate coatings, the company produced breakfast cocoa, sweet chocolate, and baking chocolate. In 1900, Hershey sold the Lancaster Caramel Company but retained the chocolate manufacturing equipment and the rights to manufacture chocolate. In 1903, he moved to the town of Derry Church, in the heart of Pennsylvania's dairy country, and began to build the world's largest chocolate-manufacturing plant, which opened two years later.

Peanuts were not among the ingredients in Hershey's earliest candy bars, but he opened the path for other manufacturers who soon combined chocolate and peanuts. Austin T. Merrill of Roxbury, Massachusetts, had employed the name Squirrel Brand since 1895. In 1899 Merrill incorporated his business as the Squirrel Brand Salted Nut Company. The following year, the company went into receivership and was sold to a group including two employees, Perley G. Gerrish and Fred S. Green. The business grew quickly and moved to Cambridge, Massachusetts. In 1905 Gerrish manufactured the first known peanut bar, called the "Squirrel Brand Peanut Bar," and followed six years later with a peanut caramel bar. By 1912, the company was roasting and salting over 1.2 million pounds of peanuts a year. Throughout the 1920s and 1930s, Squirrel Brand expanded its offerings to include additional peanut candies such as Nut Twins, Nut Zippers, Nut Chews, Nut Yippee, and Peanut Butter Kisses.[30]

Combination candy bars were manufactured beginning in 1911. The Standard Candy Company of Nashville, Tennessee, produced one of the first bars composed of caramel, marshmallow, milk chocolate, and roasted peanuts. The company was started by Howard Campbell in 1901. He named his new confection "Goo Goo Clusters" purportedly because "goo goo" was the first sound uttered by infants. Marketed mainly in the South, the hefty confection was advertised as "A Nourishing Lunch for a Nickel." Its advertisements frequently aired on country-and-western programs, including the *Grand Ole Opry.*[31]

BABY RUTH

In 1916, Otto Y. Schnering of Chicago founded a bakery, food, and wholesale candy business in Chicago. His first concoction was a bakery product called "Amerones." Schnering also launched a small candy department, which was so successful that all other lines were soon discontinued. Schnering decided to change the name of the company to reflect its new emphasis. As German names were not popular during World War I, Schnering used his mother's middle name to create the Curtiss Candy Company, which was engaged exclusively in the manufacture of candy. At this time, the company bought thirty to fifty bushel bags of peanuts a day to make its confections. In 1920, Curtiss began to make the "Baby Ruth" candy bar, which was filled with peanuts covered with nougat and a layer of chocolate. When the Babe Ruth of baseball fame sought royalties from the makers of Baby Ruth the candy bar, he was unsuccessful. The company claimed that its candy bar had been named after President Grover Cleveland's daughter, Ruth. Many observers consider this oft-repeated story to be a myth and with good reason. Ruth Cleveland was born on October 3, 1891, and died of diphtheria thirteen years later. Cleveland himself died in 1908. When the Baby Ruth candy bar was first produced, sixteen years after Ruth Cleveland's death, few youthful candy buyers would have remembered her, but they would have known Babe Ruth, who was then the nation's most popular baseball player. When Babe Ruth was informed that the company claimed that the candy bar had been named for Grover Cleveland's daughter, he reportedly retorted, "Well, I ain't eatin' your damned candy bar anymore."[32]

Whatever the reasons for the name, Baby Ruth was extremely successful, mainly due to Schnering's promotional ability. He chartered an airplane and dropped the bars by parachute over the city of Pittsburgh. He later expanded his drops to cities in more than forty states. At the same time, the company began a nationwide promotion campaign using national magazines. An advertisement in *Collier's* magazine in 1926 proclaimed that Baby Ruth, the "Sweetest Story Ever Told," was "the world's most popular candy."[33]

In the same year, Curtiss introduced its second candy bar, the Butterfinger. It promoted both products through four-color advertising in leading popular magazines. This sales drive was so successful that the company shifted to manufacturing only these two products. Another factory was soon needed to keep up with demand for Baby Ruth, which rapidly became the largest-

selling five-cent confection in America. Within a few months, another factory had to be opened as demand continued to increase. These plants consumed five or six train carloads or about 150,000 pounds of peanuts every
day, and Baby Ruth emerged as the largest-selling candy bar in the world. By
1927, the Curtiss peanut-roasting facility was the largest of its kind in the
world. To keep pace with demand, it roasted peanuts twenty-four hours a day.
In addition, Curtiss operated a fleet of fifty-four five-ton trucks, which
brought in raw materials and distributed finished candy bars.[34]

The Curtiss Company opened offices in New York, Boston, Los Angeles,
and San Francisco. Within two years of its creation, the Baby Ruth was "found
on candy counters throughout the entire country," making it one of the first
candy bars available nationwide. This position was solidified in 1929, when
Curtiss began advertising the Baby Ruth on the Columbia Broadcasting System's radio program the *Baby Ruth Hour*.[35]

OH HENRY!

George H. Williamson, a salesman for a candy broker in Chicago, knew little
of candy making, but in 1914 he opened his own store and began to make his
own candy himself. He had saved $1,000 and leased a store in Chicago's Loop
that cost $750 for the first month. He made candies in the kitchen in the back
of the store and doubled as salesman during the day and janitor at night. His
sales grew steadily. Williamson questioned customers when they bought his
candy and evaluated what they liked. Based on customer preferences, he
opened a second store, which was also successful. Rather than continue to make
the candies by hand, he decided to mass produce them. In 1919, he had closed
both stores and begun manufacturing the candies that customers had preferred
most. He soon had orders from jobbers in Illinois and surrounding states for
one candy bar in particular, from which he concluded that this was the product to launch nationally. All he lacked was a catchy name for his potential star
candy bar. Several stories subsequently circulated as to how he chose the name.
One was that the candy was named after a suitor of a young woman who
worked in Williamson's shop. Every time the man came into the candy shop
to flirt, the salesgirls would squeal, "Oh, Henry!"—or so the story goes. The
other story was that Williamson liked the short stories of William Sydney Porter, whose pen name was O. Henry. In fact, Porter under his pen name had
written about peanuts in an article, which Williamson might have read.[36]

Whatever the reason for the name, Williamson launched the Oh Henry!
candy bar in 1920. It was originally a log-shaped bar with a fudge center sur-

rounded by a caramel and peanut layer and coated in pure milk chocolate. The Oh Henry! sold for a dime—twice the going rate of the competition. Williamson knew that he would have to convince people to pay twice as much for his product. Advertising was the answer. He first advertised in newspapers in one city, then expanded to others. Oh Henry! ads appeared on posters in the same cities targeted by newspaper ads and finally hit national women's magazines, telling how women cut Oh Henry! bars into dainty slices and served them for dessert at home. The result was that by 1923 Oh Henry! was the largest-selling candy bar in America.[37]

The Williamson Candy Company moved to a larger factory in 1925; it had an output potential of 500,000 Oh Henry! candy bars every nine hours. The company issued a cookbook in 1926 titled *Sixty New Ways to Serve a Famous Candy*, in which the candy bar, sliced, diced, chopped, or melted, was used in salads, cakes, cookies, desserts, puddings, sauces, sweet breads, and "tea dainties." It even included a recipe using Oh Henry! candy bars as a topping for sweet potatoes. By 1927, plants had been opened in Oakland and New York and millions of Oh Henry! bars were manufactured each day.[38]

REESE'S PEANUT BUTTER CUP

Milton Hershey finally smelled the aroma of roasted peanuts and in November 1925 began manufacturing a chocolate-peanut-based confection christened "Mr. Goodbar." The company also employed peanuts as an ingredient in its Krackel bar, but peanuts were discontinued in 1940. Hershey supplied chocolate to the H. B. Reese Candy Company, which produced one of the most famous early peanut-chocolate confections. The founder of the company was Harry B. Reese, a former Hershey employee. Reese experimented at first with molasses and coconut candies called Johnny Bars and Lizzie Bars. Reese moved his operation to Hershey, Pennsylvania, in 1923 and began purchasing chocolate from Hershey. In 1928 Reese came out with chocolate-covered peanut butter cups, which were sold in five-pound boxes for use in candy assortments. Ten years later, Reese marketed these cups separately for a penny apiece. These subsequently became known as "Reese's Peanut Butter Cup," and they were extremely popular. Increased demand meant factory expansion, and Reese's became the second-largest buyer of chocolate in the United States. During World War II, difficulties in acquiring sugar and chocolate prompted Reese to discontinue his other lines to concentrate on the peanut butter cups, "a product that both the young and old alike can eat and enjoy."[39]

SNICKERS AND M&M'S

In 1911, Frank and Ethel Mars of Tacoma, Washington, tried to start a candy bar business but had little success. They moved to Minneapolis and in 1920 started up again using the name Mars, Inc. This time they used a technique developed at Minneapolis's Pendergast Candy Company, which had created a fluffy, chewy nougat center for its "Fat Emma" bar by increasing the quantity of egg whites. Three years later, Mars, Inc., introduced the Milky Way bar, which received local distribution. Facing financial problems, the Marses shut down their business and the Schuler Candy Company of Winona, Minnesota, produced the Milky Way for several years. In 1929, Frank and Ethel Mars bought back the rights to the bar and their company began producing it again.[40]

One year later, Frank Mars introduced the Snickers Bar, a combination of peanut butter nougat, peanuts, and caramel encased in milk chocolate. The nougat was made by whipping egg whites until they were light and frothy. This was stabilized by sugar syrup, which was added to the whites along with flavoring ingredients. The caramel consisted of milk, sugar, fat, and flavorings. Snickers quickly became the most popular candy bar in America, a position it has held ever since.[41]

Another Mars success story was M&M's, which were first introduced in 1940. Mars's goal had been to create a candy that did not melt, an idea that was said to have originated during the Spanish Civil War, when soldiers ate chocolates covered with a thin layer of sugar candy that prevented melting in the heat. M&M's version of the confection quickly became the largest selling candy in the world. Mars introduced M&M Peanut Chocolate Candies in 1954, and they have been a good seller since that time.[42]

OTHER PEANUT CANDIES

Thousands of other peanut candies have been introduced over the years. Arthur Spangler of Bryan, Ohio, manufactured Cream Peanut Clusters in 1911 and later produced the Jitney Bar, a maple-flavored marshmallow-peanut bar enrobed in chocolate. Boston's William Schraft produced Milk Peanut Blocks, Peanut Chews, and the Peanut Crackel. Schraft's Bolo bar was a caramel, peanut fudge, and chocolate combination. Another early peanut-chocolate combination bar was produced in Pittsburgh by the D. L. Clark Company, which had been launched in 1886 by David Clark. In 1917 he produced a five-cent bar composed of ground roasted peanuts covered with milk chocolate. It was at first simply called "Clark" but was later renamed the "Clark Bar."

Clark introduced the Zagnut bar, composed of crunchy peanut-butter covered with toasted coconut in 1930. In 1922 the Goldenberg Candy Company produced Peanut Chews in Philadelphia, and they were soon popular all along the East Coast. The same company released Chew-ets, a chocolate-coated version of Peanut Chews, during the 1930s. The Payday candy bar was manufactured by the Pratt and Langhoff Candy Company in 1932. The following year, the company changed its name to Hollywood Candy Company. The Bolster Bar, a peanut crunch covered with milk chocolate, was manufactured by the New England Confectionery Company (NECCO). The NECCO company introduced the Sky Bar in 1937 with a dramatic campaign featuring skywriting by airplanes.[43]

The major peanut processors also introduced peanut candies. Planters created the Jumbo Block Peanut Candy Bar and the Planters Peanut Bar, composed of peanuts, sugar, corn syrup and salt. The Tom Huston Company of Columbus, Georgia, launched Tom's Peanut Bar during the 1920s.[44]

THE CONSEQUENCES OF SNACKING

Today, peanuts, popcorn, Cracker Jack, and peanut candy bars remain stars in the snack food sector of the food industry. A little over a century ago, many Americans considered between-meal snacks unhealthy. Cracker Jack and peanut candies broke down attitudes toward eating between meals by catering directly to America's sweet tooth. These groundbreaking foods forged the way for others to follow. Their initial success can be attributed to their low cost and their association with happy occasions, such as holidays, fairs, circuses, and sporting events. Snacks were also readily available on street corners, at kiosks, and in stores. Eventually, America would support a multibillion dollar snack food industry. Candies were produced by very few manufacturers in 1900 but the field became the ninth-largest food industry in America by 1940. This industry consumed $29 million worth of peanuts annually. Almost 60 percent of all American-made candy bars included peanuts or peanut products as ingredients.[45]

8 *SCIENTISTS AND PROMOTERS*

George Washington Carver's early life is shrouded in myth and legend. He was probably born in the spring of 1865 in a one-room log cabin on a farm in Newton County, Missouri. His mother had been a slave; his father was unknown to him. The owners of the farm were Moses and Susan Carver, German immigrants. Along with his mother, young George was abducted as an infant by night riders who carted him off to Arkansas. The abductors were chased and apprehended, but the rescuers found only George. Moses Carver gave a horse valued at three hundred dollars to the man who returned George—or so a legend relates.[1]

George Washington Carver never saw his mother again and the childless Moses and Susan Carver became his foster parents. George was sickly as a child, so he engaged in household chores and learned to read rather than work in the fields. The Carvers encouraged him to get an education. George Washington Carver attended school in Fayette, Arkansas, and then in Neoshe, Missouri. He worked his way through high school in Kansas. In 1884 Carver applied to a small Presbyterian college in Highland, Kansas; he was accepted by mail but was refused admission when officials found that he was an

African American. He worked on a homestead until 1890, then enrolled in Simpson College in Indianola, Iowa. In 1891, he transferred to Iowa State College of Agriculture and Mechanical Arts at Ames. Carver worked his way through college and received a bachelor's degree in 1894, after which he was given faculty status while pursuing graduate work. He received his Master of Agriculture degree in 1896. Carver was particularly interested in botany and mycology, but he also painted and was involved in extracurricular activities—such as speaking at the local YMCA.[2]

In 1896, Booker T. Washington offered Carver a position at the Tuskegee Institute in Alabama. It had been founded on July 4, 1881, as an institution of advanced education for African Americans. Washington wanted Carver to head the new agriculture department. Carver accepted and spent forty-six years at the institute. During his first twenty years, he devoted his research to a variety of food plants, including tomatoes, sweet potatoes, and cowpeas. Carver's work earned him election to membership in Great Britain's Royal Society of Arts in 1915.[3]

Despite reports to the contrary, Carver paid little attention to peanuts during his early years at Tuskegee. The minor exception was when he conducted a small experiment in 1903, using peanuts as swine feed. However, in late 1915, Carver decided to publish a bulletin on peanuts through the Tuskegee Agricultural Experiment Station. Many other agricultural experiment stations and the U.S. Department of Agriculture had previously published peanut bulletins and circulars. In fact, Carver's interest may well have been stimulated by Jessie Rich's *The Uses of the Peanut on the Home Table,* a bulletin published by the University of Texas Agricultural Experiment Station, which presented a number of peanut recipes. Rich's bulletin was very popular, and its recipes were widely distributed.[4] Whatever moved Carver to select peanuts as a topic for the bulletin, it was an excellent decision. The boll weevil had destroyed Alabama's cotton crop, and many farmers had begun to convert to peanuts. Peanuts had several distinct advantages over other potential cash crops, especially for sharecroppers. Large numbers of cotton oil mills were idle due to a shortage of cotton seeds. These mills could be converted with little effort to produce peanut oil. Because of increasing demand, the peanut was a money crop that was relatively easy to sell.[5] If the sharecroppers could not sell them, peanuts provided a sustaining food in winter, when hunger often struck. Also, the plant's foliage and unsold peanuts could be fed to livestock. Many African Americans owned small farms, and the peanut was particularly ideal for them. Many African Americans were employed picking peanuts, and many others worked in factories manufacturing peanut products. It was a well-chosen crop for Carver, Tuskegee Institute, and African Americans.

At the time the decision was made to publish the bulletin, Carver appears to have had little knowledge about peanuts. In February 1916, he wrote a letter to the chief of the plant division at the USDA, asking a basic question about peanut varieties. His bulletin, *How to Grow the Peanut and 105 Ways of Preparing It for Human Consumption,* was published the next month. The first edition included very little information about cultivating the peanut. As such, it was clearly inferior to the bulletins and circulars published by the USDA and other agricultural experiment stations around the nation. However, it was not focused on cultivating peanuts, but on consuming them: the 105 recipes take up 80 percent of the bulletin. Observers have pointed to these recipes as indicating Carver's long-standing interest in peanuts. However, in the first edition of this bulletin, Carver "gratefully" acknowledged that the recipes had been borrowed from *The Rural World, The Rural New Yorker, The Southern Ruralist, Farm and Fireside, The Country Gentleman, The Kansas Farmer, The Hearthstone, Peerless Cook Book, Home Cooking, Common-Sense Recipes, The Royal Baker and Pastry Cook, The American Agriculturalist, The Tribune Farmer, The Montgomery Advertiser, The Farm and Home, Berry's Fruit Recipes, Wallace's Farmer, Good Housekeeping,* and *The Rumford Book,* as well as from agricultural publications from West Virginia University, the University of Nebraska, Cornell University, and U.S. Department of Agriculture. As there is no evidence in Carver's records that he had personally collected these recipes, it is extremely likely that the faculty and students in Tuskegee's home economics department had done so.[6]

John Harvey Kellogg later claimed to have introduced Carver to the peanut. Kellogg once "had the pleasure of addressing the students and faculty of the Tuskegee Institute and endeavored to interest them in the use of the peanut as a meat substitute in the dietary of the institution." Carver himself claimed that his interest had been kindled when he was approached by a white woman who owned a five-thousand-acre farm. Her cotton crop had been destroyed by the ravages of the boll weevil, and she was willing to try to grow peanuts. In conversing with Carver, she asked him, "Professor, I notice you recommend peanuts as a money crop, but what on earth are you going to do with them?" At a later date Carver was quoted as saying that he was in the laboratory when he heard God's message about the peanut. "I took a handful of peanuts and looked at them, and I said to Him, 'Why did you make the peanut?' and then I tried to find out why by taking the peanut apart."[7]

Whatever its origins, Carver's peanut bulletin immediately struck a chord. Bessie C. Moore, a home economics demonstration agent, requested an additional hundred copies of the bulletin; Alice Davis, a county home demonstration agent in Talladega, Alabama, requested more copies as well. Carver reprinted the bulletin once, and then demand required that he reprint it again and again. Sometimes it was revised. Carver sent copies of the bulletin out to peanut processors, who wrote back congratulating him on his effort to promote peanuts.[8]

THE GREAT WAR

Prior to World War I, the United States imported peanut oil and raw peanuts. The war disrupted all foreign trade, and peanut shortages arose. As transportation space was limited by the war effort and unshelled nuts wasted valuable shipping space, demand grew for peanut products, such as peanut butter, that could be easily transported. Peanuts were named as one of the four most nutritious products under consideration by the Red Cross for preparing a palatable food for the soldiers. Very little of the product was wasted. The byproduct of peanut oil—called peanut cake—had previously been fed to swine, thrown away, or ground up and used for fertilizer. During the war, it was used as a wheat substitute for making bread. Peanut vines were used for fodder for cattle. Hogs rooted up any peanuts that were left in the ground after harvesting. Peanuts and shells were utilized for stock feed and fertilizer and also in the manufacture of dyestuffs.[9]

To meet these needs, farmers greatly expanded their cultivation of peanuts. In 1914, there were under cultivation in the United States 537,000 acres of peanuts. By 1918, peanut cultivation exceeded 4,000,000 acres, largely on land formerly used for cotton. Texas, Alabama, and Georgia each farmed over a million acres. The remainder were grown in Florida, Virginia, Arkansas, and the Carolinas. Oklahoma, Louisiana, and Mississippi also greatly boosted their peanut production.[10]

Some farmers grew peanuts out of patriotic duty. The National Emergency Food Garden Commission strongly encouraged gardeners to grow peanuts, and many heeded the call. When the United States declared war on Germany in 1917, a seventy-year-old Floridian raised peanuts and lived entirely on them and corn so as not to "be a tax on the resources of the State." He survived on the forty bushels he raised, eating half a pound of peanuts per day. As there were "millions of acres in Florida and Southeastern Georgia" lying idle, he hoped other retired farmers would do "their bit for the country and the world by taking up this very easy work."[11]

Others encouraged peanut consumption to demonstrate their patriotic support for the war effort. Meatless days were instituted, and dozens of cookbooks published meatless peanut recipes. The previously mentioned Dr. H. W. Wiley specifically encouraged the addition of peanut flour to bread.

Peanut flour was so closely associated with the war effort that it was re-chris-
tened "Victory Peanut Flour." The Red Cross replaced a portion of wheat
flour with peanut flour in its food programs. When the Women's Central
Committee of Food Conservation sponsored a "Patriotic Food Show" in
Saint Louis in February 1918, it published a cookbooklet with a recipe for
"Peanut and Raisin Bread." Peanut flour recipes were reprinted in other cookbooks, such as the *Victory Cook Book* published in Jersey City, New Jersey.
During the war, the Sea Island Cotton Seed Company of Charleston, South
Carolina, made peanut flour for use as a wheat substitute. However, as soon
as the war ended, one writer noted that "the demand diminished, because
many went back to the use of wheat flour."[12]

By the end of the war, many Southern farmers had replaced their cotton
crops with peanuts. The citizens of Enterprise, Coffee County, Alabama,
erected a $3,000 monument to the memory of "Billy Boll Weevil" on its main
street. Coffee County had given up on cotton but had been saved by the peanut. With $1 million peanut operations underway, the county claimed to be
the nation's "center of peanut production."[13]

During the war, the U.S. Food Administration had promoted ways in
which the peanut could be used, issuing a list of more than forty recommendations. There was quite a range: peanut hay, cosmetics, fuel, fertilizer, packing for sardines, roofing, putty, insulating material, and linoleum. Articles
extolling the patriotic nature of the peanut appeared in magazines. For instance, James Judson's 1917 "Peanuts and Patriotism" article in *The Forum*
proclaimed that peanuts served valiantly in the war effort by conserving dairy
products, substituting for meat, and feeding stock.[14] The peanut's rise to
prominence was recognized by the magazine *Table Talk* with a poem:

> The lowly peanut now at last
>   Has come into his own;
> They tell us that he stands quite high
>   In nourishment alone;
> As I have often thought before,
>   It would be well if we ate more.[15]

By the end of the war, the peanut, which had been "formerly looked upon
as a mere trifle, and recognized chiefly on the circus ground where peddled
by vendors in small lots," was classed by the U.S. Department of Agriculture
as one of the most important commercial crops in America. But one serious
problem confronted the peanut industry, and that was related to foreign
trade. Peanuts had been imported into the United States since before the Civil
War. Imports greatly increased during the first decade of the twentieth cen-

tury but then declined during World War I. With the war over, global trade patterns returned to their normal configuration, and in 1920 imported peanuts flooded into the American market. The price for peanuts dropped, and American peanut growers were threatened. The major competition was from China and Japan, which exported 132 million pounds of peanuts annually to the United States with an additional 165 million pounds of oil. As the cost of producing peanuts in China was 1½ cents per pound, compared with 7½ to 8½ cents in the United States, American peanut growers demanded a tariff on imports. Those who imported peanuts and those who used cheap foreign peanuts and peanut oil supported free trade. They claimed that free trade benefited the consumer through lower prices for peanut products. Those who grew and processed peanuts complained that they would lose money; many African Americans who harvested and processed peanuts faced losing their jobs.[16]

CARVER GOES TO CONGRESS

The peanut growers approached Congress to levy a four-cent-per-pound tariff on peanut imports. The House Ways and Means Committee, chaired by Joseph W. Fordney, agreed to hold hearings on the potential tariff. The United Peanut Growers' Association asked several peanut experts, including Carver, to testify before the committee. All the other witnesses were white, and Carver was scheduled to speak last. Everyone was allocated ten minutes to speak. By the time Carver spoke, the committee was bored, and the chairman reminded Carver that he had only ten minutes. Despite the time limitation, Carver presented his "Pandora's box," which was laden with 101 exhibits of peanut products. He slowly laid them on the stenographer's table directly in front of the chairman. As Carver began unpacking the box, the audience smiled and the committee woke up.[17]

At the time, it was unusual for an African American to address a congressional committee. The committee chairman interrupted Carver's presentation with sharp questions, but Carver responded with witty and good-natured repartee. He captured the sympathies of the committee as well as those of the audience members, who were as much interested in him as his products. When Carver's ten minutes were up, he bowed, smiled, and thanked the committee, but he was instructed to continue. During the next hour and forty minutes, Carver presented chocolate-coated peanuts, peanut candy bars, peanut flavorings for ice cream, peanut cakes, peanut gingerbread, and peanut candy bars. Carver reported that crushed peanut cake could be made into flour and meal. He presented five breakfast foods made from peanuts. Peanut hay and meal could be used to feed stock. Carver reported that the peanut hearts that were removed before processing could be fed to pigeons and that peanut skins could be used for making dyes. Carver proudly announced that he had just found out "how to extract milk from peanuts," which was "good for those who don't like dairy products." This milk could be used to make cheese with peanut curds. Carver had also found ways to make peanut relish, mock oysters, mock meat, Worcestershire sauce, and a highly flavored imitation soy sauce. He made cherry-, orange-, blackberry-, and plum-flavored punches from peanuts. He reported that peanut oil could be used in face creams and powders, ink and wood stains.[18]

When Carver finished, the audience and the committee applauded. Chairman Fordney told him he had made a valuable contribution to science, and Representative Gardener, a Democrat from Texas, declared that Carver "had made the most wonderful exhibition he had ever known to be presented the committee." According to P. D. Bain, the president of the United Peanut Growers' Association, Carver "made a very great impression as I could see it with his exhibits, and Dr. Carver has promised to be with us again when we go before the Finance Committee." In fact, it was later concluded that Carver had "attracted more attention than any other personage that had appeared before that body during the 1921 session."[19]

The opponents of the tariff also addressed the committee. Allan DeFord, representing Musher and Company in New York, reported that U.S. production of peanuts had never met demand, and that foreign imports greatly reduced the price to consumers.[20] But the tariff was passed, and peanut imports declined appreciably.

THE PEANUT BOOSTER

Shortly after the hearing, Carver's national popularity soared. The fifty-two-year-old scientist hit the lecture circuit, addressing the United Peanut Association in Chicago on the topic, "The Potential Uses of the Peanut." Carver was enthusiastic and supremely confident, announcing that he had only just begun his work on peanuts. According to the *Peanut Promoter,* Carver "surprised not only the peanut fraternity, but has done his bit toward awakening the outside world." In 1922, headlines announced "Prof. Carver to Tell White Virginians about the Peanut" at an agricultural fair. When he arrived, he was introduced as the man who knew peanuts "better than any other living person." Carver subsequently exhibited his peanut products at the Southern Exhibition in New York City. At this fair, trays displayed his peanut flour, peanut cake, stock feed, peanut shoe blacking, mock oysters, peanut sweet pickles, peanut coffee, peanut "Wooster" sauce, peanut vinegar, and orange, lemon, and cherry flavors of peanut punch. Subsequently, Carver attended Alabama's state agricultural fair and demonstrated even more ways to use the peanut.[21]

The plethora of peanut products created by Carver soon reached 145. Then it was announced that Carver had hit 150. In 1923, he added chili sauce made from peanuts, as well as candy, salad oils, bisque, oleomargarine, cheese, instant peanut coffee, peanut beverages, and four kinds of meal stock for cattle feeding. In addition, he informed readers that peanuts, like other legumes, took nitrogen from the air and deposited it into the ground, enriching the soil for future crops. *Popular Science Monthly* christened Carver "the Burbank of the south."[22]

One of Carver's first creations was peanut milk, which he used in the same way as cow's milk and was a very satisfactory substitute. According to Carver, peanut milk varied in taste from almost no flavor to a most pronounced peanut flavor. Peanut curd could be made into cheese, chocolate fillers, cream bonbons, salads, and mock meat dishes. The rich cream could be used on fruit and breakfast cereals or in coffee. It also made "a most delicious ice cream, smooth grain, fine in appearance and of a wonderful flavor. Lemon, orange, peppermint, wintergreen, vanilla, and nearly all of the fruit juices blend with it beautifully and without curdling." Finally, peanut buttermilk closely approximated fresh dairy buttermilk. Carver claimed that peanut milk cost less to produce and was in many ways superior to cow's milk. Carver again lectured widely, extolling the virtues of peanut milk. In addition to serving as a substitute for dairy milk, peanut milk was a distinct product with its own culinary characteristics that could be advantageously used in the kitchen. Carver predicted that peanut milk would "soon be introduced into every home throughout the country," and that it would markedly lower the cost of living.[23]

By 1923, Carver had achieved great visibility for his work on peanut milk and had a number of offers to manufacture it. Carver decided that it was time to patent his valuable discovery. Unfortunately, he found that he had not been the first to make peanut milk. As previously noted, Bernabé Cobo had found Incas producing peanut milk in the seventeenth century. Peanut milk had been made for decades in the United States, and recipes for making it had been published since the late nineteenth century. Finally, as Carver discovered, an Englishman held the patent on the process of making commercial peanut milk.[24] Little more was heard about peanut milk. But there were plenty of other peanut products that needed to be explored, and Carver launched a large-scale development effort.

Carver soon increased the number of peanut products he had discovered to 166. He worked on flour and also announced that raw peanut butter sandwiches alleviated stomach problems. His peanut massage cream vanished almost instantly, penetrated quickly, and was a great "beautifier." To help the Florida citrus growers, Carver announced a new drink that combined peanuts and oranges. By 1927, he had reached 195 uses for the peanut. Two years later, he hit 250 uses. By 1932, he announced 285 peanut products or processes. Carver was thereafter called the "peanut man." A list of Carver's peanut discoveries was compiled by his colleagues, who concluded that Carver had invented more than 300 uses for the peanut, and this is the statistic that is repeated in school textbooks and in biographies about Carver.[25]

COMMERCIALIZING CARVER'S DISCOVERIES

Carver was widely recognized for his peanut work, but not all of the attention was positive. Carver was criticized for the impracticality of some of his peanut discoveries. Some people claimed that his paints were of poor quality, his stains would not stain, and his synthetic rubber was too costly. Carver responded philosophically with the comment that every new invention passed through stages from total skepticism and apathy to a great awakening, when everyone suddenly became conscious of its merits.[26] He believed that his peanut discoveries were still in the "skeptical and apathetic" stages.

But Carver was also aware of other criticisms coming from those who were already committed to his discoveries: "I understand that there are a few people who are sore because they came or sent others to get my formula without money and because I would not accede to their wishes, they are trying to discredit my work." Carver claimed that he had devoted "his entire time to investigation" and did not interest himself in the business possibilities of his many discoveries. When the results of his work were of practical value to the farmer, they were "made public and may be utilized by anyone."[27]

In fact, Carver was extremely interested in the industrial applications of his discoveries. He sent off sixteen patent applications and carefully considered how to commercialize them. On August 21, 1923, the Carver Products Company was formed in Atlanta to buy, sell, and deal in the formulae and patented processes for various products. Charles W. Wickershain, the president and general manager of a railroad, was selected as president and general manager of the new company. Others involved were the vice president and general manager of a chain of grocery stores, a former governor, and congressman. The new company was capitalized at $125,000. Carver was granted a twenty-year right to his patents and he cooperated in advertising and promoting peanut products. In return, Carver received 10 percent of the net income from the manufacturing concerns growing out of the holding corporation.[28]

Shortly after the company's formation, the *New York American* announced in a full-page article that Carver's company had received "flattering reports from their first product placement on the market." Two years later, the Baltimore *Afro-American* reported that Carver's business was capitalized at $500,000, and it lamented that "blacks" had failed to capitalize on Carver's inventions. The article predicted that this would mean a fortune for Carver.[29]

Among the more important products that Carver patented were his peanut-based face cream and Penol, a cough syrup made partly from peanuts. In 1926, the Carver Penol Company was formed, involving some of the same prominent Georgia businessmen. It manufactured and distributed Penol, an emulsion for the treatment of coughs, bronchitis, and catarrh, which contained "peanut juices and creosote in palatable combination." It was advertised as a "Tissue Builder, Intestinal Cleanser, Germ Arrester, Nerve Food, Intestinal Antiseptic." A 1927 advertisement in Alabama's *Montgomery News* reported that Penol was the result of years of untiring labor by Carver, who was identified as "one of the greatest scientists of all times" and the "Czar of the Goober." Another advertisement ran the headline "Chemist Discovers Amazing Medicinal Value in Peanuts." Despite the advertisements, Carver had little contact with the company. Although Penol continued to be sold for years, it was never highly successful.[30]

Carver was also consulted about the organization of the Peanut Products Company, which was reorganized in late 1940 as the Carvoline Company. It set out "to promote the interest and distribution of a limited number of products based on Carver's discoveries." Its products included *proteina,* a cake and waffle flour made from pulverized peanuts, and a line of cosmetics, including a face cream and lotion, a hair oil, and a massage oil, all made from peanuts. Carvoline shared profits with Carver and the George Washington Carver Foundation he had created.[31]

Carver was criticized at the time for his failure to commercialize his peanut discoveries. In fact, few of his discoveries were converted into practical uses. This failure is particularly surprising in light of the potential of the peanut during World War II. When sources for rubber were cut off by the war, however, synthetic rubber made from peanuts was not even considered as a substitute. Neither were any of the other Carver peanut discoveries used during the war, when peanuts were plentiful and many other raw materials were unaccessible.

THE PEANUT CURE

Beginning in the early twentieth century, medical researchers began reporting the peanut's healthful qualities. In 1921, one researcher reported that peanuts could be used to treat pellagra, which was caused by "improper nourishment of the human body." Ten years later, a circular written by S. G. Bendon, of Montreal, Canada, stated that the consumption of generous helpings of peanut butter tends "to ward off various children's diseases, including infantile paralysis or polio." The *Peanut Journal and Nut World* encouraged peanut processors to "feature this healthful line and everyone concerned will benefit."[32]

At the time, polio was a major crippler of infants and children. Its cause was unknown until 1908, when Austrian physicians concluded that it was caused by a virus. After World War I, many individuals sought treatment for the disease. Franklin Roosevelt contracted polio in 1921, and while looking for a treatment, he discovered the healing waters of a resort in Warm Springs, Georgia, where he went regularly for swimming and other vigorous exercise to strengthen his muscles. He bought the resort and formed the Georgia Warm Springs Foundation in 1927. It emphasized hydrotherapy treatment and massage for polio victims. The only other general treatments at the time were braces or surgery to correct deformities.

Carver, an amateur masseur, frequently gave massages to his friends. His interest in peanuts led him to use peanut oil for his massage. He reported that it vanished almost instantly, penetrated quickly, and was successful as a "beautifier." Carver produced massage cream and oil from peanuts, which he gave to some women at Tuskegee to try. However, some women "inclined to be fat brought it back to me saying they could not use it because it made them gain weight." This gave Carver an idea. The Thompsons, a prominent white Tuskegee family, had an eleven-year-old boy named Foy, who was seriously underweight. After Carver's peanut oil massages, Foy gained thirty-one pounds. Carver concluded that the phenomenal results had been caused by the muscle-building qualities of the peanut oil, which had been absorbed through the skin into the bloodstream.[33]

By 1932, Carver had employed peanut oil massage on two children suffering what was thought to be infantile paralysis. They showed remarkable improvement and recovered from their ailments. In November 1933, Carver suggested that peanut oil "may prove a cure for infantile paralysis." He volunteered to give a demonstration of the peanut oil massage to Franklin Roosevelt, who had been elected president of the United States the previous year. When Carver was asked for more details about his potential polio cure, he responded that he did "not want any further publicity at this time" as he was "making more demonstrations of its efficacy."[34]

T. M. Davenport, an Associated Press writer, interviewed Carver at Tuskegee about these developments. Davenport wrote a cautious article, quoting Carver as saying, "It has been given out that I have found a cure. I have not, but it looks hopeful." The article did report the dramatic results in Carver's two polio victims: their muscles had increased in size, permitting one who had been walking with crutches to walk with the use of a cane. The other, less severely afflicted, had increased use of his affected leg and joined other boys in playing football. Davenport then reported that Carver said, "I have used it on 250 persons, and it has never failed, so far as I can find out."[35] As Carver had worked with only two individuals who were presumed to have polio, this statement caused gross misunderstanding.

Carver told an audience in Atlanta that he was "seeking a cure for infantile paralysis" and that "beneficial results had been obtained in massaging victims of infantile paralysis with an oil made from peanuts." He explained that he applied peanut oil by massaging it into the skin so that it was absorbed through the veins. He likewise exhibited an emulsion of peanut oil, bichloride of mercury, and a paste of metallic mercury "for use in treatment of a social disease." The social disease was unidentified, but Carver reported that the peanut oil had been successful in a recent test. Carver later softened this by saying that he had made no specific claims, and he was willing to permit any reputable physician to examine his methods and results. As far as the polio "cures" went, Carver said that one person had abandoned his braces and had been able to stand without aid. He believed that scientific evidence for his massage therapy was necessary and argued for sympathetic cooperation of medical authorities.[36]

Many newspapers in the United States printed these claims, and Carver was swamped with requests for treatment. Correspondents wanted to buy peanut oil from Carver, who did not manufacture it because he did not have large commercial presses. Unable to get the peanut oil from Carver, they turned to other sources, causing a peanut oil shortage in the United States. Although Carver stated that he modified the viscosity and limpidity of the oil to match the "absorptive power of the individual's skin," he had concluded that "any refined pure peanut oil will work in the hands of a skilled masseur." A Dr. Carl S. Frischkorn claimed credit for the idea of peanut oil massage and produced "Vitalized Peanut Oil" in the fall of 1934. The Rose Miller Company sought approval from the United States Food and Drug Administration (FDA) for its peanut oil "bust developer." Several Tuskegee people entered the massage oil business.[37]

Some physicians wholeheartedly endorsed peanut oil massage. Dr. L. C. Fischer, for instance, used it at Crawford Long Hospital in Atlanta, and others were strong advocates for peanut oil therapy. However, Carver was not a physician, and the medical profession in general was not happy with his pronouncements. Despite the advocacy of some physicians, Carver's peanut oil massage therapy never received the endorsement of the American Medical Association. Carver later claimed that his idea had been snubbed by medical doctors because "they regard a non-practitioner the same as a patent medicine. They will not [prescribe] a patent medicine unless they tear the label off and put it in a bottle of their own." Physicians and medical schools expressed interest in testing Carver's methods but Carver refused to discuss his procedures, so that his experiments could not be verified and replicated. When the federal government established a clinic for African-American polio victims at Tuskegee, Carver was not involved in any way.[38]

President Roosevelt visited Tuskegee in 1938 and proudly shook hands with Carver. Photographs taken of this occasion appeared in many newspapers. The president announced that he did "use peanut oil from time to time" and he was "sure that it helps." After the visit, Carver sent Roosevelt a bottle of his emulsion to use before his peanut oil massage, writing, "I am sending you this merely as a friendly gesture and am seeking *absolutely no publicity.*"[39]

Newspapers and popular magazines regularly reported the apparent recoveries of thousands of victims who believed that "peanut oil massage could aid in the cure of arthritis, muscular disorder resulting from poliomyelitis, acne, and several other diseases and health problems." Many afflicted individuals believed themselves to have been cured or helped by the peanut oil treatments. That Carver was successful where others had failed was largely due to his skill as a masseur and his ability to inspire hope, which Carver believed was extremely important. Carver continued experiments with only brief interruptions until near the time of his death.[40] While Carver's claims verged on quackery and his pronouncements raised false hopes of a miracle cure, it must be remembered that not until 1955 did Dr. Jonas Salk release his vaccine for polio.

Carver's death on January 3, 1943, ended peanut oil massages as a treatment for polio, but it did not end the association of peanuts and polio. In 1945, teenagers in Cleveland, Ohio, began selling peanuts and donating the proceeds to help care for those suffering from polio. During the next twelve years, the idea took off nationally. In 1957, the Fisher Nut Company of Saint Paul, Minnesota, donated three million bags of peanuts in bags emblazoned with the slogan "Fight Polio with Peanuts." Kiwanis clubs netted over one million dollars from a one-day street sale in which kids dressed up in pea-nut-bag costumes and sold the peanuts to generate money for medical care and other benefits for crippled children.[41]

LEGACY

Carver received many awards throughout his life. In 1923, the National As-sociation for the Advancement of Colored People awarded Carver the Spin-garn Medal "in consideration of his services in agricultural chemistry, on agriculture during the last year before white and colored audiences, partic-ularly in the South, where his clear thought and straightforward attitude have greatly increased interracial knowledge and respect."[42]

Carver's visibility led to an invitation from Bob Barry at the Tom Hus-ton Peanut Company to visit its peanut factory in Atlanta. The company had begun with three employees roasting peanuts in a frame cabin. One employee sold the nuts on the streets of Columbus, Georgia. The company was suc-cessful and moved into a permanent building during its second year of op-eration. The Tom Huston Company prided itself on its control of the pea-nuts from the time they left the farmers' hands. The firm also emphasized advertising and promotion. Barry mainly worked on improving the quality of peanuts and teamed up with Carver to improve the standards of peanut cultivation. Carver and Huston became fast friends and their friendship continued for the remainder of Carver's life. To demonstrate its respect and honor for Carver, the company donated to Tuskegee a bas relief bearing Carver's likeness. When it was unveiled during commencement ceremonies in 1931, Barry proclaimed Carver to be the "personification of true, unselfish service to mankind."[43]

At the time of Carver's death in January 1943, America was again embroiled in a world war, yet newspapers, magazines, and Americans of all races paused to show their respect for him. One early biography, titled *The Peanut Man*, was published in 1948. Ever since, school textbooks and children's books have por-trayed Carver as an African-American role model and stressed his connection with the peanut. Such works include Barbara Mitchell's *A Pocketful of Goobers: A Story about George Washington Carver* and Patricia McKissack and Fredrick McKissack's *George Washington Carver: The Peanut Scientist.*[44]

However, during the 1970s, Carver's reputation took a dive as some Afri-can Americans did not believe that he should be a role model. For instance, June Jordan's poem "Notes on a Peanut" satirized Carver's peanut work. Her opening lines were:

Hi there. My name is George
Washington
Carver.
If you will bear with me for a few minutes I will share with you
a few
of the 30,117 uses to which
the lowly peanut has been put
by me
since yesterday afternoon.[45]

Whatever the judgments about Carver's peanut research, the peanut recipes he compiled live on. Sixty years after Carver's death, *How to Grow the
Peanut and 105 Ways of Preparing It for Human Consumption* remains in print
and the recipes are still as serviceable as when they were collected in 1916.[46]

9   *WAR AND PEACE*

The world was just recovering from the Depression when war broke out in Europe in 1939, and the United States entered the conflict two years later. World War II rocked the peanut industry along with every other aspect of American life and greatly disrupted world trade patterns. There was a major disruption of the importing of vegetable oils used in many food products and for industrial applications. Coconut oil was commonly used before the war, because it could be heated for very long periods of time without turning rancid. In addition, it was the most stable oil at room temperature. The United States had imported coconut oil from the Philippines and British colonies in Asia. After Pearl Harbor, however, the Philippines and Southeast Asia were occupied by Japan and submarine warfare cut off access to other logical sources of the oil. Coconut oil imports ceased and a scramble ensued for alternative oils accessible to the United States. As in World War I, peanut oil came to fore and its production soared.[1]

Before World War II, peanut oil was a minor domestic product in American kitchens. During the early 1930s, only 1 percent of Americans used it. By 1938, this had increased to 3 percent. This shift was due primarily to the Planters Edible Oil Company, which was created in 1933. Within four years, an estimated ten million customers, mostly in metropolitan centers like New York, purchased Planters peanut oil. Planters sold three brands: Ali D'Italia, aimed at the Italian population; Hi-Hat, targeted at the general market; and Hi-Hat Kosher, which made Planters one of the first major manufacturers to mass produce products specifically targeting observant Jews.[2]

In 1941, only $71 million worth of peanut oil was produced in the United States. It was mainly used in making shortening and only to a minor extent as a cooking or salad oil. By April 1942, however, *Fortune* magazine projected that farmers would have to produce 600 million pounds of peanut oil just to meet American needs. As in World War I, peanut oil was employed in the manufacture of glycerin to make explosives, and peanut cake—the product left after removal of the oil—was used to make flour and concentrated soup. Planters peanut oil was specifically cited in cookbooks as the alternative to other vegetable oils previously used. For instance, the 1942 edition of the *Cedric Adams Cook Book on Fish and Sea-Food Cookery* included many recipes with Planters peanut oil specifically mentioned.[3]

In 1942, the United States rationed the sale of lard, salad oil, butter, and other fats but exempted peanut oil. Secretary of Agriculture Claude R. Wickard requested that farmers plant 5 million acres of peanuts, which were expected to produce 3.6 billion pounds of oil. Cotton seed oil mills were converted to produce peanut oil and meal. The Farm Credit Administration lent money to those farmers who needed assistance in purchasing equipment and supplies.[4]

Two major factors contributed to the inability of farmers to meet the goal. One was the scarcity of shipping boxes, as wood products had been rationed. The second was the lack of labor. The Selective Service sent many young farmers off to war. As soon as it became apparent that the conscription of farmers meant a decrease in food production, deferments were granted to agricultural workers. Also, German and Italian prisoners of war were employed in peanut processing plants, but they were of marginal assistance. It took time to teach prisoners what was wanted, and then they had to be supervised. The Planters Nut and Chocolate Company employed some, but Amedeo Obici groused that "they did less than half the work the colored help was doing."[5]

Another serious problem during World War II was the disruption of sugar imports. During the war some sugar-producing areas, such as the Philippines, were cut off from America. Sugar was still imported from Hawaii and the Caribbean, but cargo ships were in short supply and priorities needed to be established. Simultaneously, the demand for sugar expanded as the military commanded vast quantities for its own use, and sugar was exported to the

United Kingdom and other allies. Declining domestic supply and increased demand resulted in civilian rationing. As peanut candy manufacturers required sugar, these companies were hard-pressed by the shortages. Most continued to produce some products for civilian consumption but mainly survived on military contracts such as manufacturing. Some companies thrived. The production of Oh Henry! candy bars, for instance, set a new sales record in 1943, with more than half of the candy bars going to the armed forces.[6]

While shortages hurt the sugar-based peanut snacks, overall the lack of sugar was, paradoxically, the major factor in the peanut's continued rise to stardom. As the rationing of sugar, chocolate, and other products took effect, the supply of candy and chocolate bars for civilians dwindled. For many Americans, commercial candy could not be acquired at any price. Peanuts and peanut products were obvious alternatives. As Americans were fully employed during the war, most had some idle money in their pockets for snack foods, and peanut sales skyrocketed. The annual sale of shelled peanuts to civilians increased from 4.8 pounds per person in 1941 to 6.2 pounds in 1942, finally hitting 6.6 pounds in 1945.[7]

Likewise, peanut butter production dramatically increased. The United States manufactured 250 million pounds of peanut butter in 1941. The following year, this increased to 400 million pounds. The United States government, the largest single buyer, purchased almost 7 million pounds just for school lunches. The quartermaster general also contracted for 57 million pounds for military forces in 1943.[8]

Before the war, 1.9 million acres of peanuts were harvested, producing 1.4 billion pounds of nuts. To forestall inflation, price ceilings were established for peanut butter and salted peanuts, but these were subsequently removed at the request of peanut growers. During 1942, acreage increased to 3.5 million acres, and the production of peanuts rose by 75 percent to 2.1 billion pounds. Even this bumper crop couldn't satisfy the demand. The price for peanuts rose from 4.7 cents per pound in 1941 to 6.1 cents a year later. For many southern farmers, the returns from peanuts provided a major portion of their farm income.[9]

When the secretary of agriculture launched the "Food for Freedom" program in 1943, he exhorted farmers to plant 5.5 million acres of peanuts. The peanut was heralded as a powerful factor "in winning the war and perhaps in the peace to follow. No doubt it will help feed a famishing world." While peanut production did rise, the increase was nowhere near the initial projection. When it became clear that there would be a peanut shortage, the Office of Price Administration reinstated price ceilings on peanuts and peanut products, excluding only roasted peanuts at the retail level because of the difficulty of monitoring small stands. All peanuts were purchased by the Commodity Credit Corporation. Further restrictions were placed on the sale of peanuts and peanut products in 1944 and 1945.[10]

POSTWAR PEANUT SALES

When the war ended, peanuts and peanut products had become American staples. Yet peanut growers were worried that prices would quickly sag when normal trading and consumption patterns returned, as had happened after World War I. The government subsidized a large peanut export market with dollar grants and loans to cushion the transition from wartime to peacetime. By 1949, exports accounted for 45 percent of the total peanut market. Although peanut cultivation was cut back once the war ended, surpluses continued. The government again stepped in and established price supports. Thanks to government-funded exports and price supports, farmers actually earned more money per acre for their crops than they did during the war.[11]

Planters peanut oil was very popular during the war, but when the conflict ended, international trade recommenced and coconut oil again became the vegetable oil of choice for margarine manufacturers. As peanut oil had been used mainly in the manufacture of margarine, producers needed to find new ways to sell their product. In 1948, Planters targeted housewives with a cookbooklet titled *Cooking the Modern Way! 129 Home Tested and Proved Recipes to Please Your Family.* All the recipes included Planters peanut oil as an ingredient or a cooking medium. The booklet demonstrated that peanut oil could be used in just about any recipe. The booklet was so successful that the company released several additional cookbooklets, such as *Planters Passover Recipe Book* and *They Taste Sooo Good.*[12]

At the beginning of the twentieth century, lard was the most important frying medium in America. By the end of the century, vegetable oils, such as coconut, peanut, and safflower, dominated the field, and lard was hard to find. This shift had occurred in part because of the medical profession's conclusion that vegetable oil was healthier than animal oils. In addition, peanut oil offers a high smoking point as well as versatility in food applications, making vegetable oils the choice for many products.[13] Finally, manufacturers of vegetable oils, such as Planters, advertised and promoted their products prodigiously, but peanut oil did not become a hot commodity until the health food establishment championed vegetable oils during the 1960s.

Of the major pre–World War II peanut butter manufacturers, Beech-Nut and Heinz discontinued producing peanut butter during the 1950s. While the motives for these decisions remain obscure, surely one reason was the competition from three major peanut butter manufacturers. Skippy and Peter Pan have already been introduced. The third was Procter and Gamble's Jif. In 1955, Procter and Gamble Company entered the peanut butter business by acquiring W. T. Young Foods of Lexington, Kentucky, makers of Big Top Peanut Butter. It introduced Jif in 1958 and now turns out 250,000 jars every day. The name *Jif* seems to be a short form of *jiff* or *jiffy*. Procter and Gamble had been launched in 1836 by William Procter and James Gamble in Cincinnati. It started as a soap- and candle-making operation. By 1890, the company was selling more than thirty different types of soap, including Ivory. Fueled by innovative advertising, including full-color print ads in national magazines, consumer demand for Procter and Gamble soaps grew. To meet this increasing demand, the company expanded its operations outside Cincinnati. It also advertised extensively. When radio became an important advertising medium, Procter and Gamble sponsored radio serials, such as *Ma Perkins* in 1933. Due to the sponsorship of many serials by soap manufacturers, the programs became known as soap operas.[14]

During the 1930s, a Proctor and Gamble researcher, Victor Mills, had revolutionized the process of making Ivory Soap. He turned his attention to peanut butter during the 1950s. Mills developed a process for preventing the oil from separating in the peanut butter. He also added 10 percent honey to improve the taste. After Jif was marketed, competitors claimed that peanut butter with honey was not consistent with the USDA definition of peanut butter, which requires at least 90 percent peanuts, with the remaining 10 percent restricted to salt, sweeteners, and stabilizers. Their charge was upheld by the FDA. By the time the ruling was made, Procter and Gamble was already committed to manufacturing peanut butter, so it removed the honey and increased advertising. Like other peanut butter manufacturers, Procter and Gamble distributed peanut butter cookbooks.[15]

Procter and Gamble diversified its peanut butter products and Extra Crunchy Jif made its debut in 1974. According to Procter and Gamble, a 28-ounce jar of Jif contains about 1,218 peanuts. It takes approximately 120 billion peanuts to equal the amount of Jif peanut butter produced in one year. The Jif plant in Lexington, Kentucky, is the largest peanut butter producing facility in the world.[16]

After the war, the peanut candy market boomed. Reese's Peanut Butter Cup, distributed through wholesale jobbers, vending machine operators, and syndicated stores, gained popularity, and the company expanded its facility in 1957. Hershey assumed control of the company in 1963 and took the product national. The advertising slogan "Two great tastes that taste great together" was developed by Ogilvie and Mather in 1970 for the Reese's Peanut Butter

Cup. Perhaps the continued success of the Reese's chocolate-peanut butter combination encouraged Hershey to test market a small peanut butter candy in 1979. While the product was under development, "PB" was its proposed name but unfortunately Mars held the trademark on it, so they shifted to "Reese's Pieces," which was released nationally in 1978. Within four years, the candy was so successful that a new production line was established in Stuart's Draft, Virginia.[17]

Mars, Inc., released Peanut Butter M&M's to compete with Reese's Pieces. Its sales peaked in 1991 at $78 million, then dropped to $34 million in 1993. According to Joël Glenn Brenner's *The Emperors of Chocolate: Inside the Secret World of Hershey and Mars,* Mars then tried to relaunch the brand by copying the coloring and styling of Reese's Pieces. This resulted in a lawsuit in which Hershey maintained that Mars was capitalizing on Hershey's goodwill and substantial investment in Reese's Pieces.[18]

Following World War II, Cracker Jack sales rebounded. By 1947 annual sales reached 100 million packages worth more than $3,300,000. The Cracker Jack Company was sold in 1963 to Borden, Inc., based in New York City. By 1970, Cracker Jack was enjoyed in 24,689,000 homes, or 41 percent of all American households. It had retained its dominance of the ready-to-eat popcorn category for decades. Cracker Jack processed twenty-five tons of popcorn per day and reportedly was the largest user of popcorn in the nation. The company also expanded abroad. Cracker Jack had been introduced into the United Kingdom in 1897 and into Canada in 1901, and by 1976 Cracker Jack was sold in fifty-three countries.[19] Then, Cracker Jack's commanding lead slipped abroad and rapidly declined at home. This fall can be attributed to two major causes. The first was Borden's acquisition drive that resulted in the purchase of twenty-three companies during the 1980s. With the further acquisition of Laura Scudder's, a snack food company of Anaheim, California, and the Snacktime Company in Indianapolis, Borden's became the number-two marketer of snack foods in the nation behind Frito-Lay, a subsidiary of PepsiCo.[20] While Borden developed new Cracker Jack products, it was simply one product line among many. It did not receive a great deal of attention or major new investment from corporate headquarters.

Another reason for the decline of Cracker Jack sales was the rise of stiff competition. The competitors utilized other sweeteners in addition to molasses, including maple syrup, sugar, and caramel. With Cracker Jack losing market share to its competitors, in 1997 Borden sold the product line to Frito-Lay. The company also had a national system that could guarantee widespread distribution throughout America. Frito-Lay lost no time in investing in major new promotions and new packaging for Cracker Jack. To celebrate the acquisition, Frito-Lay announced a prize give-away of limited-edition collector jewelry. Cracker Jack replaced the customary toy surprises in sixteen packages of the caramel-coated popcorn and peanuts with certificates for the jewelry and distributed them at random. As Frito-Lay's advertising campaign has yet to move Cracker Jack back into its number-one position, one wonders how many resources will be allocated to product advertising in the future. Over 200 million boxes of Cracker Jack alone are crunched and munched annually, yet Crunch 'n Munch, a similar product, outsells Cracker Jack. Screaming Yellow Zonkers and Poppycock are fast catching up with leaders. Although the specific sales figures are not public, the total peanut-popcorn business is a multi-billion-dollar sector of the confectionery industry.

SCHOOL SALES

Well before World War II, peanut processors targeted schools for sales of their products. Beginning in the 1920s, manufacturers lobbied school cafeterias to sell their goods, particularly peanut butter, because schools had to provide students with low-cost meals. Peanuts were being used nationwide in increasing quantities. Peanut butter was regularly sold to many school cafeterias "as a healthful, inexpensive and popular spread with juveniles." In addition, large quantities of peanuts and other peanut products were sold to institutional cafeterias. Cafeterias and automats fed many more Americans than did the vast majority of other types of restaurants at this time.[21]

Peanut processors encouraged the federal government to purchase peanut surpluses and give them to schools in the 1930s. Peanuts and peanut products have proliferated in school cafeterias ever since. A 1962 study of the federally funded school lunch program reported that school cafeteria personnel believed peanut butter to be an excellent protein supplement, a fair source of calcium, iron, thiamin, and riboflavin, and an excellent source of niacin. Children liked the flavor of peanut butter. A minimum of time and equipment was required to prepare it. The unopened containers could be held for several months without deterioration. Finally, peanut butter was a versatile food that cold be served in combination with many other foods. Peanut butter sandwiches, for instance, could be prepared two hours before serving and the spread could be combined with blackberry jam and jelly, chopped prunes, sliced apples, cranberry sauce, grated carrots, grape jelly, sliced ham, mayonnaise, diced celery, chopped sweet pickles, sliced or mashed bananas, corn syrup, melted butter, strawberry jam, applesauce, evaporated milk, plum jam, brown sugar, crushed pineapple, peach jam, plum jelly, chopped onions, lettuce, maple syrup, strawberry preserves, chocolate syrup, molasses, grated cheese, peach syrup, or chopped chicken. In addition, peanut butter also went into making other foods, such as "cookies, frosting, cakes, salads, rolls, confections, salad dressing, muffins, biscuits, apples, meat loaf, cupcakes, pie, stuffed celery, soup, vegetable sauces, peanut butter rolls, corn bread, bananas, cinnamon rolls, brownies, sweet potatoes and boiled custard."[22]

During the 1970s, peanut distribution by schools soared. In 1975, schools acquired $10 million of peanuts through federal programs. The following year, this increased to $76 million, with ninety thousand schools receiving peanuts or peanut products. Recognizing the importance of this market, peanut promoters targeted schools. The National Peanut Council published folders geared for elementary schools that focused on the peanut's history, harvesting, processing, and nutrition. The folders featured "fun things" for teachers to do with students using peanuts. Tens of thousands of these folders were distributed free through *Teacher* magazine and many more were distributed at a nominal cost.[23]

PEANUT ONE

One of the most significant influences on American peanut consumption was the election of Jimmy Carter to the presidency of the United States in 1976. Born in 1924, James Earl Carter grew up on his parents' 261-acre farm in Georgia. In Carter's early years the farm began growing peanuts, a crop that made a great impact on his life. His family first raised the small Spanish peanuts, which were used as salted nuts and in candy bars, and more prolific varieties for hog feed. Beginning at the age of five, Carter sold boiled peanuts on the streets of Plains, Georgia. As peanut butter became popular, the demand for peanuts exploded and the Carter farm became dependent on peanuts. Three acres of land produced a ton of peanuts, generating about sixty dollars in income, which for the time was an excellent return. In mid-August each year, every able-bodied person was needed for the peanut harvest. Of this experience, Carter later wrote: "The key to peanut harvest was the threshing machine, which we called a 'picker' because it picked the nuts from the vines. It was most often driven by a flat belt from the rear axle or wheel of a truck, and the dried stacks were hauled to it on wooden sleds, each pulled by a mule. The nuts were collected in a basket or washtub and dumped into a pickup truck or wagon; the nutritious dried vines were baled for animal feed. This was a big and important operation, and involved all the men on the place." Later, the Carter farm grew seed peanuts, which were sold to other farmers. In addition, the family owned a peanut warehouse, which stored the nuts. After service in the navy, Carter returned to Plains and became involved in politics. He was elected governor of Georgia and in 1975 ran for president. At the time the United States was in disarray following the collapse of South Vietnam and the aftereffects of the Watergate scandal that ended the presidency of Richard Nixon.[24]

Carter's campaign workers were called the "Peanut Brigade" and one campaign symbol was a peanut with a smile. Many Carter delegates at the Democratic National Convention in New York proudly waved signs inscribed "From Peanuts to President." Others carried placards showing a peanut with a big grin and one word: CARTER. Carter's election spotlighted the peanut. On his way to his inauguration, he rode the "Peanut Special" train from Plains, Georgia, to Washington, D.C. On board the train was the reigning "Peanut Queen" and representatives of the National Peanut Council. Peanut lapel pins were worn by Carter supporters and were sought by souvenir hunters. A forty-foot, peanut-shaped, helium-filled balloon floated above Carter's inaugural parade. Inaugural balls featured peanut dishes. Subsequently, the Secret Service identified him as "Peanut One."[25]

Carter's campaign and election inspired unprecedented interest in peanuts. Reporters and columnists contacted peanut associations and asked all sorts of questions about peanuts. Peanut facts and stories appeared on the pages of the nation's magazines and newspapers.[26] A company manufactured a large windup peanut toy bearing Jimmy Carter's likeness.[27] The Georgia Peanut Commission declared 1977 the "Year of the Peanut" and launched a national peanut recipe contest.[28] In May 1977 the commission gave Carter its distinguished service award.[29] Food editors attending the National Peanut Council's conference were given recipes for Rosalynn Carter's peanut-butter pound cake and southern peanut meringue pie. Numerous papers carried the recipes, so the council followed up by sending more recipes as press releases.[30] The editor of the *Peanut Journal and Nut World* credited Jimmy Carter for making peanuts a respectable topic for parlor conversation. Carter "promoted peanuts as no association has been able to do."[31]

During the Carter administration, a host of books was published with the intention of cashing in on the peanut's newfound celebrity status. Among these were peanut cookbooks, such as Cynthia and Jerome Rubin's *Peanut One Goes to Washington: The Peanut Cook Book, Including Jimmy and Rosalynn's Favorite Recipes;* Ginnie Bedell's *Plains, Georgia: Home of Jimmy Carter: Peanut Recipes,* Leila B. Holmes's *Plain Georgia Cookin'—100 Peanut Recipes;* and *Hugh Carter's Peanut Cook-book: Over 125 Recipes Using the Very Nutritious Peanut.*[32] Likewise, peanut recipes from the Carter family, including the president's favorites, appeared in other cookbooks.

10 *REVOLUTION AND TRANSFORMATION*

     The peanut's rise from obscurity to culinary stardom in the United States was not inevitable. Indeed, in most European countries, the peanut plays a very minor role in culinary matters, with the exception of peanut oil. On the surface, it appears that the American peanut was simply the right product in the right place at the right time: its ascendancy was largely a matter of chance. While historical events such as the Civil War, World War I, the Depression, and World War II played significant roles in peanut history, undergirding any culinary shifts were five interconnected factors that spurred the peanut industry to take full advantage of unexpected opportunities. Conversely, complications related to health have retarded the growth of peanut consumption. It is the interplay of these of these forces that has been responsible for the peanut's culinary fortunes in America.

MECHANIZATION

The first influence was the increase in the supply and quality of peanuts in the United States. Between 1860 and the end of World War II, the United

States upped peanut cultivation from 10,000 pounds to 2.3 billion pounds. Initially production increased because farmers began to realize that peanuts could be grown on sandy, marginal soil that was not ideally suited for raising other crops.

At first, peanuts were cultivated by hand. The seeds were planted in separate hills. When seedlings sprouted, the rows were hoed by hand to keep weeds down. When the vines bloomed, workers would go into the field each day and cover them with earth to ensure that the downward-growing fruit-bearing stems descended into the ground. When the peanuts matured, they were dug up with a prong-hoe, and the dirt was shaken from the roots and nuts by hand. The vines were then stacked around a pole. When the peanuts had dried, the peanuts were picked off the vines by hand.[1]

Sue Eaton Pretlow, granddaughter of the early Virginia peanut processor John Pretlow, recalled "pea picking time" during her childhood. The pickers—all African Americans—were scattered in groups around the poles with the peanut vines. The foreman walked from group to group keeping order. With his pitchfork, he replaced the piles of picked vines with vines full of peanuts. Each picker had bags with his or her own name on them. In the afternoon, the bags were piled onto wagons and taken to the barn, where they were weighed by the overseer. As each bag was weighed, the name of the picker and the amount picked were entered into a ledger. On Saturday, Pretlow remembered, "the pickers were paid for the week's work—about 25 cents per 100 pounds."[2]

When it came time for processing the peanuts, the bags were emptied into a tumbler or hand cleaner, which was churned for some time to remove the dirt from the hulls. When clean, the nuts were scattered onto a table where they were hand sorted. The prime nuts were then washed in oxalic acid and dried in the sun to bleach them. Finally, the crop was hauled to the market and sold by the bushel.[3]

The cultivation of peanuts went from hand-picked and hand-processed to totally mechanized in a very short period of time. While machines for peanut cultivation and processing had been designed and built during the Civil War, most were inefficient and were promptly discarded. During the 1870s, however, several innovations in the design of the machinery were made. The peanut dotter (a wooden cylinder about eighteen inches long with protruding pegs) made holes in the soft ground. Peanut seeds were then dropped into the holes and the planter used his foot to tamp down the soil. The invention of the dotter was followed by the development of a scrapper plow and cultivator to eliminate grass and weeds while the crop matured. Later came the peanut plow, which formed ridges to improve the planting of peanuts, and a roller, which was used to cover up the seed. By 1876, peanut diggers were sold. They were a type of plow with trailing branches, which raised from the soil the vines with the nuts attached.[4]

Early machines designed to pick the seeds off the vines were unsuccessful and harvesting was done manually for years. But the peanut planter developed in 1870 by A. R. Ayers of New Jersey did greatly reduce the work of planting. Next, a peanut weeder was invented that cut the expense of cultivation. The peanut-picking machine that eventually came into use was an adaptation of the grain thresher already in general use for small grains, such as wheat, oats, and barley. By 1920, various types of planters, cultivators, diggers, and pickers were adopted. By this date, one-quarter fewer workers were needed than in the late nineteenth century.[5]

Today, peanuts are harvested 120 to 160 days after planting, usually in September and October. Harvesting can be done fairly quickly. The farmer drives a tractor with a digger-shaker attachment along the rows of peanuts. The digger's blades loosen the plants and cut their tap roots. Just behind the blade, a shaker lifts the plants from the ground, removes the soil from the peanuts, and places the plants upside-down on the ground to dry in the sun for a few days. When the plants are dry, the farmer drives a combine through the rows to pick the peanuts off the vines. The peanuts are collected in a hopper and the plants are dropped back onto the ground, where they can be baled for cattle feed or mulched into the soil. From the hopper, the peanuts are loaded into wagons fitted with forced-air dryers that remove any remaining moisture. At the buying station, the peanuts are weighed, graded, and inspected to determine quality and value.[6]

AUTOMATION

A second revolution occurred in peanut processing. At first peanuts were cleaned and shelled by hand. Around 1890, the Eureka Peanut Sheller eliminated the tedious task of removing the peanuts by hand. Subsequent shellers had suction fans and screens for separating the unshelled nuts from the shelled. Along with this came machines for sorting, grading, and eliminating bits of metal or other foreign debris. With the invention of other equipment for processing peanuts, large factories were opened, "where thousands of colored women are employed in assorting the peanuts in grades and getting them ready for market."[7] These machines also reduced the labor force required for processing peanuts.

Producing roasted peanuts from raw nuts and then packaging them now takes less than a day. Peanuts are conveyed in 2,000-pound boxes. At the beginning of the manufacturing process, these nuts are poured into stainless steel containers and are then funneled into a cleaner. After cleaning, the nuts are white-roasted, a process that heats the kernels so that they separate from their shells and skins. The peanuts are then inspected by an electric-eye sorter to remove those with imperfections. These electric eyes scan up to six hundred nuts per minute. Then, the peanuts are continuously fed into oil heated to 315° F. A computer controls the temperature to ensure that the peanuts are roasted to the same specifications and are uniform in appearance. The peanuts are then cooled, salted, and finally dispensed into jars, cans, or pouches.[8]

To some southerners after World War I, the potential scarcity of labor was a real problem. Almost from the beginning, African Americans provided most of the labor in planting, cultivating, harvesting, and processing peanuts. Needless to say, these agricultural jobs did not pay well, and many African Americans began migrating to northern cities. W. W. Long of Clemson College in South Carolina claimed that a survey he conducted showed that this migration had "reached the danger" point. During a one-and-a-half-year period in the early 1920s, fifty thousand African Americans left South Carolina headed for jobs in northern cities. Long was worried that there would be no African Americans left in the South to do the agricultural work. A bill was introduced into the Georgia legislature to prevent African Americans from leaving the state.[9] This projected labor shortfall encouraged peanut growers and manufacturers to accelerate all the more their adoption of machinery to cultivate and process peanuts.

As the supply increased, quality improved, and the price dropped, peanuts became more accessible to average Americans. In 1912, a one-pound can of peanut butter cost the consumer twenty-five cents while peanuts cost six cents per pound; in November 1942, peanut costs had doubled, but the price of peanut butter remained the same.[10]

PROMOTION

Increased supply did not translate directly into increased demand. What did lure Americans to buy peanuts was advertising and promotion, the third major contributor to the peanut's success. The earliest peanut promotion was by street vendors, who hailed passersby to buy their products. For almost three decades after the Civil War, this was pretty much the only means of peanut advertising. At the time, most foods were generic products sold in bulk, and there was no reason to promote one over another. Farmers sold their agricultural products to middlemen or brokers, who often placed their own labels on products. These labels were relatively simple at first, but toward the latter part of the nineteenth century, they became more eye-catching. At the same time, the U.S. Patent Office began registering trademarks and slogans. With brand names, food companies could advertise, thus generating demand through customers requesting the product at local stores. These stores, in turn, could order directly from the manufacturer to procure the goods, eliminating the need for middlemen. This reduced the price to the consumer and increased profits to the retailer and manufacturer.

The first major national advertising campaign for a food product was launched by the National Biscuit Company to promote its newly launched brand-named product, Uneeda Biscuits. In 1898, the first full year of its campaign, the company sold 120 million packages.[11]

The first peanut trademarks were issued to Williams and Company, in 1895.[12] The advertising success of Uneeda Biscuits was not lost on peanut sellers and peanut product makers. Advertising proved to be a powerful tool. Initially, advertising was concentrated in newspapers, reflecting the local nature of sales. New national advertising campaigns were funneled through magazines, many of which were launched in the late nineteenth century. *Good Housekeeping,* begun in 1885, focused directly on domestic arts, including food as an important component. *Table Talk* and *The Boston Cooking-School Magazine* were aimed specifically at readers interested in cookery. *American Grocer* and *Grocery World* targeted grocery store owners and managers. By the early twentieth century, advertising by food companies financially supported these magazines. Also, magazines frequently published informational articles about the companies and their products. It is no coincidence that those manufacturers who frequently advertised their products survived and thrived. The most successful peanut advertiser was the previously mentioned Planters.

ORGANIZATION

Closely connected with the advertising revolution was an organizational evolution, the fourth factor that created the modern peanut industry. Early peanut farmers were unable to tie up directly with those consuming their produce, and thus middlemen filled a need. Likewise, individual street vendors, originally the only peanut retailers, were unable to meet the new needs of a growing industry. New organizational structures were needed to propel peanuts into the mainstream. The first response was the utilization of concession merchants. These middlemen accepted goods from growers on consignment and sold what they could. In the case of peanuts, Italian concession merchants dominated the early post–Civil War peanut trade in New York and a few other major cities.

Grocery store owners at first shunned peanuts and peanut products. After the Civil War, grocery stores underwent a transformation, and the grouping of stores into chains encouraged the introduction of peanuts and peanut products. A good example of this transition involved the Great American Tea Company, a small store selling tea and other fancy food products. It had been launched by George Hartford and George Gilman in 1859. By 1865, they claimed to be operating the largest tea store in the world along with five branch stores. After the transcontinental railroad was completed in 1869, they changed the name to the Great Atlantic and Pacific Tea Company. The firm continued to open affiliated grocery stores in many different communities. Ultimately, it became the world's largest grocery store chain, more commonly known as the A & P.[13]

This shift from an establishment run by an individual proprietor or a family to a conglomerate of many stores under a management umbrella meant that the A & P could buy in bulk, thus lowering prices to consumers and underselling the competition. It also meant that when food companies conducted national advertising, they could link up with a national retail chain to offer their products.[14]

In addition to the organization of distribution systems, producers and processors began to organize. Many problems emerged with the making of peanut butter. As noted earlier, some manufacturers used inferior or rancid nuts. As these and other abuses began to harm the business of those manufacturers emphasizing high-quality products, the need for industry-wide standards became evident. In 1922, four major Chicago peanut butter manufacturers formed the National Peanut Butter Manufacturers Association. It had two major purposes: to create industry-wide standards and to promote peanut butter nationally.[15] Many standards developed by the association were later adopted by the FDA.

Other issues were faced by the peanut industry as a whole, including overproduction, foreign imports, and lack of national promotion. In 1941, the National Peanut Council was formed to improve the quality of peanut products and promote the sales of peanuts and peanut products in the United States. The council established National Peanut Week and lauded the peanut's qualities everywhere: it advertised on radio and in local and national newspapers; generated news stories and issued special bulletins; promoted peanut sales in railroad dining cars, restaurants, and hotels; distributed window streamers and offered cash prizes for the best window displays of peanuts; conducted recipe contests; and published hundreds of peanut recipes.[16]

GOVERNMENT

The fifth factor to affect the peanut industry was the influence of state and federal governments. Since the late nineteenth century, federal and state agencies have consistently helped peanut growers. State and federally funded agricultural projects developed new peanut varieties that are resistant to disease and more productive. Thanks to these efforts, the supply of peanuts was greatly increased by the work of agricultural experiment stations and the U.S. Department of Agriculture, who conducted peanut experiments beginning in the 1890s and promoted their findings and recommendations through circulars and bulletins. These research efforts were mainly attempts to improve peanut cultivation, prevent disease, and improve varieties. When farmers increased their production of peanuts, stations and extension services promoted the consumption of peanuts by the public through the publication of peanut recipes and cookbooklets.[17]

Another way that government assisted peanut growers was through tariffs restricting foreign imports. James H. Platt, the first member of the United States House of Representatives after Virginia's readmission to Union, had procured the passage of a peanut tariff in November 1879. In 1921 Congress passed another tariff that amounted to four cents per pound on shelled peanuts and three cents on unshelled. Imports promptly decreased but a few years later surged to 79 million pounds annually. In 1929 and 1930, farm lobbyists pressured Congress to increase the tariff to seven cents a pound on shelled peanuts and four cents on unshelled peanuts. Imported peanuts promptly plunged to about 2.5 million pounds. Despite this decrease in foreign competition, the price of peanuts continued to fall. American farmers simply produced more peanuts than the market could absorb.[18]

As prices of peanuts began to drop during the early 1930s, the United States government instituted programs in 1934 to regulate the acreage, production, and price of this food item. Federal government production controls were lifted during World War II to meet the heavy demand for fats and oils required for the war efforts, but controls were reestablished after the war. In 1977, a two-tier price support system was instituted. Although this system has been revised, the last time by the 1995 Farm Bill, peanut farmers and processors have successfully fended off all attempts to end this subsidy.[19]

HEALTH MATTERS

Not every influence on the peanut industry has been totally supportive; health issues have positively and negatively affected peanut consumption. From the beginning, the popularity of peanuts and peanut products was enhanced by the unsolicited testimonials offered by food authorities, particularly medical and health food luminaries. Agricultural experiment stations and USDA researchers jumped on the peanut bandwagon and likewise extensively promoted the peanut. Testimonials and research reports often found their way into magazines and newspapers; in turn, commercial enterprises repeated these claims in their advertisements, reaching an even wider audience.

Many manufacturers and dealers promoted the idea of the peanut's healthfulness, as well as their own products, in their advertisements. When grocery stores failed to embrace peanuts and peanut products, manufacturers and promoters conducted in-store demonstrations to pique the interest of managers and customers. The peanut was proclaimed an extremely healthful food. Dr. Walter H. Eddy claimed that the peanut was a "virtually a nutritive gold mine." George Washington Carver declared that "a pound of peanuts has a little more body building nutriment than a pound of steak and nearly twice as much heat and energy producing nutriment."[20] To promote the peanut's healthful qualities, Carver helped M. M. Osborn, the editor of the *Peanut Journal,* to create this peanut advertisement, which was circulated to hundreds of thousands of Americans:

Protein is the most necessary and most costly food element.

4 OUNCES OF PROTEIN
Are Contained in
One pound of Roasted Peanuts
One pound of Salted Peanuts
Fourteen ounces of Peanut Butter
A man must put away two ounces of Protein a day
to maintain Strength of body and mind
You cannot buy PROTEIN in any cheaper or more
wholesome form than in Peanuts or Peanut Products.[21]

Peanuts are indeed nutritious, but the industry and its supporters oversold their case. The Center for Science in the Public Interest (CSPI), founded by Michael Jacobson, targeted the snack food industry. Jacobson popularized the term "junk food" in 1972 to describe the many snack foods that contain "empty calories." Candy consumption dropped by 25 percent in the 1970s. The confection industry went on the offensive with even more advertising and promotion. Mars, for instance, responded to the CSPI by advertising that "Snickers really satisfies."[22] Indeed, peanuts are heavy on the calories—not surprising, because they're high in fat. One cup of salted peanuts weighs in at 840 calories, with 500 of those calories coming from fat. That cup of peanuts also contains 680 mg of salt. One ounce of honey-roasted peanuts contains an estimated 180 calories. Writing just before and during the Depression, George Washington Carver had stressed the consumption of peanuts as a way to put flesh on bones. In calorie-conscious America today, however, most people are not interested in gaining weight.

Many manufacturers have attempted to reduce the calories in peanuts and peanut butter by removing a portion of the oil. Unfortunately, when the oil is removed, the aroma, taste, and texture are adversely affected. The peanut's rich, nutty flavor is produced by a blend of about a dozen natural compounds that are present mainly in the oil. To maintain the rich creaminess of peanuts and peanut products, additives were required. In reduced-fat peanut butter, the peanuts are mixed with a variety of bulking agents, including corn syrup solids, maltodextrin, and polydextrose. The reduced-fat Koogle peanut spread contained 60 percent peanuts. This and other reduced-fat products had to be termed "peanut spreads" as FDA guidelines require at least 90 percent peanuts for a product to be labeled "peanut butter." The reduced-fat spreads lack flavor, have a gritty texture, and are excessively sweet. These problems may be resolved by further research.[23]

Another problem to adversely affect the healthful image of peanuts was the possible presence of aflatoxin, a powerful yet tasteless, odorless, and colorless mycotoxin produced by strains of *Aspergillus flavus,* a common fungus that can be found in soil, air, and decaying plant residues. These mold spores require specific temperature, moisture, and nutrient conditions to germinate. Most reports indicate that infection occurs in the field where aflatoxin germinates and then the mold flourishes in poor storage conditions. Aflatoxin is extremely toxic to animals and humans and can cause death. As aflatoxin is also a known carcinogen, contamination remains a potential health hazard and a major problem for the peanut industry.[24]

The *Aspergillus* fungi have proven largely immune to pesticides. In attempts to minimize aflatoxin contamination in crops, farmers have resorted to a variety of methods, including using insecticides to control the insects that spread the fungal infestations. Aflatoxin-causing fungi live on dead plant debris, producing spores that are distributed by wind and insects. The prevention of aflatoxin contamination of peanuts and other commodities has been a major research objective since 1960, when farmers in Georgia reported that their swine had been poisoned after consuming peanuts with aflatoxin, as were more than one hundred thousand turkeys in England. Even though extensive testing procedures have been in place to detect aflatoxin in peanuts, the scare has periodically reemerged. The aflatoxin problem is particularly acute in peanut butter. A 1974 study found that 4 percent of the samples of peanut butter it tested exceeded FDA guidelines. Two years later, two peanut butter brands were recalled because of aflatoxin contamination.[25]

Another urgent health concern is that ingesting peanuts leads to allergic reactions among many people. According to the American Academy of Allergy, Asthma and Immunology, six to eight of every one hundred children have food allergies. Peanuts are one of the leading causes of food-allergic reactions and one of the leading causes of fatal and near-fatal food-induced anaphylactic reactions, which occur when the body's immune system responds abnormally to a food protein or proteins. The body overreacts, flooding the system with histamines and other chemicals to battle what is perceived as a threat or invader. While physicians report that peanut allergies are on the rise, there is no epidemiologic evidence to indicate why. Allergists, pediatricians, and emergency-room physicians are reporting more cases than ever. Researchers surmise that in today's environment, children are exposed to more peanut products at a younger age, when their immune systems may not be mature enough to tolerate allergens found in peanut proteins. Physicians recommend that parents withhold peanuts from children under five years old who have asthma, or a family history of peanut sensitivity, or if either parent has hay fever, eczema, asthma, or other food allergies.[26]

While many people outgrow food allergies, the peanut allergy may be lifelong and, like allergies to shellfish, can be quite violent. Researchers are identifying which of the many peanut proteins are responsible for allergic reactions and how the immune system responds to them. Allergic reactions to peanuts can result in hives, swelling of the throat, difficulty breathing, vomiting, abdominal cramps, and anaphylactic shock, which can be fatal if not treated immediately. Many children and adults with known peanut allergies have been encouraged to carry an injectable form of epinephrine, which relaxes constricted airways for a while, giving the patient time to get help. While the Center for Disease Control reported ten deaths in 1996 due to all food allergies, deaths due to peanut allergies have doubled during the last ten years and the incidence of allergic reactions to peanuts has dramatically increased.[27]

Some experts estimate that as many as 5 to 10 percent of American children may have food allergies, the most common of which are related to milk and eggs. But the diagnosis of peanut allergies among young children has been increasing at a disturbing rate. The problem is that allergic reactions may be generated not only by ingesting peanuts, but simply by coming into contact with them or consuming dishes made with peanut products. Simply removing peanuts from a dish does not remove the contaminating protein. Hydrolyzed peanut proteins are present in many cookies, crackers, baked goods, enriched cocoa, Chinese restaurant dishes, gravies, ice cream, and other sweets. Even food prepared with utensils or dishes that were used to prepare a food containing peanuts or their derivatives can cause an allergic reaction.

Schools where students have been diagnosed with life-threatening forms of peanut allergies have removed peanuts from their cafeteria menus. Some schools have tried to ban peanuts altogether, forbidding students to bring peanuts or foods containing peanuts into the school. Elementary school principals have even banned peanut butter and other peanut-based foods from students' lunch boxes.[28] While at the present time there is no remedy for peanut allergies except avoidance, researchers are attempting to identify the proteins that cause the reactions in hopes of developing a cure. Likewise, manufacturers have made extensive improvements in labeling peanut ingredients in products.

In additions to schools, airplanes have also been a battleground. One researcher published a report of an inhalation reaction on an airliner, and another study documented that small amounts of peanut allergen had been collected in the ventilation filters of commercial airplanes. Airlines have decreased their distribution of peanuts as snacks and the U.S. Department of Transportation has proposed that airplanes create "peanut-free zones"; the idea was shelved after extensive criticism that there was not enough scientific data to support this proposed regulation. Still some airlines have created peanut-free rows.[29]

Despite these problems, there are many promising signs that offset concerns about the peanut's possible negative characteristics. Some new research studies have revealed that ingesting peanuts and peanut products five times a week helped reduce the risk of coronary heart disease by 35 percent. Consuming peanuts also may lower cholesterol levels and encourage weight loss. More research is underway.[30]

11 AN AMERICAN ICON AND A GLOBAL FUTURE

During the early 1990s, the demand for peanuts plunged, as weight-conscious Americans stopped buying them and allergy-conscious schools cut back or eliminated peanuts from their menus. In the last twenty years, the number of peanut farmers has dropped by 50 percent because of skyrocketing land costs, increased foreign competition, and the economies of scale that favor large agribusiness conglomerates. Some observers have wondered whether the American peanut industry will survive. While the industry is rapidly changing, however, reports of its demise are greatly exaggerated.

PEANUT COOKERY

The peanut remains one of cookery's most versatile foods. It has a mild taste and can easily be combined with other ingredients. The prime market for American peanuts is edible consumption. United States per capita peanut consumption is approximately 6.5 pounds, which is far greater than that of other countries, where the end products are peanut oil, cake, and meal. Only 15 percent of U.S. peanut production is normally crushed for oil.[1]

More peanut cookbooks and booklets were published during 1976 and 1977 than during any other years, the culmination of a decades-old tradition of books focusing solely on peanuts or peanut products. As previously mentioned, the first cookbook totally devoted to peanuts was published in 1920; it took forty-five years for the next one to be published, and it focused solely on peanut butter. William Kaufman's *"I Love Peanut Butter" Cookbook* set a trend for subsequent peanut butter cookbooks, such as Annabelle Simon's *The Gourmet Peanut Butter Cookbook,* which was published in 1975.[2]

The most important peanut cookbook published in 1976 was Dorothy C. Frank's *The Peanut Cookbook.* It featured one hundred recipes from soups to sweets. It included interesting recipes for Indonesian "Gado Gado" and "African Peanut Soup." Frank observed that "to study peanut cookery is a delicious way of 'traveling' and learning about far-off places and tastes!" Her first recipe is "Jimmy Carter's Favorite Peanut Brittle," evidently supplied by the president's mother, Lillian Carter, who also provided other "authentic Plains Georgia recipes." The book also boasted recipes for traditional "Georgia Boiled Peanuts" and "Peanut Butter Pie." Some of Frank's recipes combine peanuts with some novel ingredients: chilies, avocados, curry, and spaghetti. Three years later, Frank wrote *Cooking with Nuts,* which also included peanut recipes.[3]

Sandra Fenichel Asher's *The Great American Peanut Book,* published in 1977, was the most comprehensive peanut work at that time. She included sections about growing peanuts, roasting peanuts, the history of the peanut, and numerous recipes as well as several pages of resources. Larry and Honey Zisman's *The Great American Peanut Butter Book* featured such interestingly named treats as "Jimmy Carter's Favorite Peanut Butter Pie," "Annette Funicello's Peanut Butter Cookies," "Singapore Salad," "Peanut Butter and Potato Chip Cookies," "Frozen Yogurt Squares," and "Tortoni Pudding."[4]

In the 1990s, Norman Kolpas's *The Big Little Peanut Butter Cookbook* included fifty recipes "for delicious, easy-to-make desserts, snacks, and sandwiches." Kolpas proclaimed that peanut butter had high nutritional value and had been approved by Weight Watchers and the American Diabetic Association as rich in niacin, vitamin E, phosphorus, and copper, along with some zinc, thiamin, iron, riboflavin, and calcium. Besides the usual sandwich recipes, he offered ones for "Indonesian Gado Gado Salad with Warm Peanut Butter Dressing," "Thai Chicken Satay with Peanut Butter Dipping Sauce," "Malted Peanut Butter and Banana Smoothie," "Peanut Butter Shake," and "Hot Peanut Butter Milk."[5]

Linda Romanelli Leahy's *The World's Greatest Peanut Butter Cookbook* was one of the more attractive peanut cookbooks. After recognizing that peanut butter manufacturers target their products at children, Leahy paraphrased George Bernard Shaw with "It's a shame that peanut butter has to be wasted on the young." She believes that peanut butter "is America's favorite food. It's not only delicious, but packed with vitamins and fiber, and versatile as well." Her book featured catchy recipes with peanuts as ingredients, such as "Huevos Rancheros with Peanut Butter Salsa," "Peanut Butter Humus," "Potato Pancakes and Caviar," "Real Texas Chili," "Southwest Pizza," "Beef Wellington in Pumpkin Brioche," "Peanut-Crusted Mahimahi," and "Peanut Butter Mousse in Phyllo Cups."[6]

In addition to these cookbooks, dozens of cookbooklets have been issued by peanut organizations and federally funded agricultural extension centers. The Growers' Peanut Food Promotions, headed by Betsy Owens, published 100,000 copies of its recipe books in 1976 alone. These cookbooklets incorporated peanuts into dishes with ham, chicken, veal, macaroni, pepper steak, Salisbury steak, pizza, meat loaf, hamburgers, liverwurst, fondue, cheese loaves, rarebits, shrimp, pork chops, potato balls, barbecue sauces, sweet potatoes, eggplants, cauliflower, meat balls, teriyaki sauce, and avocado dip, as well as calling for them in casseroles, soups, salads, dressings, pies, ice creams, cakes, and confections of all kinds. Many more peanut recipes have been featured in cooking magazines and other publications. *Gourmet,* for instance, has published hundreds of recipes utilizing peanuts, including ones for "Oriental Peanut Popcorn," "Chocolate Chip Bars," "Chocolate Truffles," "Frozen Chocolate-Covered Peanut Banana Clusters," and "Oriental Peanut Sauce."[7]

Creative recipe writers have combined peanuts with almost every conceivable ingredient. The versatile legume is used in soups, salads, vegetable dishes, main courses, and desserts. It is a breakfast, lunch, and dinner food. It can be served in its original state, in pieces, creamed, or liquefied. It can be served hot, at room temperature, or in ice cream. Peanut butter can be used on virtually every conceivable sandwich and in most recipes. Even peanut confections, such as Baby Ruth candy bars and Peanut M&M's, have been included in other dishes. Peanuts and peanut products, particularly peanut oil, are found in many packaged and convenience foods. Peanut oil can be used by itself as a salad dressing or ingredient, or it can be used to fry or heat foods. In the near future, peanut oil consumption is projected to increase at an average annual growth rate of 0.5 percent.[8]

Perhaps the most interesting cookbooks are those with recipes from nontraditional sources. Monica Bayley's *Black Africa Cook Book* contains a recipe for "Ground Nut Stew," and Carolyn Quick Tillery's *The African-American Heritage Cookbook* proudly offers "Dr. Carver's Peanut Cake with Molasses," "Dr. Carver's Peanut Cookies #3," and many other peanut recipes.[9] Numerous Chinese, Thai, and other Asian cookbooks include recipes with peanut sauce. These trends have been encouraged by thousands of national and ethnic restaurants that have served mainstream Americans nontraditional peanut dishes.

THE PEANUT AS ICON

In America, peanuts are more than just a consumable food. They have graduated into the broader culture and have become an American icon. Peanuts have been employed as a medium for crafts, music, and sculpture. As early as 1908, Lina Beard designed peanut toys that could be made by children. She provided directions on how to make rabbits, eagles, squirrels, storks, horses, grasshoppers, beavers, and other animals, using peanuts embellished with materials such as wooden toothpicks, roots, glue, and tissue paper. She suggested that these toys could also be made by adults, who could use them as party favors. In 1974, Natalie Donna built on this tradition in her *Peanut Craft*, which told how to turn peanuts into people, puppets, flowers, decorations— and almost everything else.[10]

Peanuts and peanut products have frequently appeared in songs. Sheet music for a song called "The Peanut Stand," written by Joe Bowers, was regularly published beginning in 1860. It was described as a traditional African-American song. James Unsworth's "The Peanut Gal: Comic Song Banjo Song" was also published around this time. In 1864, Tony Pastor's *Combination Songster* included a song about a "blackguard by the name of McCarthy," who was a "book-keeper to a peanut-stand." In 1894 Charles J. Wilson composed the "Peanut Dance," which was "Played with Great Success by all the Leading Bands and Orchestras." The cover to the sheet music included seven anthropomorphized peanut figures with arms, legs, and faces.[11]

The slogan "Peanuts! Five cents a bag" was immortalized in the chorus of a 1923 song of the same title composed by George Weinberg. Another tune, "Peanut Vendor," with music by Moises Simons and lyrics by L. Wolfe Gilbert, was popularized by Don Azpiazu's Havana Casino Orchestra. It was advertised as a "musical portrait of a street merchant and his steaming hot peanuts." Azpiazu combined the lyrics with a new Cuban melody, "as unique and sensational in the world of dance rhythm as Ravel's 'Bolero' is in the concert field." The song quickly became popular in the United States and was picked up by jazz musicians, including Stan Kenton and Duke Ellington. The music has been regularly published, played, and recorded since 1930. The song was so popular that Queen Mary of the United Kingdom requested that it be played at a ball in Buckingham Palace, much to the surprise of the string band of the Royal Artillery, who obliged her. In addition, "Peanuts" was the name of a polka that has been frequently recorded. Peanuts and peanut butter have regularly also appeared in the names of songs, such as "Peanut Butter" on Chubby Checker's 1962 *Let's Twist Again* album and "Peanuts" on Herb Alpert's *Whipped Cream and Other Delights,* released in 1965. One 1960s rock music group called itself "The Peanut Butter Conspiracy."[12]

Peanuts have appeared in sculptures around peanut-growing areas. Residents of Ashburn, Georgia, erected the "World's Largest Peanut." Designed by A. R. Smith Jr., it was surrounded by floodlights, and bicycle reflectors were placed on its crown to catch the light. The giant figure was visible from route I-75. But citizens of Plains, Georgia, quickly erected the world's second-largest peanut at the Davis E-Z Shop. Manufactured by three Carter admirers in Evansville, Indiana, the ten-foot-high sculpture was sent to President Carter in 1977. As it was made primarily of Styrofoam, and souvenir hunters quickly began gouging out pieces of the peanut once it was installed in Georgia, a small fence was constructed to protect it. It remains the "most photographed place in Plains."[13]

Lesser peanut sculptures were constructed by the townspeople of Pearsall and Floresville, Texas, and Dothan, Alabama, which considers itself the "Peanut Capital of the World." Other also-rans are found in Sylvester, Georgia, and on the grounds of the county courthouse in Blakley, Georgia. An even smaller peanut monument was erected in Durant, Oklahoma, on top of a time capsule. Inscribed on the monument is the claim that it is the "World's Largest Peanut." The Oklahoma Peanut Commission placed a peanut cookery booklet in the time capsule, which is scheduled to be opened in June 2023.[14]

Peanut ephemera have become popular collectibles and several organizations have been launched to promote the collection of these items. The Cracker Jack Collector's Association was established through the effort of Ann Brogeley of Philadelphia in 1993. It publishes a newsletter, *The Prize Insider,* ten times a year and holds an annual conference, where its two hundred members meet annually to sell, buy, discuss, and exhibit Cracker Jack prizes. The group even has two members from France and one from Belgium. The first listing of Cracker Jack prizes and ephemera was published in 1976 by James D. Russo. Alex Jaramillo, a spokesman for Cracker Jack during the early 1980s, collected over five thousand items and in 1989 published a price guide to Cracker Jack collectibles. This was followed by Ravi Piña's *Cracker Jack Collectibles with Price Guide* in 1995 and Larry White's *Cracker Jack Toys: The Complete, Unofficial Guide for Collectors* in 1997.[15]

Since Mr. Peanut was adopted as a corporate symbol, he has appeared on virtually every Planters package, container, premium, and advertisement. As a result, the caricature has become one of the most familiar images in advertising history. Today, Mr. Peanut's likeness graces mugs, pencils, pens, and tote bags that are available by redeeming product wrappers. Planters has offered a variety of premium items with its products: glass jars, charm bracelets, clocks, metal tins, wristwatches, ashtrays, plastic whistles, and display figures of Mr. Peanut in which the monocle lights up. Collectors of Planters Peanut ephemera have joined in a group called Peanut Pals. This organization publishes *Peanut Papers for Peanut Pals,* edited by Joyce Spontak, and currently has more than eight hundred members. The first book devoted to Planters Peanuts ephemera was published in 1978 by Richard D. Reddock. This was followed in 1995 by two comprehensive volumes by Jan Lindenberger and Joyce Spontak, the first of which advanced into a second edition four years later.[16]

In addition to Cracker Jack and Planters, containers for peanut butter have also made it into the collectible and organizational arena. Barbara E. Mauzy published a listing and price guide for peanut butter glasses in 1997, and peanut butter containers and ephemera are frequently listed in collectible price guides. The Adult Peanut Butter Lovers' Fan Club was formed more than ten years ago. It publishes *Spread the News* and currently counts over sixty thousand members from all fifty states as well as Ireland, Germany, Saudi Arabia, and Israel. The fan club also boasts quite a number of honorary members, including Little Richard, Bonnie Blair, Barbara Bush, Dan Rather, Julia Child, Madonna, Larry King, Cher, Jack Nicholson, William F. Buckley, Tom Selleck, Kim Basinger, Julia Roberts, Barbara Walters, Bill Cosby, Jerry Falwell, and Michael J. Fox.[17]

PEANUT CHILDREN

Peanuts have become an American icon primarily because children have been the target of extensive advertising and promotion. Peanuts have been considered a childhood favorite according to the earliest records of the nineteenth century. As previously mentioned, peanuts were given as gifts to children at Christmas. During the mid-nineteenth century, boys sold peanuts on trains, at circuses, on street corners, at political rallies, in stadiums, at fruit stands, and in many other venues. In 1868, William N. White of Athens, Georgia, recommended that farmers grow a few hills of peanuts "for the sake of the little folks." By the turn of the twentieth century, magazines suggested that children make peanut recipes. For instance, a 1903 issue of *Good Housekeeping* recommended that parents permit their children to make peanut brittle as a Christmas candy, because the candy was the "hard, peanut variety which cannot be swallowed hurriedly or without masticulation."[18]

Table Talk magazine heralded peanut butter as good for children, who liked it "spread on bread for lunch or supper."[19] Peanut poetry appeared in children's books. Elizabeth Gordon's *Mother Earth's Children* included a poem as well as an illustration of friendly peanut people. The poem reads:

> Said Mrs. Peanut, in a flutter,
> "I quite forgot to salt the butter";
> The little Peanut children said:
> "Why then, Mama, we'll salt the bread."[20]

Early commercial manufacturers of peanut products created brand names, slogans, and trademarks that would appeal to children, such as School Boy Peanut Butter, manufactured by the Rogers Company of Seattle, and Brer Rabbit Peanut Bread, made by National Bakers Service of Chicago. Advertisements were also targeted at parents, who were expected to buy these products for their children. In 1913, a Heinz advertisement asked, "Do You Know that Heinz Peanut Butter Is Good for Children?" Two years later, Heinz published a promotional book aimed directly at children titled *The Story of Peanutville: A Tale for Little Children*. In Saint Paul, Minnesota, the Fisher Roasting Company's major slogan was "Eat Peanuts for Health's Sake," an effort to educate many parents who were "under the false impression" that peanuts were "injurious to children."[21]

The makers of Nut-Let Butter asked parents, "Why give the children dairy butter that often costs about forty cents a pound, when NUT-LET Butter costs half as much, and is liked better?" In 1921 H. H. Thompson, a Department of Agriculture official, observed that peanut butter was gaining great popularity with children. The following year, *Spice Mill* published an article titled "What an Appeal to Children Did for Peanut Butter." According to the author, the demand from children was the reason for the rapid increase in peanut butter sales in the United States: "Being ready to eat from the package as a spread for bread and crackers, it is needed in every home where growing children require some nourishing food between meals." Some manufacturers sold the peanut butter in lacquered pails, which served as toys when empty. The author declared that tin pails were "the greatest stimulant the peanut butter business ever had." Peanut butter advertising had been so successful with children that it was used as a model by other advertisers. Many advertisements were placed in children's magazines, such as *Boy's Life* and *Scholastic*. Likewise, large budgets went into ads in picture books, stamp albums, and comic strips. At the request of Planters, Ham Fisher, the creator of the comic strip "Joe Palooka," drew an unsigned comic strip titled "Mr. Peanut's

Nutty History." Years before, Fisher had been a struggling advertising solic-
itor in Wilkes-Barre, and Mario Peruzzi of Planters had helped him out.[22]

Films and filmstrips about peanuts were produced and dispatched to the
schools. An Eastman-Kodak film originally created in 1928 for classroom use
was revised in 1945 and showed the preparation of the ground for planting
peanuts, followed by harvesting, cooking, and salting as well as the manufacture of peanut butter and peanut candy. In 1938, the North Carolina State
Board of Conservation and Development made its own movie about peanuts. The film opened with thirteen "society girls" harvesting peanuts with
pitchforks. It then followed the bagged peanuts to Raleigh, where the Sells-
Floto Circus was appearing with its thirty-four elephants. The unroasted
peanuts that circus attendees refused to eat were fed to the elephants. The
film took three days to shoot and was shown in the nation's schools. In 1960,
peanut growers released a filmstrip for classroom audiences to promote the
sales of peanut butter. In the mid-1970s, a fifteen-minute film titled *Food: The
Story of a Peanut Butter Sandwich* traced the history of the peanut, food processing, and market research as an aid to improving both products and advertising. It was targeted for use in primary grades. Peanut butter manufacturers have also distributed educational filmstrips for classroom use to point
out the nutritional benefits of their product.[23]

By far the most successful promotion of a peanut product on film was in
a big-budget feature movie. In 1981, Hershey was approached by Universal
Studios for assistance with making a new film. The main character was to be
a lovable alien, and the film makers wanted to have the children in the film
lure the creature with a trail of candy. The producers had previously contacted
Mars, Inc., requesting to use M&M's, but Mars refused. So Universal turned
to Hershey to use Reese's Pieces instead, and Hershey agreed. Reese's Pieces
consequently received "national visibility in the blockbuster film *E.T.*, which
set box office records; it was a cheap marketing triumph."[24]

Peanut processors and peanut product makers have issued children's
coloring and comic books. The manufacturers of Peter Pan Peanut Butter had
produced peanut coloring books by 1960, comic books by 1963, and games
by 1969. Not long ago it spent $400,000 on posters associated with the *Res-
cuers* television program. Planters excelled at similar promotions. In 1960
alone, Planters published one million copies of a Mr. Peanut coloring book
telling the story of the peanut. The company also issued numerous toys and
games for children.[25]

The peanut industry has also supported peanut promotions through
children's shows on television. In 1972, for instance, the Peanut Associates
supported an hour-long program in the *Captain Kangaroo* series. At the time,

Captain Kangaroo was the only national children's telecast, and an estimated five million viewers watched the program, which dealt with peanut growing, harvesting, shelling, and peanut butter making, as well as presenting
peanut foods throughout the episode.[26]

Because the peanut was closely associated with children, peanuts and
peanut butter have frequently appeared in juvenile songs and books. Peanuts
have been used as a vehicle to teach science, and the history of the peanut
has appeared in several children's books. Even "Billy Boll Weevil," the pest
that became a hero as southern farmers shifted from growing cotton to peanuts, was the subject of one book. Likewise, peanuts and peanut butter have
been also been featured in many children's fiction and humor books, and
biographies aimed at children have also emphasized peanuts. For example,
George Washington Carver was the subject of several biographies for young
people. Just as Jimmy Carter election to the U.S. presidency brought numerous adult books on peanuts, so did it generate children's books. The previously mentioned Natalie Donna, the author of *Peanut Craft*, published the
first children's peanut cookbook in 1976.[27]

The word *peanut* has denoted something insignificant or of little value
since the 1830s. Because *peanut* implied small size, it came to mean a small
person by 1919. The term *peanut gallery*, which originally referred to the cheapest seats in a theater, came to refer to a section of seats reserved for children,
especially after the visibility of the children's "peanut gallery" on television's
Howdy Doody Show, first broadcast on radio in 1943. In 1950, Charles M. Schulz
selected the name "Peanuts" for his comic strip, which was peopled only by
small children and animals. His comic strip lasted fifty years and inspired the
development of dozens of books associated with it, including several cookbooks featuring peanut recipes. The comic strip ended with Schulz's death in
February 2000. In honor of his service, the U.S. Congress awarded a Congressional Gold Medal posthumously to Schulz in June of that year.[28]

CENTRALIZATION

Despite the popularity of peanut-related ephemera, the field that produced
this culinary star is rapidly changing. Even before World War II, segments
of the peanut industry had begun to merge, a trend that will likely continue
to have a major impact on the peanut's future. The consolidation of the peanut processing industry greatly accelerated toward the end of the twentieth
century. In 1961, the Planters Nut and Chocolate Company was acquired by
Standard Brands, the forerunner of Nabisco Brands. In 1985, Nabisco Brands
and R. J. Reynolds merged; the company became known as RJR Nabisco.

Nabisco then separated from RJR and in June 2000 Philip Morris made a bid for Nabisco. The new peanut division was called the Planters LifeSaver Company. The Cracker Jack Company has gone through similar reorganizations. In 1963, the Cracker Jack Company was sold to Borden, Inc., based in New York City. In 1997, Borden sold Cracker Jack to Frito-Lay, America's largest snack food business and a subsidiary of PepsiCo.

The Tom Huston Company bought out the McAfee Candy Company, Inc., in Macon, Georgia, and moved into the candy business in 1962. It changed its name to Tom's in 1970, and today is a wholly owned subsidiary of General Mills. The Williamson Candy Company, makers of the Baby Ruth candy bar, was sold to Standard Brands in 1930, then bought by Nabisco. In 1990, the candy bar was acquired by the Nestlé Food Corporation, the world's largest food company.[29]

When Harry Reese died in 1956, the Reese company went through a bitter battle for control among the six brothers who inherited it. With annual sales at $14 million, the company was acquired by Hershey Chocolate Company in 1963 for $23.3 million. Under Hershey's ownership, Reese's Peanut Butter Cup sold steadily during the 1970s. In 1976, Reese's Crunchy Peanut Butter Cup, with a different flavor and a texture of chopped peanuts, was introduced. The Hollywood Candy Company, makers of Payday, was sold to Consolidated Foods Corporation (Sara Lee) in 1983. Hollywood Brands was then purchased by Huhtamaki Oy and became part of Leaf, Inc., which was in turn purchased by the Hershey Foods Corporation in 1996.[30]

On the positive side of such consolidation, the food giants, such as Nestlé, ConAgra, Hershey, Nabisco, and PepsiCo, have the funds to invest in nationwide distribution and marketing. They also have a national system that can guarantee widespread distribution throughout the United States and the world. On the down side, giant corporate structures often make decisions based almost entirely on profit margins and projected future growth. As the American peanut and peanut product industry is considered mature and unlikely to grow at high rates in the near future, multinational companies may not be willing to make the investment sufficient to improve equipment and promotion. The peanut industry grew so fast largely because of individuals who made timely decisions and were willing to take risks. Large corporate structures often discourage flexibility and initiative.

The Clark family continued to manage the D. L. Clark Company, makers of the Clark Bar, until 1955, when it was sold to the Beatrice Food Company, which operated the company until 1983, when Leaf, Inc., acquired the confectionery division of Beatrice foods. When Leaf announced plans to move the candy operations from Pittsburgh, the city protested. The candy plant and rights to the Clark Bar were sold to Michael Carlow, and D. L. Clark became part of the Pittsburgh Food and Beverage Company. The company slowly declined in sales and market position and in February 1995 was thrown into bankruptcy. In June of that year, Jim Clister purchased the D. L. Clark Company, renaming it Clark Bar America. But this company also went bankrupt and was acquired by NECCO in 1999.[31]

Like other segments of the industry, peanut butter producers have undergone structural change. Peter Pan Peanut Butter had previously been acquired by Swift and Company. Swift was sold to Beatrice/Hunt-Wesson in 1984, which in turn was acquired by ConAgra in 1988. Peter Pan Peanut Butter is currently manufactured at plants in Sylvester, Georgia, and Dallas, Texas. In 1955 Best Foods purchased Rosefield Packing Company, makers of Skippy Peanut Butter. Best Foods subsequently was bought out by Corn Products Refining Company in 1958, which changed its name to CPC International. In 1998 CPC International spun off its corn refining business to shareholders. The new corn refining business changed its name to Bestfoods.[32] In 2000, Bestfoods became a target of a takeover bid by Unilever, the Anglo-Dutch multinational food giant.

GLOBALIZATION

The final major shift in the peanut industry is toward globalization. To an extent, peanuts have been a global product for the past five hundred years. Originally, peanuts were uniquely a food of the Western Hemisphere, but Europeans introduced them to Africa and Asia. Peanuts have been an important component of international trade since the mid-nineteenth century. Since World War II, peanuts and peanut products have been increasingly exported abroad.

Today, world exports total approximately 1.3 million metric tons of shelled peanuts. The major exporters are the United States, China, and Argentina. Although U.S. peanuts represent only 8 to 10 percent of the world's peanut production, the United States is one of the leading world exporters, accounting for about one-fourth of world's peanut trade. Sixty percent of U.S. raw peanut exports are destined for the European Union (EU). The major markets for peanuts within the EU are the United Kingdom, the Netherlands (which serves as the primary port of entry for peanuts), and Germany. Demand in Europe for peanuts has been steady, although competition within a dynamic snack market has put considerable pressure on peanuts to compete with a growing range of products such as potato chips, pretzels, and popcorn. Exports of processed peanuts and specialty peanut products have steadily increased, representing approximately 25 percent of total United States peanut exports by value. The largest U.S. export market for processed peanut butter is Saudi Arabia, followed by Canada, Japan, Germany, and Korea. Major peanut snack markets are the Netherlands, Spain, the United Kingdom, France, and Germany.[33]

American candy with peanuts has had particular success in the global marketplace. Other American candy companies expanded within the United States, but Mars, Inc., has grown through global expansion of M&M's, Snickers, and Milky Way. Although several of its products were known abroad by different names (Snickers was originally called the "Marathon Bar" and M&M's were initially called "Treets" in the United Kingdom), Mars relaunched all of its major brands with the American names in the 1990s. The company also creatively used opportunities to promote its products. For instance, during the Gulf War in 1991, while U.S. troops were assembling in Saudi Arabia, a Snickers bar was on every American soldier's meal tray on Thanksgiving Day. Mars has continued to promote its candy throughout the world. Today, for example, Snickers is the number-one-selling candy bar in Russia.[34] Likewise, in a turnabout, foreign-owned multinational corporations such as Nestlé operate in the United States and now distribute candy with peanuts.

In addition to world trade and multinational corporations, trade agreements, such as the North American Free Trade Association (NAFTA), will greatly affect various sectors of the American peanut industry. Protection was eliminated and replaced with minimum import access levels and tariffs for edible peanuts and peanut butter. Under NAFTA, Mexico is granted duty-free access for some sales. For peanut butter, access was restricted during the early stage of the agreement. An *ad valorem* tariff was levied on amounts above the minimum levels for shelled edible peanuts and peanut products. NAFTA eliminates all tariffs over a fifteen-year period. While Mexico is presently not a significant peanut-producing country, economics may change this in the future.

JUST PEANUTS?

During the last ten years, American peanut production has hovered between 3.6 and 4.9 billion bushels. Peanuts rank eighth among primary field crops produced in the United States, with an average farm value of $1.2 billion. Production is concentrated in nine states comprising three major production regions: Georgia, Florida, Alabama, and South Carolina, which produced 60 percent of the total; Texas, Oklahoma, and New Mexico, which averaged 20 to 25 percent; and Virginia and North Carolina, which averaged 15 to 20

percent.[35] The American retail market for peanuts and peanut products to-
tals $2.5 billion annually, and consumption has increased 2 to 3 percent over
the last few years.

Today, Americans consume annually about 857 million pounds of peanut butter, or 3.36 pounds per person. According to one market tracker, Information Resources of Chicago, the top seller in the $810 million peanut
butter category is Jif, with sales of $271.9 million, compared with $158.6 million for Skippy brand and $153.5 million for private-label brands. The con-
fectionery industry uses about 25 percent of the American peanut crop to
make candy. Five of the eight top-selling chocolate confections contain peanuts or peanut butter. Peanut butter and chocolate seem to be among America's favorite pairs.[36]

The peanut remains a significant food in Asia, Africa, and the Americas.
Roasted peanuts and other peanut snacks have growth potential far into the
future. Peanut oil is the sixth most popular vegetable oil in the world, accounting for 5.7 percent of the world's production of major vegetable oils.
Peanut oil thus maintains its place as an important frying medium, and hydrolyzed peanut products are present in many processed foods. Peanuts as
an ingredient in cooking have seen a recent renaissance and this trend may
well point in new directions for the future. The culinary versatility of the
peanut permits its integration into almost any cuisine. Peanuts still enthrall
people, young and old. The aroma of roasting peanuts is celestial. Peanut
butter remains a favorite food among America's youth and those young at
heart. The chocolate-peanut combination is a marriage made in heaven.
Peanut confections still dominate the candy charts and remain some of
America's favorite candies.

New technological advances, such as the Internet, may help peanut sales
to maintain stardom in the snack world. The peanut industry may be mature in America, but it has just begun to expand abroad. The reasons for its
potential global success are the same as those behind the peanut's success in
North America: peanuts are easily grown, inexpensive, and readily available
in many different forms. Peanuts and peanut products are basically healthful foods, and research is underway to make them even more so. As American snack foods continue their rise in popularity around the world, peanuts
will continue to make gains.

Whatever peanuts' future global success, they are firmly embedded in
America's social and cultural life. In the eighteenth century, African slaves introduced them into America's cuisine. The nation's upper classes eschewed
them but the privations of the Civil War encouraged many Americans to adopt
peanut cookery. European immigrants sold peanuts on the streets, and ma-

jor peanut processing and retailing businesses emerged. Vegetarians adopted peanuts and promoted peanut butter throughout America. In the twentieth century, peanuts moved into the culinary mainstream. Boosted by George Washington Carver and advertisements such as those featuring Mr. Peanut, peanuts became a staple. Yet peanuts also remain a major snack food, enjoyed at fairs, sporting events, and picnics. Nowhere else in the world are peanuts consumed in so many ways or in such quantities as in the United States. This long social history has converted peanuts into a mainstream culinary icon. As such, peanuts help define what it means to be an American.

Historical Recipes

As I worked on this book, I located more than five thousand recipes for preparing peanuts or using them as an ingredient. I found these recipes in cookbooks, agricultural and horticultural journals, newspapers, almanacs, medical journals, magazines, and a host of other sources. Of these, a thousand substantially differed from one another. This section represents a sampling of those recipes. I have selected some because they were typical, others because they were unusual. As a collection, they reflect diversity of handling and demonstrate the great variety of sources in which peanuts recipes appeared.

These historical recipes differ markedly from those that appear in modern cookbooks. Because of the state of cooking technology in the early nineteenth century, cooks were unable to control temperatures easily, and thus exact cooking times were difficult to specify. Quantities often depended upon what was available. As peanuts were not uniform, quantities also depended upon their size and shape. When quantities were listed, they were often in very large amounts. Proportionally scaling back the quantities in these recipes will often result in finished products similar to the original, although doing so can be a fairly tricky business.

Spelling, capitalization, punctuation, and directions in these recipes have been left in their original form. There are a few measures and terms in the recipes that are not commonly used today. For instance, a *gill* is a liquid measure equal to a quarter of a pint. A *peck* is equal to eight quarts. A *bushel* is equal to four pecks, or thirty-two quarts.

The phrase "peanut butter" was not in common use until the second decade of the twentieth century. Several other words were used, including "peanutine." Some recipes identify commercial products such as "nutora" and "peanut meal." Try substituting freshly ground, unsweetened peanut butter if you try recipes that call for these ingredients.

PEANUT BEVERAGES

Peanut Coffee

Here again the Peanut fills a useful end, especially in times of scarcity, or high prices for coffee. Taken alone, and without any addition whatever of the pure berry, the Peanut makes a quite good and palatable beverage. It closely resembles chocolate in flavor, is milder and less stimulating than pure coffee, and considerably cheaper than Rio or Java. If mixed, half and half, with pure coffee before parching, and roasted and ground together, the same quantity will go as far and make about as good a beverage as the pure article, and a better one than much of the ground and adulterated coffee offered in the market. Indeed, if people will adulterate their coffee, it were much to be wished that they would use nothing more harmful than the Peanut for this purpose.

For making the beverage, the Peanut is parched and ground the same as coffee, the mode of decoction the same, and it is taken with cream and sugar, like the pure article.

Source: Brian W. Jones, *The Peanut Plant: Its Cultivation and Uses* (New York: Orange Judd, [1885]), 58.

Peanut Chocolate

True chocolate is made by roasting and grinding to a paste, by the aid of heat, a very oily seed, the Cocoa-bean. In the preparation of chocolate a great variety of articles are used to adulterate it and diminish its cost. Some of these, such as sugar and starchy substances, are harmless, while others, such as mineral coloring matters are injurious. Peanuts are largely used to adulterate chocolate, and so far as wholesomeness is concerned, are not objectionable. In containing a great deal of starch and oil, peanuts resemble the Cocoa-bean, though without the nitrogenous principle . . . to which its nutritive qualities are largely due. Peanut chocolate is made in some Southern families by beating the properly roasted nuts in a mortar with sugar, and flavoring with cinnamon or vanilla as may be desired. Peanut chocolate, on so high an authority as the author, the late William Gilmore Simms, is vastly superior to peanut coffee.

Source: Brian W. Jones, *The Peanut Plant: Its Cultivation and Uses* (New York: Orange Judd, [1885]), 58–59.

Peanut and Cereal Coffee

Take 1 cup of coarsely ground peanuts, 2 cups of wheat bran, ½ cup of cornmeal, ⅓ cup of malt dissolved in ⅓ cup of boiling water. Mix all together, and bake in the oven to a nice brown.

Source: Almeda Lambert, *Guide for Nut Cookery* (Battle Creek, Mich.: Joseph Lambert and Co., 1899), 382.

Raw Peanut Milk and Cream

Put the peanuts in the oven or peanut roaster, and let them stay until they are hot, but not the least browned; the skins will then be loose enough to blanch quite easily. Tick out those that will not blanch without extra effort, and save them to roast. They can be put with raw nuts, as it will take just as long to roast them after they have been once cooled, as it will to roast those that have not been heated. Look the raw nuts over carefully, as every speck or dark spot will show in the unroasted nuts. Grind them to a meal; if they are ground until buttery and oily, it is hard to get the milk out. Then to 2 cups of the meal add 3 cups of lukewarm or cold water; beat ~ well with a spoon for four or five minutes, then line an earthen pan or bowl with two thicknesses of cheese-cloth, and pour in the mixture; fold the edges of the cloth together, and squeeze out the milk. It will look like dairy milk. The last will look quite thick, and some of the finest part of the pulp will go through, but that will do no harm as it will settle to the bottom when left to stand. The cream will also rise to the top. If the nuts are properly ground, the cream should be from one half to three fourths of an inch thick on a dish where the milk was three inches deep. It is richer than dairy cream, and can be used for all purposes for which dairy cream is used in seasonings and shortenings.

This cream diluted with water to the consistency of milk, and a very little salt and sugar added, makes a milk which tastes like, and closely resembles, dairy milk. The residue can be made into nut meal by steaming and then drying, or made into nutmeatose, sausages, etc. Raw peanuts are considered beneficial in some forms of dyspepsia. The milk, if cooked in a double boiler for two or three hours, has none of the raw taste left; but the cream, cooked for any length of time, becomes oily. The raw taste is not noticeable when used in cake, crisps, rolls, or pie crust. The housewife will find this recipe invaluable.

Source: Almeda Lambert, *Guide for Nut Cookery* (Battle Creek, Michigan: Joseph Lambert and Co., 1899), 72–73.

Peanut Cream
(Crème aux Pistaches)

4 Ounces of Fresh Peanuts.
The Zest of 1 Lemon.
1 Gill of Water.
½ Pints of Milk and Cream.
1 ½ ounces of Powdered White Sugar.
1 Ounce of Gelatine.

Peel four ounces of fresh peanuts, and pound them into flour. The quantity must equal four ounces shelled. Add the grated zest of a lemon, and a little water, sufficient to make all into a thick paste. Boil equal quantities of milk and cream to equal a pint and a half, and add an ounce and a half of white powdered sugar. Let it cool, and add a piece of gelatine, blended with one spoon of water. Mix well, and then strain through a sieve. Put the cream back on the fire to heat, and add the peanuts. Let all come to a good boil, take off and set it to cool in a cool place, and serve cold.

Source: *The Picayune Creole Cook Book,* 2d ed. (New Orleans: The Picayune, 1901), 291.

Peanut Butter Milk

Reduce Cream brand peanut butter to consistency of milk by the continued addition of water. Heat to the boiling point and drink like milk. This drink will agree with the weakest stomach. A drink of peanut butter milk will insure a sound refreshing sleep.

Source: *Peanut Promoter* 3 (January 1920): 171.

PEANUT BISCUITS, BREAD, CRACKERS, AND ROLLS

Peanut Bread

If peanuts are first mashed or ground into a pulp, and then worked into the dough in the process of kneading, no lard will be required to make good biscuit, and the bread will have an agreeable flavor, different from that imparted by lard, but of such a mild and pleasant taste as to be entirely unlike the peanut flavor. The skin of the kernel must first be removed, or it will impart a bitterish and nutty taste. There is some difficulty doing this. Scalding does not do it very well. Strong soda water or lye, will quickly loosen it, so that it may be readily removed by rubbing with the hands, but either fluid would soon convert the Peanut unto soap, and is, therefore impracticable for this purpose. Could some cheap and handy machine be invented, that would remove the skin from the kernel without loss, no doubt large quantities of peanuts would be used for bread-making purposes. Whether or not it would be economical, we cannot at present say.

Source: Brian W. Jones, *The Peanut Plant: Its Cultivation and Uses* (New York: Orange Judd, [1885]), 59–60.

Peanut Crackers

1 qt. peanuts, whites of two eggs; ½ cup of sugar; roll the peanuts fine, beat whites of eggs stiff, and add sugar. Spread on butter thin crackers, and brown in oven a few minutes. (1 quart peanuts makes 1 cup meats.)

Source: Women of the First Church, *Tour of Nations Cook Book* (Springfield, Mass.: F. A. Bassette, 1907), 27.

Peanut Butter and Fruit Rolls

Sift together two cups of pastry flour, half a teaspoonful of salt and four level teaspoonfuls of baking powder; work in one-half a cup of shortening, then mix to a dough with sweet milk (about half a cup of milk will be needed). Turn upon a floured board, and pat and roll into a thin rectangular sheet. Mix about one-third a cup of peanut butter into a tablespoonful of ordinary butter that has been beaten to a cream, and use this to spread over the dough; sprinkle with sultana raisins or dried currants; roll up like a jelly roll. Cut the roll into pieces about an inch and a half long. Set these on end close together in a buttered baking pan. Bake about twenty-five minutes.

Source: *Boston Cooking-School Magazine* 16 (November 1911): 192.

Peanut Butter Biscuits

1 quart flour, sifted
1 level teaspoon Rumford Baking Powder
2 rounded tablespoons shortening
1 ½ cups milk, or milk and water
1 egg
¼ cup sugar.

Mix the same as for Rumford biscuits, roll thin, spread with the nut butter, place two rounds together and bake.

Source: Henrietta C. Beeks, comp., *Rumford Cook Book* (Providence, R.I.: Rumford Chemical Works, 1914), 3.

Aunt Nellie's Peanut Brown Bread

1 ½ cups white flour
1 ½ cups Graham flour
1 ½ cups blanched and ground peanuts
½ cup sweet milk, or just enough to make a soft dough
2 teaspoons baking powder
1 teaspoon salt

Mix well together and bake in a moderate oven.

Source: George Washington Carver, *How to Grow the Peanut and 105 Ways of Preparing It for Human Consumption,* Bulletin No. 31 (Tuskegee, Ala.: Tuskegee Institute Experiment Station, 1916), 9.

Oat Meal Peanut Bread (Delicious)

2 cups liquid yeast
2 cups rolled oats
2 teaspoons sugar
1 teaspoon salt
1 tablespoon butter

Add white flour as long as you can stir it; beat well; let rise over night; stir up well in the morning; add one cup of chopped or ground peanuts; pour into buttered baking-pan and set in a warm place to rise; when light bake in a moderate oven for one hour.

Source: George Washington Carver, *How to Grow the Peanut and 105 Ways of Preparing It for Human Consumption,* Bulletin No. 31 (Tuskegee, Ala.: Tuskegee Institute Experiment Station, 1916), 10.

Swedish Nut Rolls

1 pint milk, scalded
½ cup butter
¼ cup sugar
½ cup yeast [f]or 7 or 8 cups flour
2 eggs (whites)
1 scant teaspoon salt

Mix early in the morning a sponge with the milk, sugar, salt, eggs, and yeast, using flour enough to make a drop batter. Place in a pan of warm water, and when light add the butter (softened) and enough more flour to thicken it. Knead well, and let it rise again. When light roll out into a large triangular piece one-third of an inch thick. Spread all over with soft butter and a sprinkle of sugar, cinnamon, and a generous coating of finely ground peanuts. Roll over and over; cut off slices an inch thick; lay them on a well-buttered pan with the cut-side down: Let it rise again, and bake in a moderate oven.

Source: George Washington Carver, *How to Grow the Peanut and 105 Ways of Preparing It for Human Consumption,* Bulletin No. 31 (Tuskegee, Ala.: Tuskegee Institute Experiment Station, 1916), 10.

Peanut Butter Raisin Bread

Flour 4 cups
Salt 2 teaspoons
Baking Powder 8 teaspoons (level)
Peanut Butter 1 cup
Raisins 1 cup
Sugar ½ cup
Milk

Sift flour, salt, and baking powder into a bowl; add sugar, and raisins; beat peanut butter in lightly; mix well, and pour in milk to make soft dough. Grease pan. Bake in moderate over 40 minutes. Best when 24 hours old. Margaret Fulton.

Source: Ladies of the First Congregational Church, *Victory Cook Book* (Jersey City, N.J.: Ladies of the First Congregational Church, 1919), 40.

Peanut Butter Corn Bread

¾ cup yellow corn meal
¾ cup rye flour
½ cup sugar
1 cup milk
1 egg well beaten
1 tablespoon shortening (rounded)
½ teaspoon salt
2 teaspoons baking powder
½ cup peanut butter

Cream peanut butter and shortening, add sugar, milk, and egg and turn into well greased shallow pan. Bake about 30 minutes in moderate oven.

Source: Women's Club of Hackensack, *Women's Club Cook Book* (Hackensack, N.J.: Home Economics Department of the Women's Club of Hackensack, 1924), 44.

PEANUTS BOILED

Boiled Peanuts

First blanch the peanuts, which can be done by heating in the peanut roaster or in the oven until they are quite hot, but not browned in the least. Let
them cool in a dry place, and when nearly cold, the skins can easily be removed by rubbing in the sieve or between the hands, or they can be blanched
by pouring boiling water on them, and letting them stand in it until the skins
become loosened; then rub off with the hands. When blanched, put into cold
soft water to cook, as they cook quicker in soft water than in hard water—in
about one-half the time. When perfectly tender, salt and let stew until they
are well seasoned throughout. Serve hot.

Source: Almeda Lambert, *Guide for Nut Cookery* (Battle Creek, Mich.: Joseph Lambert and Co.,
1899), 251–52.

Peanut Beans

Take the raw peanuts and shell them. Put the meats into hot water until you
can "blanch" them; that is, till the brown skin will rub off. Then treat them
exactly as you would beans. Boil them till soft, then bake, make soup, or eat
them boiled, as you prefer. They are very rich in oil and taste so much like
baked beans that it is difficult to realize that you are not eating beans.

Source: *Peanut Promoter* 3 (May 1920): 66.

PEANUT BUTTER

Peanut Butter

The first step is to roast the peanuts to a nice brown, being careful not to over-
brown or scorch them, as too much cooking spoils the flavor. They can be
roasted in an ordinary oven, but can be better done in a peanut roaster made
especially for this purpose. As soon as they are roasted and cool, the skins or
bran should be removed by rubbing them in the hands, or what is better, a
coarse bag; or take a square piece of cloth and fold the edges together, forming a bag of it. The chaff can then be removed by the use of an ordinary fan,
or by pouring from one dish to another where the wind is blowing. The process of removing the skins is called blanching. Next look them over carefully, remove all defective nuts and foreign substances, and they are ready for
grinding. If a fine oily butter is desired, adjust the mill quite closely, and place

in the oven to warm. Feed the mill slowly, turn rapidly, and always use freshly roasted nuts; after they have stood a day or two they will not grind well nor make oily butter. If the butter is kept in a cool place in a covered dish, and no moisture allowed to come in contact with it, it will keep several weeks; and if put in sealed jars or cans, will keep indefinitely.

Source: Almeda Lambert, *Guide for Nut Cookery* (Battle Creek, Mich.: Joseph Lambert and Co., 1899), 70–71.

Raw Peanut Butter

Heat the peanuts just sufficiently to remove the skins but do not allow them to get brown; prepare them as described in a former recipe, and grind in a nut mill. Although the raw peanut butter is not as palatable as the roasted butter, it is considered more healthful and easier of digestion. It is also preferable to use in making soups and puddings, in cooking grains, and in seasoning vegetables. Food seasoned with this butter does not have that objectionable taste that the roasted peanut butter imparts; and if it is properly used, the peanut taste is almost entirely eliminated.

Source: Almeda Lambert, *Guide for Nut Cookery* (Battle Creek, Mich.: Joseph Lambert and Co., 1899), 71.

Peanut Meal

Peanut meal may be used as thickening for soups or sauces, or may be added in small quantities to our breakfast muffin, sally lunn, or griddle cakes. Add but little flour; the peanuts contain starch, which will take the place of flour, and fat to take the place of shortening. Procure raw peanuts; shell the nuts and put into the oven just long enough to loosen the brown skins. Rub these off and grind the nuts. Adjust the grinder so that you will have a meal rather than an oily mixture. Put this aside in glass jars; it will keep for several weeks in a cool place, if properly covered.

Source: Sarah Tyson Rorer, *Mrs. Rorer's New Cook Book* (Philadelphia: Arnold, 1902), 535.

Process

Put a layer of peanuts about one-half inch deep in a dripping-pan and place on perforated shelf in a moderate oven. Allow them to bake slowly for about one hour. Cook them until they are a light brown or straw color. Shake the pan or stir the peanuts every few minutes. When the kernels begin to crack and pop they brown very quickly and should be watched closely.

A splendid way to cook them is to fill a tight-covered dish about two-thirds full, place in the oven and shake occasionally. When cooked this way, they are not so liable to burn, and they retain their flavor better. When they have cooked sufficiently, spread out at once. When they have become quite cool, blanch as follows: This can be done by rubbing them in the hands, or what is better, a coarse bag, or take a piece of cloth and fold the ends together, forming a bag. Another good device is a screen made of coarse wire. Rub them until the skins are loose. The chaff can be removed by using a fan or by pouring them from one dish to another where the wind is blowing. Look them over carefully, removing defective nuts and foreign substances.

The next step is to grind them. The most practical family mill we know of for grinding nuts, etc., is the Quaker City Mill.

Always grind freshly cooked nuts, as they do not make good butter when left a day or two after being cooked.

Source: E. G. Fulton, *Vegetarian Cook Book; Substitutes for Flesh Foods* (Mountain View, Calif.: Pacific Press Publishing Association, 1904), 241–42.

PEANUT BUTTER AND PEANUT SANDWICHES

Peanut Sandwiches

Remove the skin from roasted peanuts, put them in a meat chopper, and grind them to a paste. Spread a thick layer on unbuttered bread, adding a light sprinkle of salt before folding the slices together.

Source: Anna Churchill Carey, "Some New Sandwiches," *Good Housekeeping,* May 1896, 205.

Peanut Sandwiches

Mash peanuts in a mortar to a paste, or chop as fine as possible. Thoroughly mix with Worcestershire sauce; spread on thin slices of bread and butter cut small. A good "appetizer" and nice to serve at "5 o'clock tea." Mrs. Nathaniel Waldo Emerson, Boston.

Source: Women's Guild of Saint Mark's Church, *Clever Cooking* (Seattle: Metropolitan Printing and Binding Company), 218.

Peanut Sandwiches

Peanuts make fine sandwiches. One way of making them is to roll the meats very fine and stir them in mayonnaise dressing and spread between thin slices of bread. Another method is to roll or pound the shelled and skinned Peanuts and spread them thickly upon thin slices of buttered bread.

Sprinkle lightly with salt before putting the slices together. Still another is made by salting the powdered nut meats and mixing them with enough cream cheese to hold them together. Spread this on squares of thin bread or crackers. These sandwiches are particularly nice to serve with lettuce salad.

Source: "Peanuts. Palatable Peanuts. Since Physicians Have Declared the Nut Nutritious, It Is Popular," *Philadelphia Press,* in John R. Parry, *Nuts for Profit: A Treatise on the Propagation and Cultivation of Nut-Bearing Trees* (Parry, N.J.: By the Author, 1897), 151.

Peanut Sandwiches

Three quarts shelled peanuts rolled and mashed very fine. One cup weak vinegar, one cup butter, three teaspoons flour, two teaspoons mustard, two large tablespoons sugar, salt to taste. Mix flour, mustard, and butter together, heat the vinegar, and pour it slowly over the mixture, and boil, stirring constantly five minutes. Remove from stove and add yolks of two eggs well beaten, then pour over the peanuts. Spread the bread using no butter. This will make 110 sandwiches quite small. Mrs. S. N. Briggs.

Source: Young Lady Workers of the Methodist Episcopal Church, *The Carbondale Cook Book of Tried and Tested Recipes* (Carbondale, Pa.: Methodist Episcopal Church, 1898), 54.

Peanut Sandwiches

Use freshly roasted peanuts if possible. Mash the meats with a rolling pin; sprinkle with a little salt; and mix with enough Neuchatel or other cream cheese to make a paste. Spread between very thin slices of unbuttered bread, and serve with a salad. Mrs. Ralph Sollitt.

Source: Young Woman's Auxiliary, *Tested Recipes* (Chicago: 41st Street Presbyterian Church, c. 1910), 44.

Daphne Sandwiches

Mix ground pop-corn with just enough peanut butter or cream cheese to form a paste. Spread on a thin slice of buttered bread; lay a few stoned dates on top and cover with another slice of bread.

Source: May Belle Brooks, "Meals from the Corn-Popper; Attractive Dishes for the New Year's Table," *Good Housekeeping,* January 1913, 119.

Beech-Nut Peanut Butter and Nasturtium Sandwich
From Cosey Tea Shop
(Alma B. Cosey, 19 East Thirty-third Street, New York)

Cut thin slices of bread in circle sandwiches to fit the small leaves of the nasturtium. Mix Beech-Nut Peanut Butter with a few drops of French dressing, spread between the slices or bread, then place on the leaves. Dress with a few petals of the flower.

Source: Beech-Nut Packing Company, *Beech-Nut Peanut Butter: The Great Tea and Luncheon Delicacy as Served in New York Tea-Rooms* (Canajoharie, N.Y.: Beech-Nut Packing Company, 1914), 7.

Beech-Nut Peanut Butter–Pimento–Cheese Sandwich

Mix equal quantities of Beech-Nut Peanut Butter and cream cheese with finely chopped Pimento. Spread between thin slices of brown or white bread, or on crackers.

Source: Beech-Nut Packing Company, *Beech-Nut Peanut Butter: The Great Tea and Luncheon Delicacy as Served in New York Tea-Rooms* (Canajoharie, N.Y.: Beech-Nut Packing Company, 1914), 10.

Nut-Let Apple Sandwich

Take two nice, crisp crackers (preferably Salted Banquet Wafers) or fresh toast; spread evenly with Nut-Let. Insert a thin slice of good apple or other favorite fruit. This makes a delicious sandwich tempting to a lagging appetite.

Source: Bosman and Lohman Co., *The Story of Nut-Let Peanut Butter; From the Vine to the Table* (Norfolk, Va.: Bosman and Lohman, c. 1914], 32.

Peanut and Egg Sandwich

12 hard-cooked eggs
¾ teaspoon celery salt
1 teaspoon paprika
¼ cup minced green pepper
¾ cup peanut butter
Salt to taste

Mash eggs until quite smooth; add seasonings and peanut butter, and mix thoroughly. Add minced pepper, and water enough to make spread well. Spread thickly on slices of bread, and put together with lettuce. The bread may be buttered, but it is not necessary.

Source: Frances Lowe Smith, *More Recipes for Fifty* (1918; reprint Boston: Whitcomb and Barrows, 1921), 184.

Peanut Butter and Onion Sandwiches

Spread one slice of bread with butter, and another one with peanut butter. Put together with thinly sliced Bermuda onion which has been marinated with French Dressing.

Source: Frances Lowe Smith, *More Recipes for Fifty* (1918; reprint Boston: Whitcomb and Barrows, 1921), 184.

Peanut-butter Sandwich Cream

Perhaps the best known use for peanut butter as a sandwich filling. The butter may be used as it comes from the jar, but many prefer to thin it with a little cream or other liquid. This sandwich filling is delicious.

1 cup milk.
1 tablespoon flour.
1 tablespoon water.
1 egg.
1 cup peanut butter.
1 teaspoon salt.
¼ teaspoon paprika.
2 tablespoon vinegar.
½ cup chopped stuffed olives.

Heat the milk in a double boiler. Blend the flour, water, and peanut butter to a smooth paste, add salt and paprika, and the egg beaten slightly. Mix with the hot milk and cook for 5 minutes in the double boiler. Add the chopped olives and vinegar. Cool and spread on sandwiches.

Make only the quantity needed for immediate use, as this sandwich cream does not keep well.

Source: Homer Columbus Thompson, *The Manufacture and Use of Peanut Butter*, Circular No. 128 (Washington, D.C.: USDA, 1920), 14.

Peanut Butter and Ginger Sandwich

Thin slices white or whole wheat bread, buttered; mixed preserved ginger, lemon juice, and peanut butter.

Mince preserved ginger fine, and mix to a paste with the ginger syrup and a little lemon juice. Spread one slice of the bread with a layer of peanut butter, the second slice with the ginger paste. Press slices together and trim and cut in triangles.

Source: Betty Barclay, *Trenton, New Jersey Gazette*, as reprinted in *Peanut Journal* 4 (March 1925): 13.

PEANUT CAKES

Groundnut Cheese Cake

Blanch one pound of groundnuts; beat them very fine in a marble mortar, adding a little brandy while pounding, to prevent oiling; then add ten eggs, one pound of sugar, and one pound of butter; beat the whole well together; make a puff paste, lay it on your tins, fill them with this mixture, grate sugar over them, and bake in a slow oven.

Source: [Sarah Rutledge], *The Carolina Housewife* (Charleston: W. R. Babcock, 1847), 117.

Ground Nut Cakes

Boil two pounds of light brown sugar in a preserving kettle, with enough water to wet it thoroughly, and form a syrup. Have prepared a quarter of a peck of groundnuts, roasted in the shell, and then shelled and hulled. When the sugar begins to boil, throw in the white of an egg to clear it; strain it, and try, by dropping a little of the syrup from a spoon into cold water, if it is done enough. If the sugar hardens and becomes brittle, it is sufficiently boiled, and must be taken from the fire; if not, boil it longer, and try it again. When it has become brittle in the water, remove it from the fire, and stir the nuts thoroughly through the sugar. Then wet with a brush a pasteboard or marble slab, free from all grease, and drop the hot mixture upon it from a spoon, in little lumps, which must be flattened into thin cakes, the size of a tumbler top. When cold take them off the board with a knife; the white of egg may be omitted if clearness is not desired.

Source: Women's Centennial Committees, *National Cookery Book* (Philadelphia: Women's Centennial Committees, 1876), 269.

Peanut Cake

One-half cup butter, one and one-half cups sugar, one-half cup milk, two and one-half cups flour, whites of four eggs, one-half tea-spoonful cream tartar, one-fourth tea-spoonful soda; just before putting into the oven, sprinkle over the top one cup of peanuts broken in pieces.—*Mrs. Geo. B. Hooper.*

Source: Ladies of the First Baptist Church, *Exeter Cook Book*, rev. ed. (Exeter, N.H.: Ladies of the First Baptist Church, 1889), 101.

Peanut Pound Cake

3 large or 4 small eggs, a scant cup granulated sugar, 1 tablespoonful lemon juice, 1 tablespoonful ice-water, 1 cup sifted Nut Meal, ½ cup sliced citron, if desired, ½ to ⅔ cup pastry flour, sifted once before measuring, salt.

Have the ingredients as nearly ice-cold as possible. Sift the sugar; sift the flour twice, and leave it in the sifter. Beat the yolks of three eggs, adding the sugar gradually. When stiff, add part of the water and more sugar. Beat, add more water, sugar, and half the lemon juice until all the sugar is in. Stir into this mixture half the Nut Meal, a good pinch of salt, and the citron. Beat the whites of the eggs to a moderately stiff froth. Add the remainder of the lemon juice, and beat until dry and feathery. Slide the beaten whites on to the yolk mixture, sprinkle part of the Nut Meal over them, sift a little flour, and chop in lightly. Add more meal and flour, chop; continue until the flour is all in. Take care not to mix too much. Put into a pan at once, and bake slowly in an oven that bakes well from the bottom. Handle carefully when taking from the oven. If a gasoline oven is used, the fire may be turned off, and the cake allowed to cool in the oven.

Source: E. E. Kellogg, comp., *Healthful Cookery: A Collection of Choice Recipes for Preparing Foods, with Special Reference to Health* (Battle Creek, Mich.: Modern Medicine Publishing Company, 1904), 230–31.

Peanut Roll Cake with Jelly

4 eggs
⅔ cup flour
½ cup powdered sugar
¼ teaspoon salt
½ teaspoon baking powder

Beat egg yolks and sugar till light; add mixed dry ingredients, then stiffly beaten whites; mix lightly together. Bake in thin sheet in a quick oven. As soon as done turn quickly on a towel wrung out of water; spread with jelly; sprinkle liberally with coarsely chopped peanuts; roll up and dust with powdered sugar.

Source: George Washington Carver, *How to Grow the Peanut and 105 Ways of Preparing It for Human Consumption*, Bulletin No. 31 (Tuskegee, Ala.: Tuskegee Institute Experiment Station, 1916), 14.

Peanut Layer Cake

Make cake exactly the same as for roll cake, except bake in jelly cake tins. Make the pastry cream as follows:

2 cups sugar
1 ½ pints milk
3 tablespoons corn starch
1 tablespoon butter
2 teaspoons extract of lemon
1 pint coarsely ground peanuts

Add peanuts to the milk; let simmer 5 minutes; with sugar add the starch dissolved in a little cold water; as soon as it recoils [*sic*] take from the fire;

beat in the yolks; return to the fire two or three minutes to set the eggs; when cold spread between the layers of cake, and finish with clear icing garnished with blanched peanuts.

Source: George Washington Carver, *How to Grow the Peanut and 105 Ways of Preparing It for Human Consumption,* Bulletin No. 31 (Tuskegee, Ala.: Tuskegee Institute Experiment Station, 1916), 14.

Peanut-Butter Cake Filling

½ cup sirup.
1 tablespoon vinegar.
¾ teaspoon salt.
2 tablespoons peanut butter.
The white of 1 egg.

Cook the sirup with the vinegar until it forms a hard ball when dropped in cold water. Pour over the beaten egg white and beat until stiff. Add the peanut butter the last thing. Spread between the layers of a simple 1-egg cake or sponge cake. Serve with a fork.

Source: Homer Columbus Thompson, *The Manufacture and Use of Peanut Butter,* Circular No. 128 (Washington, D.C.: USDA, 1920), 16.

Johnny Cake

Large Recipe	Small Recipe
Popped corn, chopped before measuring, 1 ½ cups	Popped corn, chopped before measuring, ¾ cup
Shelled peanuts, ½ cup	Shelled peanuts ¼ cup
Brown sugar, 1 ½ cups	Brown sugar, ¾ cup
Light corn syrup, ½ cup	Light corn syrup, ¼ cup
Water, ¾ cup	Water, ½ cup
Molasses, 2 tablespoons	Molasses, 1 tablespoon
Butter, 2 tablespoons	Butter, 1 tablespoon
Soda, ¼ teaspoon	Soda, ⅛ teaspoon
Salt, ½ teaspoon	Salt, ¼ teaspoon

Brown the peanuts in the oven and break them into pieces. Chop the popped corn in a chopping bowl. It should be quite coarse.

Put the sugar, corn syrup, and water into a saucepan and cook, stirring, until the sugar is dissolved. Continue cooking, until the temperature 270° F.

Remove from fire, add soda (free from lumps), and stir until it ceases to bubble. Add chopped, popped corn and nuts, mixed with the salt, and stir until well mixed. If using the large recipe have the corn warm. Turn into small, greased patty tins, making cakes one-fourth of an inch thick. On top of each little cake place a half peanut. When cold remove from the pans.

It is necessary to work rapidly when turning the mixture into the pans, as it hardens very quickly. If it begins to become hard it is better to set the saucepan of candy into a pan of hot water while dipping out the cakes.

Cold water test when the candy reaches 270° F.: hard, almost brittle.

Yield (large recipe): number of cakes—thirty-two (one and one-fourth inches in diameter and one-fourth of an inch thick).

Source: May B. Van Arsdale, Day Monroe, and Mary I. Barber, *Our Candy Recipes* (New York: Macmillan, 1922), 172–73.

Peanut-Prune Shortcake

Prepare a crust for the peanut biscuit, make in layers, one baked on top of the other, and for the filling cut one-half pound of prunes which have been soaked overnight in cold water after being well washed, then simmered in the same water until tender, add half a cupful of sugar and cook until thick. Cool, add lemon juice and grated rind if desired or orange juice and rind. Serve over the shortcake as one does any fruit.

Source: *Peanut Journal* 4 (July 1925): 26.

PEANUT CANDIES AND CONFECTIONS

Molasses Candy

As all children are fond of this article, the following directions may be acceptable. Boil the molasses (maple is best) till it will, if dropped in cold water, become crisp. Then, for each quart, put into it an even teaspoonful of saleratus dissolved in a little warm water, and stir it till well mixed. This makes it tender and crisp. Take a part and cool it in a buttered pan, to work white and draw into sticks. Into the remainder stir roasted corn, either pounded or whole, or peanuts or almonds, or walnuts or hazelnuts.

Whole Popped corn made into cakes with candy is excellent. Roasted corn pounded and mixed with half the quantity of maple sugar is good, and some eat it thus with milk.

Source: Catharine Esther Beecher, *Miss Beecher's Domestic Receipt Book* (New York: Harper, 1846), 292.

An Excellent Receipt for Groundnut Candy

To one quart of molasses add half a pint of brown sugar and a quarter of a pound of butter; boil it for half an hour over a slow fire; then put in a quart of groundnuts, parched and shelled; boil for a quarter of an hour, and then pour it into a shallow tin pan to harden.

Source: [Sarah Rutledge], *The Carolina Housewife* (Charleston: W. R. Babcock, 1847), 219.

Pea-Nut Taffy

1 pound of brown sugar, ¼ pound of butter, 1 quart of peanuts, nicely toasted a light brown. Put the sugar and butter in a skillet with 2 tablespoons of water; let them boil until the taffy is of a clear, dark color, then stir in the peanuts; let it boil for 15 minutes and then have ready the griddle on which breakfast cakes are baked, and drop a spoonful of taffy on at a time, it will cool very quickly, and makes very pretty little cakes.

Source: M. L. Tyson, *The Queen of the Kitchen: A Collection of Old Maryland Receipts for Cooking from a Receipt Book Used for Many Years. All Tried and Approved* (Baltimore: Lucas Brothers, 1870), 234.

Pea-nut Candy

(1) Dissolve 2 lb. of sugar and 1 saltspoonful of cream of tartar in ½ pint of cold water, then set it over a moderate fire and cook till brittle, adding and stirring in about ½ oz. of butter. Shell some Pea-nuts, a layer of them, two deep, at the bottom of some well-buttered tins, and when the candy is ready, pour it over them, and leave till cold. Then cut it or break it into pieces of a convenient size.

(2) Shell 1 qt. of Pea-nuts (measured in their shells). Put in ½ lb. of molasses in a saucepan over the fire, boil it, stirring constantly till a little dropped from the spoon hardens in cold water. Then stir in 1 table-spoonful of extract of vanilla, 1 saltspoonful of bicarbonate of soda (dry), and lastly the shelled Pea-nuts. When these are well mixed in, turn the candy into buttered shallow tins, and press it down smooth with the back of a wooden spoon.

Source: Theodore Francis Garrett, ed., *The Encyclopaedia of Practical Cookery: A Complete Dictionary of All Pertaining to the Art of Cookery and Table Service*, 8 vols. (London: L. Upcott Gill, Bazaar Buildings, W.C., [1890]), 5:131.

Peanut Nougat

1 lb. sugar.
1 quart peanuts.

Shell, remove skins, and finely chop peanuts. Sprinkle with one-fourth teaspoon salt. Put sugar in a perfectly smooth granite saucepan, place on range, and stir constantly until melted to a syrup, taking care to keep sugar from sides of pan. Add nut meat, pour at once into a warm buttered tin, and mark in small squares. If sugar is not removed from range as soon as melted, it will quickly caramelize.

Source: Fannie Merritt Farmer, *Boston Cooking-School Cook Book* (New York: Little, Brown, 1896), 449.

Peanut Candy

One cup granulated sugar, one cup rolled Peanuts. The Peanuts are prepared by chopping or by rolling with a wooden pin. Heat the sugar in a hot oven; when it has melted remove to back of range and add the Peanuts, mixing them thoroughly with the sugar. Spread on a tin and press into shape with knives. The tin does not need greasing. Cut into bars. It hardens immediately.

Source: John R. Parry, *Nuts for Profit: A Treatise on the Propagation and Cultivation of Nut-Bearing Trees* (Parry, N.J.: By the author, 1897), 152.

Peanut Bars

Three lbs. confectionery sugar, put on the fire dry and stirred very fast until it becomes a liquid, drop in 3 quarts raw peanuts, boil until peanuts snap, stir constantly, turn out on buttered pans; just before hard, block in bars.— Mrs. S. Talmage.

Source: Ladies Aid Society, Methodist Episcopal Church, Monroe, N.Y., *The Cook's Counsellor* (Newburgh, N.Y.: Newburgh Journal Print., 1900), 91.

Peanut Pralines
(Pistaches Pralinées)

1 Pound of Peanuts.
1 Pound of Brown Sugar.
4 Tablespoonfuls of Water.
1 Tablespoonful of Butter.

Shell the peanuts and break into bits. Then set the sugar and water to boil, and as it begins to simmer add the peanuts and the butter. Stir constantly and as it bubbles up once take from the fire, pour from the spoon on the marble slab or a buttered plate, and set away to harden.

Source: *The Picayune Creole Cook Book,* 2d ed. (New Orleans: The Picayune, 1901), 376.

Peanut Candy

To one pound brown sugar, add one cup Karo corn Syrup and one cup water. Boil until it hardens when dropped in cold water. Just before taking from fire, add two ounces butter and three-quarters pound peanuts. Pour into well-buttered tin. Be careful in preparing the meat that none of the brown skin is left on. Some candy-makers prefer to put the peanuts in a well-greased pan and pour the syrup mixture over them, instead of stirring them in, as it makes the taffy more even in appearance.

Source: Emma Churchman Hewitt, *Karo Cook Book* (New York: Corn Products Refining Co., 1909), 37.

Peanut Sticks

Roll to a paste sufficient shelled and blanched peanuts to make a cupful. Add the grated rind of a lemon, the well beaten yolks of four eggs, six tablespoonfuls of sugar, and a good half cupful of shifted flour. Mix smooth, add the stiffly beaten whites of the eggs, and roll out on a board, cut in strips, twist, and fry in hot cooking oil.

Source: Elma Iona Locke, "The Peanut as Food," *Table Talk* 26 (October 1911): 576.

Beech-Nut Peanut Butter Fudge
From The Clover Tea Shop
(Dorothy Howard, 640 Madison Avenue, New York)

Two Cups Sugar
One Cup Milk
Two Squares Chocolate
Four Tablespoons Beech-Nut Peanut Butter

Boil until it makes soft ball in cold water. Take from fire and stir. Cool and cut in squares.

Source: Beech-Nut Packing Company, *Beech-Nut Peanut Butter: The Great Tea and Luncheon Delicacy as Served in New York Tea-Rooms* (Canajoharie, N.Y.: Beech-Nut Packing Company, 1914), 14.

Beech-Nut Peanut Butter Caramels

Two Cups Brown Sugar
One Cup Granulated Sugar
One Cup Fresh Milk
Two Squares Chocolate
Four Tablespoons Beech-Nut Peanut Butter

Cook until waxy. Stir occasionally. Remove from fire and beat to a cream. Turn into buttered pan and cut into squares.

Source: Beech-Nut Packing Company, *Beech-Nut Peanut Butter: The Great Tea and Luncheon Delicacy as Served in New York Tea-Rooms* (Canajoharie, N.Y.: Beech-Nut Packing Company, 1914), 14.

Peanut Bon-Bons

Take one part peanut butter and one part fondant, blend them thoroughly, press out and cut into squares, allow to harden, and then coat with dipping cream. The dipping cream may be colored a little with caramel.

Source: Sherwood Snyder, *The Art of Candy Making Fully Explained* (Dayton, Ohio: Health Publishing Co., 1915), 30.

Peanut Tutti-Frutti Caramels

2 cups light brown sugar
½ cup milk
1 cup peanuts, blanched and ground
1 cup corn syrup
1 tablespoon butter
1 teaspoon lemon extract
½ cup raisins, seeded and chopped
½ cup preserved watermelon rind, chopped very fine
¼ cup chopped figs
½ cup chopped dates
¼ cup candied pineapple

Place all the ingredients in a sauce-pan together, and boil to the hard-boil stage; stir only enough to keep the mixture from sticking. If the double boiler is used, the candy will not stick much. Remove from the fire; add the extract; pour into buttered pans, and mark off into squares.

Source: George Washington Carver, *How to Grow the Peanut and 105 Ways of Preparing It for Human Consumption*, Bulletin No. 31 (Tuskegee, Ala.: Tuskegee Institute Experiment Station, 1916), 27.

Peanut Nougat with Honey

⅜ cup honey
½ cup brown sugar
1 pound blanched peanuts
2 egg whites

Boil the honey and sugar together until drops of the mixture hold their shapes when poured into cold water; add whites of two eggs, well beaten, and cook very slowly, stirring constantly until the mixture becomes brittle when dropped in cold water; add the peanuts and cool under a weight, break in pieces or cut and wrap in waxed paper.

Source: George Washington Carver, *How to Grow the Peanut and 105 Ways of Preparing It for Human Consumption*, Bulletin No. 31 (Tuskegee, Ala.: Tuskegee Institute Experiment Station, 1916), 24.

Peanut Brittle

The success of this brittle depends upon cooking the peanuts in the candy to just the right degree and, too, upon spreading the brittle as thin as possible. The recipe makes two pounds and one-fourth.

Look over three cups of Spanish raw peanuts, number one, and put into a shallow pan in a moderate oven while candy is cooking. Into an iron frying kettle or an enamel saucepan, if preferred, put one pound, each, of white Karo and sugar and one cup and one-third of cold water. Boil to 275 deg. Fah. Then remove the thermometer and add four tablespoonfuls of butter, the peanuts and one-half teaspoonful of salt. Stir constantly until the peanuts are light brown in color. Remove from fire and add one tablespoonful of vanilla, also three-fourths a tablespoonful of soda, which has been dissolved in one tablespoonful of cold water. Stir thoroughly and pour on buttered marble as thin as possible. With a spatula spread thinner, and as soon as one can touch the mixture with the hands, pull the brittle apart to make it thin and lacy.

Source: *American Cookery* 30 (December 1925): 358.

Peanut Chips

7 lbs. granulated sugar
1 lb. molasses sugar
2 lbs. corn syrup
6 lbs. peanut butter

Place in kettle the sugar, molasses sugar, corn syrup, and sufficient water to dissolve the sugars. Cook the batch to a temperature of 295 degrees F. and pour it on a well oiled cooler. Fold in the edges and work so as to keep it smooth and free from lumps. When sufficiently cooled, pull until light, then twist out the air. Knead the batch so as to make it smooth, then form it into a jacket and add the peanut butter which has been warmed to the same temperature as the jacket. After folding the jacket around the center and closing the ends, stretch the batch out, then throw back bringing the ends together while stretching them. Throw back again keeping the batch in three pieces placing them alongside one another flat on the table and stick their edges together. If any large portion of the ends has been squeezed solid while working, cut this off, then stretch out the batch keeping it flat. When of sufficient length, fold one end of the batch back on itself so as to cover two-thirds of the whole length, then fold over the other making a batch that is quite wide and three rows high. Form the ends which were cut off into rolls and place one on each side of the batch, then spin out into thin chips and mark with either a chip or adjustable cutter. When cold, break apart and coat with chocolate. The molasses sugar mentioned in this formula is the sugar which settles to the bottom of molasses tanks. If this is not obtainable a good grade of New Orleans molasses can be used.

Source: Matthew Berman [pseud. for James P. Booker, Clifford Clay, James A. King, and others], *The How and Why of Candy Making* (Chicago: Emmet Boyles, 1925), 275–76.

PEANUT CEREAL

Peanut Butter with Cereals

Left-over cream of wheat, wheatena, oatmeal, cornmeal, or other cereals is excellent if mixed with half the quantity of peanut butter, turned, turned into a bread pan, allowed to cool, then sliced and dipped in egg and cracker crumbs and fried in hot fat. Serve with maple syrup.

Source: *Peanut Promoter* 3 (May 1920): 65.

PEANUT COOKIES

Ground-nut Macaroons

Take a sufficiency of ground-nuts, that have been roasted in an iron pot, over the fire; remove the shells; and weigh a pound of the nuts. Put them into a pan of cold water, and wash off the skins. Have ready some beaten white of egg. Pound the ground-nuts, (two or three at a time,) in a marble mortar, adding, frequently, a little cold water, to prevent their oiling. They must be pounded to a smooth, light paste; and, as you proceed, remove the paste to a saucer or a plate. Beat, to a stiff froth, the whites of four eggs, and then beat into it, gradually, a pound of powdered loaf-sugar, and a large tea-spoonful of powdered mace and nutmeg mixed. Then stir in, by degrees, the pounded ground-nuts, till the mixture becomes very thick. Flour your hands, and roll, between them, portions of the mixture, forming each portion into a little ball. Lay sheets of white paper on flat baking-tins, and place on them the macaroons, at equal distances, flattening them all a little, so as to press down the balls into cakes. Then sift powdered sugar over each. Place them in a brisk oven, with more heat at the top than at the bottom. Bake them about ten minutes.

Source: Eliza Leslie, *Miss Leslie's New Receipts for Cooking* (Philadelphia: T. B. Peterson, 1854), 209.

Peanut Cookies

2 tablespoons butter.
¼ cup sugar.
1 egg.
1 teaspoon baking powder.
¼ teaspoon salt.
½ cup flour.
2 tablespoons milk.
½ cup finely chopped peanuts.
½ teaspoon lemon juice.

Cream the butter, add sugar, and egg well beaten. Mix and sift baking powder, salt, and flour; add to first mixture; then add milk, peanuts, and lemon juice. Drop from a teaspoon on an unbuttered sheet one-inch apart, and place one-half peanut on top of each. Bake twelve to fifteen minutes in a slow oven. This recipe will make twenty-four cookies.

Source: Fannie Merritt Farmer, *Boston Cooking-School Cook Book* (New York: Little, Brown, 1896), 408–9.

Peanut Flour Drop Cookies

1 ½ cups peanut flour
1 ½ cups sifted flour
1 teaspoon salt
1 egg
2 teaspoons baking powder

¾ cup corn sirup (brown)
3 tablespoons fat

Bake 10 minutes.

Source: *Use Peanut Flour to Save Wheat, 1918,* Circular No. 110 (Washington, D.C.: USDA, 1918), n.p.

Oatmeal-peanut-butter Drop Cookies

½ cup sugar.
¼ cup sirup.
8 tablespoons peanut butter.
¾ teaspoon salt.
2 eggs, well beaten.
2 ½ cups rolled oats.

Mix together and drop by the spoonful on a greased baking sheet. Bake until brown.

Source: Homer Columbus Thompson, *The Manufacture and Use of Peanut Butter,* Circular No. 128 (Washington, D.C.: USDA, 1920), 16.

Delicious Oatmeal Drop Cakes or Hermits

1 cupful *School Boy Peanut Butter* or shortening
1 cupful brown sugar, free from lumps
2 cupfuls rolled oats
1 beaten egg
1 cupful milk of cold coffee
2 ½ cupfuls flour
3 ½ teaspoonful *Rogers' Baking Powder*
1 teaspoonful salt
1 teaspoonful cinnamon
½ teaspoonful each cloves, nutmeg, and ginger
1 cupful seeded or seedless raisins
½ to 1 cupful nuts

Cream peanut butter and sugar, add rolled oats and beaten egg. Sift together the flour, baking powder, salt, and spices and add alternately with milk, stirring raisins and nuts in with part of flour. Drop from teaspoon onto buttered shallow pans and bake in a rather hot oven.

Source: Isabelle Clark Swezy, comp., *My One Hundred Best Recipes with Cooking Helps* (Seattle: The Rogers Company, 1923), 30.

PEANUT DOUGHNUTS, WAFERS, GRIDDLE CAKES

Peanut Butter Doughnuts

Peanut butter doughnuts offer a novelty for the table and will be found to be especially good. They are made without sugar.

Directions: one-half cup peanut butter, 1 well beaten egg, 5 tablespoons molasses, 1 teaspoon salt, 1 cup sweet milk, 1 cup cold water, 1 teaspoon cinnamon, ½ teaspoon nutmeg or mace, 3 heaping teaspoons baking powder, about 3 cups flour, amount sufficient varying according to the flour. Mix as given. The doughnuts will be somewhat richer than ordinary ones and should be cut out somewhat thicker than usual and should be cooked a little more slowly. As a variation of this recipe one can add 3 tablespoons of cocoa to the mixture.

Source: *Peanut Journal* 1 (May 1922): 24.

Peanut Wafers

Mix a half cup of peanut meal with a half cup of peanut butter; beat thoroughly, then add gradually one and a half cups of sugar. Dissolve a half teaspoonful of soda in a half cup of warm water; add to the nut mixture and then work in about three cups of Graham meal. The dough must be rather hard. Roll out into a very thin sheet, and cut into squares of two inches. Bake in a very slow oven until a golden brown.

Source: Sarah Tyson Rorer, *Mrs. Rorer's New Cook Book* (Philadelphia: Arnold, 1902), 535.

Peanut Butter Griddle-Cakes

Stir together two cups flour, two teaspoons baking powder, one-half teaspoon salt. Add one egg and four tablespoons Larkin Peanut Butter. Beat vigorously, add two cups milk. Bake on a hot greased griddle. Mrs. Jos. E. Culver, New Haven, Conn.

Source: Larkin Co., *Larkin Housewives' Cook Book: Good Things to Eat and How to Prepare Them* (Buffalo: Larkin Co., 1915), 67.

PEANUT ICE CREAM AND SYRUPS

Ice Cream

Peanut meringue shells are nice to serve with plain ice cream. Beat the whites of four eggs very light and stir in three-quarters of a pound of sugar, one tablespoonful of flour, and one cup of finely chopped Peanuts. Drop the mixture by the spoonful upon buttered papers and bake in a rather cool oven.

Place a shell on each side of a large spoonful of ice cream and put a little whipped cream over the top in serving.

Source: "Peanuts. Palatable Peanuts. Since Physicians Have Declared the Nut Nutritious, It Is Popular," *Philadelphia Press*, in John R. Parry, *Nuts for Profit: A Treatise on the Propagation and Cultivation of Nut-Bearing Trees* (Parry, N.J.: By the author, 1897), 151.

Peanut Frappe

Make one pint of good gelatine; set aside to harden. Stir 1 cup of granulated sugar into one pint of whipped cream, when the gelatine is just on the point of setting, stir into the whipped cream by beating with a fork; add ¾ cup of peanut meal; serve in sherbert glasses with fresh or preserved fruit.

Source: George Washington Carver, *How to Grow the Peanut and 105 Ways of Preparing It for Human Consumption*, Bulletin No. 31 (Tuskegee, Ala.: Tuskegee Institute Experiment Station, 1916), 21–22.

Peanut and Prune Ice Cream

2 cups milk
3 eggs (yolks)
½ pound pulp from well-cooked and sweetened prunes
1 quart cream cup blanched and ground peanuts. (Peanut meal can be used)
1 teaspoon vanilla extract and a pinch of salt

Heat the milk; pour it into the well-beaten egg yolk; blend all the other ingredients thoroughly; freeze and serve in dainty glasses.

Source: George Washington Carver, *How to Grow the Peanut and 105 Ways of Preparing It for Human Consumption*, Bulletin No. 31 (Tuskegee, Ala.: Tuskegee Institute Experiment Station, 1916), 22.

Chocolate Peanut Butter Syrup

One-half pound cocoa, one and one-half pounds brown sugar, one quart evaporated milk, one pound peanut butter.

Mix thoroughly the first three ingredients and cook to boiling point, stirring constantly. When cold mix the peanut butter in with the first ingredients. Serve over ice cream either hot or cold.

Source: *The Soft Drink Journal*, as reprinted in *Peanut Journal* 1 (May 1922): 24.

PEANUTS AND THE MAIN COURSE

Peanut Hash

Cream one tablespoonful of peanut butter with enough cold water to make a smooth paste, add three-quarters of a cupful of ground peanuts, and two cupfuls of finely chopped cooked potatoes. Mix well, then add one-half a teaspoonful of salt and one-quarter teaspoonful of pepper, with sufficient milk or water to moisten. Melt one tablespoonful of butter in a hot frying pan, simmer in it a teaspoonful of finely minced onion for two minutes; add the potatoes and nuts and cook, with moderate heat, until a brown crust has formed over the bottom, as in making corned beef hash. Turn out upon a platter and serve.

Source: Gertrude R. Lombard, "The Food Value of the Peanut," *Good Housekeeping,* December 1912, 843.

Peanut Omelet

Make a cream sauce with one tablespoonful of butter, two tablespoonfuls of flour, and three-quarters of a cupful of milk poured in slowly. Take from fire, season, add three-quarters of a cupful of ground peanuts and pour the mixture on the lightly beaten yolks of three eggs. Fold in the stiffly beaten whites, pour into a hot, buttered baking-dish and bake for twenty minutes.

Source: *Good Housekeeping,* October 1912, 567.

Macaroni and Peanuts

Cook one cupful of macaroni, broken into one inch pieces, in boiling salted water until tender; drain and pour cold water through it to separate the pieces. Then add cream sauce made with four tablespoonfuls each of butter and flour, one teaspoonful of salt, one-fourth teaspoonful of pepper, and two cupfuls of milk, and two cupfuls of chopped peanuts. Pour into a buttered baking dish, cover with buttered crumbs, and bake until golden brown in color.

Source: Gertrude R. Lombard, "The Food Value of the Peanut," *Good Housekeeping,* December 1912, 843.

Liver with Peanuts

Boil the liver from two fowls or a turkey; when tender mash them fine; boil one pint of blanched peanuts until soft; mash them to a smooth paste; mix and rub through a puree-strainer; season to taste with salt, pepper, and lemon juice; moisten with melted butter; spread the paste on bread like sandwiches, or add enough hot chicken stock to make a puree; heat again and season with salt, pepper, and lemon juice.

Source: George Washington Carver, *How to Grow the Peanut and 105 Ways of Preparing It for Human Consumption,* Bulletin No. 31 (Tuskegee, Ala.: Tuskegee Institute Experiment Station, 1916), 15–16.

Peanut and Cheese Roast

1 cup grated cheese
1 cup bread crumbs
1 teaspoon chopped onion
1 cup finely ground peanuts
1 tablespoon butter
Juice of half a lemon
Salt and pepper to taste

Cook the onion in the butter and a little water until it is tender. Mix the other ingredients, and moisten with water, using the water in which the onion has been cooked. Pour into a shallow baking dish, and brown in oven.

Source: George Washington Carver, *How to Grow the Peanut and 105 Ways of Preparing It for Human Consumption,* Bulletin No. 31 (Tuskegee, Ala.: Tuskegee Institute Experiment Station, 1916), 17.

Peanut Flour–Cottage Cheese Loaf

1 cup cottage cheese
1 cup peanut flour
1 egg
1 teaspoon salt
1 cup chopped nuts
1 cup cooked salted rice
2 tablespoons chopped onion cooked until soft in 8 tablespoons water
1 tablespoon fat
$\frac{1}{4}$ teaspoon pepper

Cook 35 minutes. Serve hot with tomato sauce.

Source: *Use Peanut Flour to Save Wheat 1918,* Circular No. 110 (Washington, D.C.: USDA, 1918), n.p.

Scalloped Rice with Peanut-butter Sauce

2 cups milk.
2 tablespoons flour.
6 tablespoons peanut butter.
2 teaspoons salt.
2 teaspoons onion juice.
2 ½ cups cooked rice.

Blend the flour and the peanut butter with a little cold milk. Add to the hot milk with the seasonings. Cook until it thickens. Put a layer of rice in a baking dish and cover with a layer of the peanut sauce. Repeat until the dish is full. Bake in oven for 20 minutes.

Source: Homer Columbus Thompson, *The Manufacture and Use of Peanut Butter*, Circular No. 128 (Washington, D.C.: USDA, 1920), 15.

Peanut Stuffing for Poultry

2 cups hot mashed white potatoes
½ cup ground peanuts
1 teaspoon grated onion
1 teaspoon salt
4 tablespoons cream
1 tablespoon butter
Yolks of 2 eggs
¼ teaspoon paprika

Mix and blend all the ingredients together, adding any herbs desired.

Source: Bessie R. Murphy, *Peanuts for Breakfast, Dinner, Supper* (Chicago: Rand McNally, 1920), 9.

Mashed Potatoes with Peanut Butter

6 medium-sized potatoes
2 tablespoonfuls butter
About ½ cupful hot milk
1 ½ tablespoonfuls peanut-butter
1 teaspoonful salt
⅛ teaspoonful pepper

Boil, mash, and beat to a cream the potatoes, adding salt and pepper, one tablespoonful butter, and milk. Heap in a hot buttered baking-dish. Blend the peanut-butter and remainder of butter, dot over potatoes, and brown in a 500° F. oven.

Source: Good Housekeeping, *Good Housekeeping's Book of Menus, Recipes and Household Discoveries*, 10th ed. (New York: Good Housekeeping, 1922), 223.

Stuffed Sweet Potatoes and Peanut Butter

Bake as many potatoes as needed of uniform size. Take off slice from end to be used as the top, about ¼ the potato, scoop out end and put into bowl and season for each potato a pinch of salt, 1 teaspoon sugar, 1 tablespoon Southern Brand peanut Butter, 1 tablespoon seeded raisins, a little milk or water may be added to mixture to be able to mix well. Refill the shells and heat and serve in place of candied potatoes or as a dish for dinner or lunch.

Source: *Peanut Journal* 1 (January 1922): 25.

PEANUT MISCELLANY

Canapes

Rub the yolks of hard-cooked eggs to a paste with equal quantities of sardines and chopped peanuts. Moisten with lemon juice, season, and serve on rounds of toast.

Source: *Good Housekeeping*, October 1912, 567.

Nut Oil

Take 2 cups of medium brown peanut butter, add to it 1 scant cup of malt extract; mix well, and knead like bread until it is very oily; then grind it through the nut-butter mill, and squeeze out what oil you can with the hands, and grind it through the mill the second time. Squeeze again thoroughly. This ought easily to make one cup of oil.

The remainder can be used in making malt food. Oil can be extracted from butter made from other nuts by the foregoing method. If there is any sediment or particles of the nuts in the oil, let it stand, and they will settle, when the top can be poured off, and will be clear, nice oil.

Source: Almeda Lambert, *Guide for Nut Cookery* (Battle Creek, Mich.: Joseph Lambert and Co., 1899), 82.

Nutora with Peanuts and Eggs

Take 2 cups of raw peanut butter, 1 cup of water, the white of 1 egg, and salt to taste. Add the water to the butter, a little at a time, until it is smooth. It should be thin enough to beat with an egg beater; if it is not, add more water, and beat for five minutes. Then take the white of 1 egg, and beat to a stiff froth; add it to the nut butter, and beat again for a few minutes; put it in cans, and cook for three hours.

Source: Almeda Lambert, *Guide for Nut Cookery* (Battle Creek, Mich.: Joseph Lambert and Co., 1899), 86.

Peanut Mayonnaise

Into a cupful of mayonnaise dressing beat sufficient peanut butter, a little at a time, to flavor it. Place a teaspoonful of the dressing on any desired salad. This is especially good for halved tomatoes.

Source: Gertrude R. Lombard, "The Food Value of the Peanut," *Good Housekeeping,* December 1912, 843.

Marguerites

From Nova Club Tea-Room (Florence B. Wilson, 47 Church Street, New York) Boil one cup of granulated sugar and one half cup water. When it threads remove to back of stove and drop in six marshmallows. Let stand until the marshmallows are dissolved, then pour on to the whites of two eggs, stiffly beaten. Beat until thick, then add some cocoa-nut and flavor with vanilla. Spread fresh saltines with Beech-Nut Peanut Butter and then spread with the mixture. Brown in a hot oven. Delicious for afternoon tea.

Source: Beech-Nut Packing Company, *Beech-Nut Peanut Butter: The Great Tea and Luncheon Delicacy as Served in New York Tea-Rooms* (Canajoharie, N.Y.: Beech-Nut Packing Company, 1914), 18.

Malted Peanuts

Take 1 ½ cups peanut meal, ½ cup of malt extract, a small pinch of salt; rub all together, and dry in the oven door where it is warm, being careful not to scorch it. The malt scorches very easily. When perfectly dry, grind through the mill to a meal, and it is ready to eat. When mixed with malt, the peanut dries more easily than any other nut.

Source: *Spice Mill* 38 (October 1915): 1128.

Peanut Timbales

½ pint of peanuts cooked until soft in salted water; drain and mash.
2 well beaten eggs and two cups thin cream, added to the nuts.
½ teaspoon of salt, and a dash of pepper.

Turn into custard cups; put the cups in a basin; surround them with boiling water; cover the tops with buttered paper, and bake in a moderate oven for 20 or 25 minutes; then unmould and serve with a little cream sauce poured around them.

Source: George Washington Carver, *How to Grow the Peanut and 105 Ways of Preparing It for Human Consumption*, Bulletin No. 31 (Tuskegee, Ala.: Tuskegee Institute Experiment Station, 1916), 18.

Peanut Butter Cups

Take one pound of peanut-butter, place in a double boiler and heat.
Place in kettle
10 lbs. sugar.
1 teaspoonful cream of tartar.
2 qts. water.
Set on fire and mix.

When batch starts to boil remove paddle and wash off the sides of the kettle with a wet brush. Place cover on kettle and allow to steam for a few minutes. Remove cover, place thermometer in batch and cook to 335°, then add about a tablespoonful of burnt sugar color and when boiled in well, pour batch on greased slab. Turn edges in, place gloves on, knead up and when stiff enough to handle pull hard and fast until very shiny. Flavor vanilla while pulling. Knead up good and form in flat square piece about 16 inches square. Spread peanut-butter on batch and roll up, seal both ends and pull out about as large as your finger. Cut on butter-cup cutter.

Source: William M. Bell, comp., *The Pilot: An Authoritative Book on the Manufacture of Candies and Ice Creams*, 3d ed. (Chicago: Wm. M. Bell, 1918), 99.

Peanut-butter Fondue

3 eggs.
6 tablespoons peanut butter.
½ cup milk.
1 teaspoon salt.
1 cup dry bread crumbs.

Blend the peanut butter with the milk and add the beaten yolks and the bread crumbs. Fold in the stiffly beaten whites. Pour into a baking dish or individual baking cups, surround with hot water, and bake until firm.

Source: Homer Columbus Thompson, *The Manufacture and Use of Peanut Butter,* Circular No. 128 (Washington, D.C.: USDA, 1920), 15.

PEANUT MOCK DISHES

Turkey Legs

Take ½ cup of water, 2 hard-boiled eggs, 2 tablespoonfuls of pecan meal, 1 teaspoonful peanut butter, a little sage and salt, 2 tablespoonfuls of zwieola, and 2 tablespoonfuls of gluten. Boil the eggs until the yolks are dry and mealy, and then rub both the whites and yolks through a fine wire sieve. Mix with it the nut meal and butter, rubbing until smooth; then add a very little water. Pour ½ cup of water over the zwieola, let it soak for a few minutes; add the other mixture, beating well, and lastly add the gluten. It should be stiff enough to handle well. Take a large, heaping tablespoonful, press it around the piece of macaroni, which should be four or five inches long, forming it in the shape of a turkey leg, leaving an inch or more of the macaroni to stick out to represent the bone. Roll in beaten egg, and bake on an oiled tin until a nice brown. This makes a pretty dish, and is very palatable. Serve with a pecan gravy with egg.

Source: Almeda Lambert, *Guide for Nut Cookery* (Battle Creek, Mich.: Joseph Lambert and Co., 1899), 103.

Mock Tenderloin Steak

The better way to do is to make a quantity of this, put into cans and cook it, then cut it off and broil or heat it when needed. The following ingredients will be sufficient for several meals.

1 quart nut meats (English walnuts, peanuts, pine nuts, and almonds in equal quantities)
1 quart bread crumbs
1 pint water
1 tablespoonful salt
2 saltspoonfuls pepper

Put the nuts through the meat chopper, mix them with crumbs, add the seasoning and the water, pack into tin cans, and steam or boil three hours. Stand in a cold place with the lid off until perfectly cold, then cover and keep them in the refrigerator. When ready for use, turn them out, cut in slices, and heat in the oven or broil quickly. Serve plain or with tomato sauce.

Source: Sarah Tyson Rorer, *Mrs. Rorer's Vegetable Cookery and Meat Substitutes* (Philadelphia: Arnold, 1909), 44.

Mock Veal Roast

½ pint shelled roasted peanuts
½ pint lentils
½ pint toasted bread crumbs
1 teaspoonful salt
1 saltspoonful pepper

Soak the lentils over night, drain, bring them to a boil; throw the water away; cover with fresh water, and boil until tender; drain again; press them through a colander. Add nuts, chopped or ground; the bread crumbs and the seasoning with sufficient milk to make it the consistency of mush. Pour into a baking-dish, and bake in a moderate oven for one hour.

Source: Sarah Tyson Rorer, *Mrs. Rorer's Vegetable Cookery and Meat Substitutes* (Philadelphia: Arnold, 1909), 43.

Peanut Sausage

Grind ½ pound of roasted peanuts, ½ pound pecans, 1 ounce hickory nuts, and ½ pound walnut meats. Mix with six very, ripe bananas; pack in a mould, and steam continuously for two hours; when done remove lid of kettle or mould, and when mixture is cold turn out and serve the same as roast meat sliced thin for sandwiches, or with cold tomato sauce or other sauce.

Source: George Washington Carver, *How to Grow the Peanut and 105 Ways of Preparing It for Human Consumption,* Bulletin No. 31 (Tuskegee, Ala.: Tuskegee Institute Experiment Station, 1916), 16.

Peanut and Lentil Roast

½ cup shelled roasted peanuts
½ cup lentils
½ cup toasted bread crumbs
Milk
½ tablespoon butter
½ teaspoon salt
½ teaspoon pepper

Soak lentils over night; in morning drain, cover with cold water and allow to come to a boil. Drain again and cook in fresh water until tender. Drain and put through colander. Add peanuts (chopped), butter, bread crumbs, and seasoning. Mix with sufficient milk to make like mush. Bake in a buttered baking dish one hour over a medium flame. Garnish with parsley. Serve with brown sauce or Sauce Piquante. Gwen Lowrey.

Source: *Celebrated Actor Folks' Cookeries: A Collection of the Favorite Foods of Famous Players* (New York: Mabel Rowland, 1916), 199.

PEANUT PUDDINGS AND PIES

Peanut Custard Pie

Rub one rounded tablespoonful of peanut butter smooth with one-half cupful of water, adding but a few drops at a time at first, until well blended. Then add one well beaten egg, two tablespoonfuls of sugar, and one-fourth teaspoonful of salt. Beat all well together, then add another half cupful of water, pour into a paste-lined pie tin, and bake. Or the custard may be poured into custard cups, set into a pan of hot water, and baked until set in a slow oven.

Source: Elma Iona Locke, "The Peanut as Food," *Table Talk* 26 (October 1911): 576.

Date and Peanut Pudding

Dates and peanuts make an exceptionally good combination. Beat two eggs well, add one cupful of granulated sugar, one cupful of peanuts finely chopped, one-third of a cupful of flour sifted with one teaspoonful of baking powder and one-eighth teaspoonful of salt. Turn into a large layer cake pan, buttered, and bake in a moderate oven about one hour. When cool turn out upon a flat serving dish, sprinkle with two tablespoonfuls of lemon juice and cover with whipped cream.

Source: Gertrude R. Lombard, "The Food Value of the Peanut," *Good Housekeeping*, December 1912, 843.

Chocolate Nut Pudding
From Ye Olde English Coffee House
(Alice Arencibia, 20 West Forty-third Street, New York)

One Cup Soft Bread Crumbs
Two Cups Scalded Milk

Three-quarters Cup Beech-Nut Peanut Butter
One-half Teaspoon Salt
Two Squares Chocolate (melted)
Two Egg Yolks
Three-quarters Cup Sugar
One Lemon (juice and rind)
Two Egg Whites (beaten)

Mix all the ingredients but the egg whites. When well blended, cut and fold in the egg whites. Pour into individual moulds and bake twenty or thirty minutes. Serve hot with sauce or whipped cream.

Source: Beech-Nut Packing Company, *Beech-Nut Peanut Butter: The Great Tea and Luncheon Delicacy as Served in New York Tea-Rooms* (Canajoharie, N.Y.: Beech-Nut Packing Company, 1914), 16.

Peanut Butter Pie

One and one-half cups sweet milk, one cup sugar, two tablespoons cornstarch, one-third cup peanut butter, one teaspoon vanilla, two eggs, a pinch of salt.

Put milk and sugar in a double boiled. When at the boiling point, add cornstarch moistened with a little cold milk. Stir until smooth. Add beaten yolks of eggs and flavoring, stirring well all the time. Add the peanut butter, mix well. Pour this custard into a baked crust. Make a meringue with the whites of eggs and sugar. Put on top of the pie and brown in a warm oven.

Source: *Peanut Promoter* 3 (May 1920): 65.

PEANUTS ROASTED AND SALTED

Roasted Peanuts

Peanuts may be cooked in the same manner as parched corn, or baked in a stove or oven. They are healthful food as a part of the regular meal—at all events, to stomachs accustomed to plain living.

Source: R[ussell] T[hatcher] Trall, *The New Hydropathic Cook-book* (New York: Fowlers and Wells, 1855), 187.

Salted Pea-nuts

Shell and skin about 1 qt. of Pea-nuts, melt 1 oz. of butter before the fire, put the nuts into it, and stir them about some as to oil them well with it. Put them on another dish, brown them in the oven, sprinkle with fine salt, and serve hot.

Source: Theodore Francis Garrett, ed., *The Encyclopaedia of Practical Cookery: A Complete Dictionary of All Pertaining to the Art of Cookery and Table Service,* 8 vols. (London: L. Upcott Gill, Bazaar Buildings, W.C., [1890]), 5:131.

PEANUT SALADS

Cabbage and Peanut Salad

Shred a small cabbage very finely or chop if desired. Mix thoroughly with a boiled salad dressing. Just before serving, add one cupful of salted peanuts freed from their skins. Serve very cold.

Source: Gertrude R. Lombard, "The Food Value of the Peanut," *Good Housekeeping,* December 1912, 843.

Cherry and Peanut Salad

Use the large white California cherries. Remove the pits and substitute a salted peanut for each one, letting the nut show a little. Place on lettuce hearts and dress with mayonnaise.

Source: *Good Housekeeping,* February 1913, 261.

Celery, Apple, and Beech-Nut Peanut Butter Salad
From Happen Inn
(Ella C. Emerson, 65 East Fifty-ninth Street, New York City)

Cut apples and celery in cubes. Sprinkle with lemon juice and let stand until cold. Mix one-half cup Beech-Nut Peanut Butter with one cup mayonnaise. Arrange the apples and celery on endive and decorate with stars of the dressing. Serve cold.

Source: Beech-Nut Packing Company, *Beech-Nut Peanut Butter: The Great Tea and Luncheon Delicacy as Served in New York Tea-Rooms* (Canajoharie, N.Y.: Beech-Nut Packing Company, 1914), 10.

Grape, Orange, and Beech-Nut Peanut Butter Salad
From the Garden Tea-Room
(Ada Mae Luckey, Twenty-first Street, New York)

Remove skins from California grapes. Cut in halves and remove seeds. Remove peel from several oranges and cut lengthwise.

Dress with oil and lemon juice and a little powdered sugar if desired.

Place on a bed of lettuce and garnish with balls of Beech-Nut Peanut Butter.

Source: Beech-Nut Packing Company, *Beech-Nut Peanut Butter: The Great Tea and Luncheon Delicacy as Served in New York Tea-Rooms* (Canajoharie, N.Y.: Beech-Nut Packing Company, 1914), 11.

Pineapple and Beech-Nut Peanut Butter Salad
From Colonia Tea-Room (Ida L. Frese, 400 Fifth Avenue, New York)

Surround one slice of pineapple with small inside leaves of lettuce, and squeeze over this the juice of quarter of a lemon. Then pour over it French dressing made of olive oil and lemon juice, sweetened and highly seasoned with paprika, which has been beaten until thick and creamy. Mix Beech-Nut Peanut Butter with equal part of cream cheese, roll into ball and place in center of pineapple. Sprinkle finely chopped English walnuts over salad.

Source: Beech-Nut Packing Company, *Beech-Nut Peanut Butter: The Great Tea and Luncheon Delicacy as Served in New York Tea-Rooms* (Canajoharie, N.Y.: Beech-Nut Packing Company, 1914), 13.

Nut-Let Chicken Salad

Beat up three raw eggs, add a dash of pepper, six tablespoonfuls vinegar, two tablespoonfuls prepared mustard, two tablespoonfuls Nut-Let, salt to taste; mix thoroughly and boil to consistency of cream. Cut cold boiled chicken into half-inch cubes and mix with an equal quantity of celery cut in small pieces, then combine with the above dressing. Serve on lettuce leaves and garnish with sections of hard-boiled eggs and more celery.

Source: Bosman and Lohman Co., *The Story of Nut-Let Peanut Butter; From the Vine to the Table* (Norfolk, Va.: Bosman and Lohman, c. 1914), 32.

Peanut Salad with Bananas

Slice bananas through center; spread out on lettuce leaves, and sprinkle liberally with chopped peanuts; serve with mayonnaise or plain salad dressing.

Source: George Washington Carver, *How to Grow the Peanut and 105 Ways of Preparing It for Human Consumption,* Bulletin No. 31 (Tuskegee, Ala.: Tuskegee Institute Experiment Station, 1916), 21.

Beechcroft Salad

8 Neufchatel cheeses
2 cups peanut butter
1 tablespoon salt
12 to 14 large, red apples

Put cheese, peanut butter, and salt into bowl; mix well. Oil fingers slightly with salad oil, and form mixture into small balls. Wash apples, remove centers with corer, and cut each apple crosswise into four or five slices. Place on watercress or lettuce, fill center with cheese balls, and serve with Bretton Woods Dressing. Cook cores in small amount of water; strain, and use juice in dressing. Cottage instead of Neufchatel cheese may be used. As fast as apples are cut, moisten with French Dressing or put in salted water to prevent discoloration.

Source: Frances Lowe Smith, *More Recipes for Fifty* (1918; reprint Boston: Whitcomb and Barrows, 1921), 169–70.

Potato and Peanut Salad

9 quarts potato cubes
1 quart diced celery or cucumber
5 tablespoons salt
2 teaspoons pepper
3 finely minced onions
1 ¼ cups vinegar
1 cup oil or margarine
1 quart peanuts
California Mayonnaise

Mix carefully all ingredients except nuts and Mayonnaise; let stand an hour or more. Use freshly roasted or reheated peanuts, in halves or large pieces. Just before serving, mix with potato; arrange in salad bowl, garnish with watercress, and serve with California Mayonnaise.

Source: Frances Lowe Smith, *More Recipes for Fifty* (1918; reprint Boston: Whitcomb and Barrows, 1921), 172.

Peanut Butter Ball Salad

1 cup of cream cheese
6 tablespoons peanut butter
2 teaspoons lemon juice

seasoning of salt and pepper
½ cup chopped seeded raisins
beat together until smooth

Form mixture into small tablespoon-size balls on a bed of shredded lettuce and serve with a lemon French dressing. Mrs. Edward D. Easton.

Source: Women's Club of Hackensack, *Women's Club Cook Book* (Hackensack, N.J.: Home Economics Department of the Women's Club of Hackensack, 1924), 34.

Three P's Salad

Chopped sweet pickles
Chopped peanuts
Peas

Serve equal amounts of above on lettuce with mayonnaise.

Source: Seattle Women, *Fruit and Flower Mission Cook Book* (Seattle: Seattle Fruit and Flower Mission, 1924), 154.

PEANUT SAUCE AND GRAVY

Pea-nut Sauce

Remove the shells from 1 pint of Pea-nuts, blanch, and break them in halves, put them in boiling stock, and boil till soft; then mash them fine in the stock in which they were cooked. Brown 1 tablespoonful of flour in 2 tablespoonfuls of butter, then stir it in with the nuts and cook for five minutes. Season to taste with salt and pepper, and serve.

Source: Theodore Francis Garrett, ed., *The Encyclopaedia of Practical Cookery: A Complete Dictionary of All Pertaining to the Art of Cookery and Table Service,* 8 vols. (London: L. Upcott Gill, Bazaar Buildings, W.C., [1890]), 5:131.

Nut-Let Gravy

To one tablespoonful Nut-Let Butter take one pint of boiling water; add the water slowly and rub smooth until it becomes like milk; add to this two tablespoonfuls of lightly browned flour rubbed to a smooth paste in cold water. Let it boil for a few minutes and salt to taste.

Source: Bosman and Lohman Co., *The Story of Nut-Let Peanut Butter: From the Vine to the Table* (Norfolk, Va.: Bosman and Lohman, c. 1914), 33.

PEANUT SOUPS AND PUREES

Ground-Nut Soup

To half a pint shelled ground-nuts, well beaten up, add two spoonsful of flour, and mix well. Put to them a pint of oysters, and a pint and a half of water. While boiling, throw on a seed-pepper or two, if small.

Source: [Sarah Rutledge], *The Carolina Housewife* (Charleston: W. R. Babcock, 1847), 45.

Cream of Peanut Soup

1 quart of milk
1 teaspoonful of grated onion or onion juice
A tablespoonful of cornstarch
A dash of paprika
½ pint of peanut butter
A bay leaf
A saltspoonful of celery seed or a little chopped celery
½ teaspoonful of salt
A dash of white pepper

Put the milk, peanut butter, onion, and celery seed into a double boiler; stir and cook until hot. Moisten the cornstarch in a little cold milk, add it to the hot milk, and stir until smooth and thick. Strain through a sieve; add the salt, pepper and paprika, and serve at once with croûtons.

Source: Sarah Tyson Rorer, *Mrs. Rorer's New Cook Book* (Philadelphia: Arnold, 1902), 75.

Tomato Soup

Take 1 pint of sifted tomatoes, 1 grated onion, 1 tablespoonful of minced parsley, 1 tablespoonful of minced celery, 1 pint of peanut milk or cream as may be desired. Serve hot with crackers or croutons; 1 teaspoonful of sugar and a little salt should be added to the above.

Source: Almeda Lambert, *Guide for Nut Cookery* (Battle Creek, Mich.: Joseph Lambert and Co., 1899), 306.

Oyster and Peanut Soup

Take half a pound of shelled and roasted peanuts well pounded. Add two spoonfuls of flour, mix well, boil a pint of oyster water and mix with the peanuts and flour, let it thicken slowly for fifteen minutes, stirring all the time.

Add a pint of oysters and let them cook five minutes. Flavor with salt, red and black pepper.

Source: Celestine Eustis, *Cooking in Old Creole Days* (New York: R. H. Russell, 1904), 9.

Peanut Bisque

Remove the brown skin from one pint of peanuts; chop very fine, add one quart of veal or chicken stock and simmer until tender. Rub through a purée sieve, adding a little milk from time to time. Season with salt and pepper, and add enough beet juice or pink coloring paste to give a good tint. Serve with peanut crackers which have been toasted in the oven.

Source: L. L. McLaren, comp., *High Living: Recipes from Southern Climes* (San Francisco: Paul Elder, 1904), 3.

Raw Peanut Soup

Shell the raw nuts and blanch them by pouring boiling water over them. After they have stood for a few minutes the skins may be easily rubbed off. Dry them, and grind fine. Put into the Kettle with plenty of water, and boil until done. Add any vegetables and seasoning liked while cooking, and thicken with a little flour.

Source: Elma Iona Locke, "The Peanut as Food," *Table Talk* 26 (October 1911): 574.

Consomme of Peanuts

Take 1 pint of shelled peanuts; boil or steam until the skins can be removed; boil in salted water until tender and until nearly all the water boils away; add 1 quart of beef stock, a few grains of cayenne pepper, half a teaspoon salt; let boil slowly for 10 minutes; serve hot.

Source: George Washington Carver, *How to Grow the Peanut and 105 Ways of Preparing It for Human Consumption,* Bulletin No. 31 (Tuskegee, Ala.: Tuskegee Institute Experiment Station, 1916), 8.

Tomato and Peanut Soup

1 ½ cups stewed and strained tomatoes.
½ cup peanut butter.
1 teaspoon salt.
1 teaspoon paprika.
2 ½ cups boiling water.

Add tomatoes gradually to the peanut butter and when smooth add the seasonings and water. Simmer for 10 minutes and serve with croutons. Well-

seasoned soup stock may be substituted for the water; but, if used, the quantity of salt should be reduced.

Source: Homer Columbus Thompson, *The Manufacture and Use of Peanut Butter,* Circular No.
128 (Washington, D.C.: USDA, 1920), 15.

Peanut and Cheese Chowder

Into 3 qts. boiling salted water sprinkle a generous ½ cup rice, 4 good sized
potatoes, diced, and a small onion cut fine. Let boil ½ hr. or until rice and
potatoes are done. Add ½ cup or more peanuts, coarsely chopped, ½ cup
grated or finely cut cheese, and 1 can tomato soup. Let boil few minutes longer,
season with butter, pepper, and salt to taste. The chowder is in itself almost
a complete meal. Mrs. Vernon P. Squires.

Source: *Y.M.C.A. Cook Book,* 4th ed. (Grand Forks, N.D.: n.p., 1924), 6.

Notes

CHAPTER 1: ORIGIN AND DISPERSION

1. Alfred W. Crosby Jr., *The Columbian Exchange: Biological and Cultural Consequences of 1492* (Westport, Conn.: Greenwood Press, 1973); Immanuel Wallerstein, *The Modern World-System I: Capitalist Agriculture and the Origins of the European World-Economy in the Sixteenth Century* (New York: Academic Press, 1974), 41–44.

2. Bartolomé de las Casas, *Apologética Historia de las Indias,* ed. Serrano y Sanz (Madrid, 1875), as translated in Ray O. Hammons, "Early History and Origin of the Peanut," in American Peanut Research and Education Association, *Peanuts—Culture and Uses: A Symposium* (Roanoke, Va.: Stone Printing Co., for the American Peanut Research and Education Association, [1973]), 18.

3. Gonzalo Fernández Oviedo y Valdés, *La Historia general y natural de la Indias,* as translated in Hammons, "Early History and Origin of the Peanut," 19.

4. Jean Baptiste Dutertre, *Histoire générale des Antilles* (first quote) and Jean Baptiste Labat, *Nouveaux voyage aux isles de l'Amerique* (second and third quotes), both as translated in Hammons, "Early History and Origin of the Peanut," 28–30.

5. Alphonse de Candolle, *Origin of Cultivated Plants* (London: Kegan Paul, Trench, 1884), 414–15; A. Krapovickas, "The Origin, Variability and Spread of the Groundnut (*Arachis hypogaea*)," trans. J. Smartt, in *The Domestication and Exploitation of Animals and Plants,* ed. Peter J. Ucko and G. W. Dimbleby (Chicago: Aldine-Atherton, 1969), 431–32; Johnny C. Wynne and Terry A. Coffelt, "Genetics of *Arachis hypogaea* L.," in *Peanut Science and Technology,* ed. Harold K. Pattee and Clyde T. Young (Yoakum, Tex.: American Peanut Research and Education Society, 1982), 51.

6. R. O. Hammons, "The Origin and History of the Groundnut," in *The Groundnut Crop: A Scientific Basis for Improvement,* ed. J. Smartt (London: Chapman and Hall, 1994), 28–29;

(quote) Jean de Léry, *Histoire d'un Voyage faiet en la Terre du Brésil autrement dite Amerique* (quote), as translated in Hammons, "Early History and Origin of the Peanut," 19.

7. G. Soares de Souza, *Tratado Descriptivo do Brasil em 1587* (Lisbon: 1851), 175–76, as translated in Hammons, "Early History and Origin of the Peanut," 20–21 (quotes); Hammons, "The Origin and History of the Groundnut," 28.

8. Hammons, "The Origin and History of the Groundnut," 28–29.

9. Carl O. Sauer, "Cultivated Plants of South and Central America," in *Handbook of South American Indians*, ed. Julian H. Steward, 6 vols. (Washington, D.C.: USDA, 1950), 6:499–500.

10. Bernardino de Sahagún, *Historia General de las Cosas de Nueva España*, 3 vols. (Mexico: 1946), 2:262–63.

11. Francisco Hernandez, *Opera, cum edita, tum inedita (De historia plantarum Novae Hispaniae)* (Madrid, 1604), as cited in Krapovickas, "The Origin, Variability and Spread of the Groundnut," 437; R. S. MacNeish, "The Origin of American Agriculture," *Antiquity* 39 (1965): 87–94; C. E. Smith Jr., "Plant Remains," in *The Prehistory of the Tehuacan Valley*, ed. D. S. Byers (Austin: University of Texas, 1967), vol. 1, 220–25; Hammons, "The Origin and History of the Groundnut," 26; Sauer, "Cultivated Plants of South and Central America," 6:500; Sophie D. Coe, *America's First Cuisines* (Austin: University of Texas Press, 1994), 35–36.

12. E. G. (Ephraim George) Squier, *Peru Incidents of Travel and Exploration in the Land of the Incas* (New York: Harper, 1877), 81; Coe, *America's First Cuisines*, 35–36; A. Hyatt Verrill, *Foods America Gave the World* (Boston: L. C. Page, 1937), 98.

13. George Gumerman IV, "Corn for the Dead: The Significance of *Zea mays* in Moche Burial Offerings," in *Corn and Culture in the Prehistoric New World*, ed. Sissel Johannessen and Christine A. Hastorf (Boulder, Colo.: Westview, 1994), 399; Charles W. Mead, *Old Civilizations of Inca Land* (New York: [American Museum Press], 1924), 33 (quote).

14. José de Acosta, *The Naturall and Morall Historie of the East and West Indies*, trans. E. Grimeston (London: Printed by Val: Sims for Edward Blount and Williams, 1604), vol. 1, 235.

15. Garcilaso de la Vega, *Comentarios Reales de los Incas. Royal Commentaries of the Incas, and General History of Peru*, 2 parts, trans. Harold V. Livermore (Austin: University of Texas Press, 1966), part 1, 501.

16. Bernabé Cobo, *Historia del Nuevo Mundo*, ed. Jimenez de la Espada, 4 vols. (Seville: Sociedad de Bibliofilos, Andalucces, 1890–95), 1:359–60, as translated in Hammons, "Early History and Origin of the Peanut," 28.

17. Hammons, "The Origin and History of the Groundnut," 26.

18. Nicolas Monardes, *Joyfull Newes out of the Newe Founde Worlde*, trans. John Frampton (London: Wm. Norton, 1577), vol. 1, v, 177, vol. 2, 14, as quoted in Hammons, "The Origin and History of the Peanut," 27–28.

19. John Parkinson, *Theatrum Botanicum: The Theater of Plants* (London: T. Cotes, 1640), 1069–70 (first quote); Augustus Trinchinetti, "Observations and Experiments on the Property Possessed by some Plants, Particularly the A'rachis hypogae'a [*sic*], of Ripening their Fruit under Ground," *Gardener's Magazine* 12 (1836): 396 (second quote).

20. Hammons, "The Origin and History of the Groundnut," 26; Trinchinetti, "Observations and Experiments," 396; George Everhard Rumpf, *Herbarium amboinense*, 5 vols. (Amsterdam: Francisum Chaguion, Hermannum Uytwere, 1747), 5:426–28; A. F. M. Willich, *The Domestic Encyclopedia: or, a Dictionary of Facts and Useful Knowledge, Chiefly Applicable to Rural and Domestic Economy*, ed. James Mease, first American ed., 6 vols. (Philadelphia: William Young Birch, and Abraham Small, 1804), 2:438; Friedrich A. Flückiger and Daniel Hanbury, *Pharmacographia: A History of the Principal Drugs of Vegetable Origin Met with in Great Britain and British India*, 2d ed. (London: Macmillan, 1879), 187; William Dymock, C. J. H. Warden, and David Hooper, *Pharmacographia Indica: A History of the Principal Drugs of Vegetable Origin, Met with in British India*, 3 vols. (London: K. Paul, Trench, Trubner, 1890), 1:495; L. Carrington Goodrich, "Early Notices of the Peanut in China," *Monvmenta Serica: Journal of Oriental Studies of the Catholic University of Peking* 2 (1936–37): 405–9.

21. Ibn Battuta's "Travels" (1352), as quoted in Tadeusz Lewicki, *West African Food in the Middle Ages* (Cambridge: Cambridge University Press, 1974), 20. I am indebted to Charles Perry for locating this citation.

22. Jerom Merolla de Sorrento, "A Voyage to Congo," 1682, in A[wnsham] Churchill, *A Collection of Voyages and Travels*, 6 vols. (London: Printed by Messra. Churchill, 1744), 1:563 (first quote); "Ground-nuts," *Gardeners' Chronicle*, n.s 14 (September 4, 1880): 293–94; Joachim John Monteiro, *Angola and the River Congo*, 2 vols. (London: Macmillan, 1875), 2:111 (other quotes); Stephen Facciola, *Cornucopia II: A Source Book of Edible Plants* (Vista, Calif.: Kampong Publications, 1998), 114; Alan Davidson, *The Oxford Companion to Food* (New York: Oxford University Press, 1999), 357.

23. The account of the Alvares de Almada exploration was not published until 1594, as cited in Francisco Manuel de Melo, Conde de Ficalho, *Plantas úteis da Africa Portugueza* (Lisbon: Imprensa nacional, 1884), 136; Charles Perry, "The Peanut's Pilgrimage," *Los Angeles Times*, June 9, 1999, ID 0990051625 at <http://www.latimes.com>, accessed July 23, 2001.

24. C. W. Greene, "Origin of the Name Goober for Peanut," *Gardener's Monthly and Horticulturalist* 27 (July 1885): 216; A. M. Bacon, "Proposal for Folk-Lore Research at Hampton, Va.," *Journal of American Folk-Lore* 6 (1893): 307; Perry, "The Peanut's Pilgrimage."

25. Monteiro, *Angola and the River Congo*, 2:110–11 (first quote); "Ground-nuts," 293–94 (other quotes).

CHAPTER 2: SLAVE FOOD TO SNACK FOOD

1. John Brereton, *A Briefe and True Relation of the Discouerie of the North Part of Virginia* (London: Impensis G. Bishop, 1602), 7 (first quote); Francis Parkman, *Pioneers of France in the New World* (Boston: Little, Brown, 1865), 274 (French leader's comment); Lewis Cecil Gray, *History of Agriculture in the Southern United States to 1860*, 2 vols. (Washington, D.C.: Carnegie Institution of Washington, 1933), 1:4; Alexander Young, *Chronicles of the Pilgrim Fathers of the Colony of Plymouth, from 1602–1625. Now First Collected from*

Original Records and Contemporaneous Printed Documents (Boston: C. C. Little and J. Brown, 1841), 329 (quote about Pilgrims).

2. Peter Kalm, *The America of 1750: Peter Kalm's Travels in North America*, ed. Adolph B. Benson, 2 vols. (New York: Wilsonn-Erickson, 1937 [1772]), vol. 1, 254; George H. Loskiel, *History of Missions of the United Brethren* (London: Brethren's Society for the Furtherance of the Gospel, 1794), 67; Edwin James, *Account of an Expedition from Pittsburgh to the Rocky Mountains*, 2 vols. (London: Printed for Longman, Hurst, Rees, Orme, and Brown, 1823), 1:199–200; Joseph Correa de Serra, "Notice Respecting Several Vegetables, Used as Esculents, (or Food,) in North America, in a Letter to Richard Anthony Salisbury," *London Horticultural Society,* July 17, 1821, as in the *New England Farmer* 3 (August 14, 1824): 28; Henry D. Thoreau, *Journal of Henry D. Thoreau,* ed. Bradford Torrey and Francis H. Allen, 14 vols. (Boston: Houghton Mifflin, 1906), 4:384, 10:19, 12:358 and 385; Henry D. Thoreau, *Walden,* ed. J. L. Lyndon Shanley (1854; Princeton: Princeton University Press, 1971), 239 (quote); Almeda Lambert, *Guide for Nut Cookery* (Battle Creek, Mich.: Joseph Lambert and Co., 1899), 30; Facciola, *Cornucopia II,* 102.

3. William Watson, "Some Account of an Oil, Transmitted by Mr. George Brownrigg, of North Carolina," *Philosophical Transactions of the Royal Society of London* 59 (October 1769): 379–80.

4. Marion Francis Shambaugh, "The Development of Agriculture in Florida during the Second Spanish Period" (M.A. thesis, University of Florida, 1953), 71.

5. Watson, "Some Account of an Oil," 381.

6. Gonzalo Fernández de Oviedo y Valdés, *Historia general y natural de las Indias, islas y tierra-firme del mar Océano, por el capitán Gonzalo Fernández de Oviedo y Valdés . . . Prólogo de J. Natalicio González, notas de José Amador de los Ríos,* 5 vols. (Asunción, Paraguay: Editorial Guaranía, [1944]-45), 2:176; Carolus Clusius, *Rariorum plantarum historia* (Antwerp: Ex officina Plantiniana apud Ioannem Moretum, 1601), 79; Hans Sloane, *A Voyage to the Islands Madera, Barbados, Nieves, St. Christophers, and Jamaica,* 2 vols. (London: For the author, 1707), 1:lxxiii (first quote); Henry Barham, *Hortus Americanus* (Kingston, Jamaica: Alexander-Aikman, 1794), 184–85 (second quote); Patrick Browne, *The Civil and Natural History of Jamaica* (London: T. Osborne and J. Shipton, 1756), 295 (third quote); Edward Long, *The History of Jamaica, or General Survey of the Ancient and Modern State of That Island with Reflections on Its Situations, Settlements, Inhabitants, Climate, Products, Commerce, Laws and Government,* 3 vols. (London: T. Lowndes, 1774), 3:788–89 (last quotes); Fusée Aublet, *Histoire des plantes de la Guiane Françoise* (Paris: P. F. Didot jeune, 1775), 765.

7. "Pea-Nuts," *Harper's Weekly* 14 (July 16, 1870): 449; W. F. Tomlinson, "The Peanut as a Food Constituent," *Table Talk* 10 (April 1895): 109; [E. M. Morrison], *A Brief History of Isle of Wight County, Virginia, Compiled for Distribution at the Jamestown Tercentenary Exposition* (Norfolk, Va.: Branch A. P. V. A., 1907), 30; Edward Mott Woolley, "Tom Rowland—Peanuts," *McClure's Magazine,* December 1913, 186; "Peanuts in the Americas," *Bulletin of the Pan American Union* 48 (January 1919): 28; "Thomas B. Rowland," *Peanut Promoter* 3 (January 1920): 108; Julia A. Brinkley, "The Peanut," *Suffolk Herald,* reprinted in *Peanut Promoter* 6 (December 1922): 23–24; Wilbur E. MacClenny, *History of the Pea-*

nut (Suffolk, Va.: The Commercial Press, 1935), 21; Clarence J. Hylander and Oran B. Stanley, *Plants and Man* (Philadelphia: Blakiston, 1941), 183; G. W. Ray, "Peanuts and the Peanut Industry," *Peanut Journal and Nut World* 22 (November 1942): 24–26; letter from Abraham Pereira Mendes to Aaron Lupec, November 29, 1767, as in Elizabeth Donnan, *Documents Illustrative of the History of the Slave Trade to America,* 4 vols. (Washington, D.C.: Carnegie Institution of Washington, 1930–35), 3:324, 327.

8. Willich, *Domestic Encyclopedia,* 2:438 (first quote); David Ramsay, *The History of South Carolina,* 2 vols. (Charleston: David Longworth, 1809), 2:564–65 (second quote).

9. Mary Reynolds, quoted in B. A. Botkin, ed., *Lay My Burden Down: A Folk History of Slavery* (Chicago: University of Chicago Press, 1945), 121.

10. Northcote W. Thomas, *Anthropological Report on Sierra Leone,* 3 vols. (London: Harrison and Sons, 1916), 1:50; Newbell N. Puckett, *Folk Beliefs of the Southern Negro* (Chapel Hill: University of North Carolina Press, 1926), 15; Benjamin G. Brawley, *Negro Builders and Heroes* (Chapel Hill: University of North Carolina Press, 1937), 43–44 (quote); Elsie Clews Parsons, *Folk-lore of the Sea Islands, South Carolina* (New York: American Folk-Lore Society, G. E. Stechert, 1923), vol. 16, 209; Daniel Lindsey Thomas and Lucy Blayney Thomas, *Kentucky Superstitions* (Princeton: Princeton University Press, 1920), 223.

11. *Ballou's Pictorial Drawing-Room Companion,* February 24, 1855, 120–21 (quote).

12. Thomas Jefferson, *Notes on the State of Virginia; Written in the Year 1781, Somewhat Corrected and Enlarged in the Winter of 1782* ([Paris]: n.p., [1785]), 69; idem, *Thomas Jefferson's Garden Book, 1766–1824, with Relevant Extracts from His Other Writings,* ed. Edwin Morris Betts (Philadelphia: American Philosophical Society, 1981), 208, 211 (quote), 306.

13. *The American Museum or Universal Magazine* 5 (March 1789): 253; Henry Wansey, *The Journal of an Excursion to the United States of North America, in the Summer of 1794* (Salisbury, Eng.: J. Easton, 1798), 250–51.

14. Bernard McMahon, *The American Gardner's Calendar; Adapted to the Climates and Seasons of the United States* (Philadelphia: Printed by B. Graves for the author, 1806), 581; Women's Centennial Committees, *National Cookery Book* (Philadelphia: Women's Centennial Committees, 1876), 269.

15. *Morning Chronicle* (New York City), January 23, 1803 (first quote); ibid., February 1, 1803; Washington Irving, *Letters of Jonathan Oldstyle, Gent. Salmagundi; or the Whim-whams and Opinions of Launcelot Langstaff, Esq. and Others,* ed. Bruce I. Granger and Martha Hartzog (1807; Boston: Twayne, 1977), 22; ibid., 209 (second quote).

16. New York *Sun,* April 2, 1834, 2 (first quote); William Dunlap, *Memoirs of a Water Drinker,* 2 vols. (New York: Saunders and Otley, 1837), 2:25 (second quote); *New York Herald,* January 4, 1845, 2; "Pea-Nuts," 449.

17. *Miner's Journal,* August 17, 1836, 4; *New England Farmer* 11 (August 15, 1832): 38 (first and second quotes); Francis Peyre Porcher, "A Report of the Indigenous Medicinal Plants of South Carolina," *Transactions of the American Medical Association* 2 (1849): 743 (third quote).

18. "Instruction to Captain John L. Gallop of the Bark *Remer* 1843," "Enoch Richard Ware's Voyage to West Africa, 1844–1845," and "Enoch Richard Ware's Voyage to West Africa, 1845–1846," all in *New England Merchants in Africa: A History through Documents,*

1802 to 1865, ed. Norman Robert Bennett and George E. Brooks Jr. (Brookline, Mass.: Boston University Press, 1965), 279–80 (quote), 328, 338; *Gambian Blue Books,* 1835–42, as quoted in George E. Brooks, "Peanuts and Colonisation: Consequences of the Commercialisation of Peanuts in West Africa, 1830–70," *Journal of African History* 16 (1975): 34, 37; George E. Brooks, *Yankee Traders, Old Coasters, and African Middlemen: A History of American Legitimate Trade with West Africa in the Nineteenth Century* (Brookline, Mass.: Boston University Press for Africana Publishing Co., 1970), 100; *Colonization Herald,* March 1839, 124, as cited in U.S. House of Representatives, 27th Cong., 3d Sess., Report No. 283, *Report of Mr. Kennedy of Maryland from the Committee on Congress of the House of Representatives,* February 28, 1843, 996.

19. *Annual Report of the Commissioner of Patents for the Year 1847, Part 2: Agriculture* (Washington, D.C.: Wendell and Van Bentbuysen, 1848), 190–91 (quotes); J. C. Paulette, "Culture of the Ground Pea," *Southern Cultivator* 6 (April 1848): 53–54; R. L. Allen, *The American Farm Book* (New York: C. M. Saxton, 1849), 168.

20. Emily P. Burke, *Reminiscence of Georgia* (Oberlin, Ohio: Jas. M. Fitch, 1850), 126 (first quote); John Dent, in *Report of the Commissioner of Patents for 1849, Part 2: Agriculture* (Washington, D.C.: Office of Printers, 1850), 148–49; W. B. Easby, in *Report of the Commissioner of Patents for 1851,* Part 2: Agriculture (Washington, D.C.: Robert Armstrong, 1852), 353–55; George Noble Jones, in *Florida Plantation Records from the Papers of George Noble Jones,* ed. Ulrich Bonnell Phillips and James David Glunt (St. Louis: Missouri Historical Society, [c. 1927]), 115, 119, 127, 129, 163, 170, 202, 525; M. W. Philips, "Letter to Commissioner of Patents," *Report of the Commissioner of Patents for 1852* (Washington, D.C.: Robert Armstrong, 1853), 65–67 (second quote); John B. C. Gazzo, "The Pea-nut, or Pindar," *Annual Report of the Commissioner of Patents for the Year 1855, Part 2: Agriculture* (Washington, D.C.: A. O. P. Nicholson, 1856), 259; *Country Gentleman* 9 (May 7, 1857): 302 (third quote); *Country Gentleman* 9 (June 11, 1857): 382–83 (fourth quote); *Country Gentleman* 12 (December 23, 1858): 401; "Cultivation of the Pea-nut," *Sacramento Times,* as quoted in the *Southern Cultivator* 14 (March 1859): 79; Fearing Burr, *The Field and Garden of America* (Boston: Crosby and Nichols, 1863), 557 (final quote).

21. Willich, *Domestic Encyclopedia,* 2:438; Ramsay, *History of South Carolina,* 2:349; (quote) John Lunan, *Hortus Jamaicensis,* 2 vols. (Jamaica: St. Jago de la Vega Gazette, 1814), 2:348; Trinchinetti, "Observations and Experiments," 396; Porcher, "Report of the Indigenous Medicinal Plants," 743.

22. Eliza Leslie, *Directions for Cookery; being a System of the Art, in its Various Branches* (Philadelphia: E. L. Carey and A. Hart, 1837), 352, 365; Mrs. A. L. Webster, *The Improved Housewife, or Book of Receipts* (Hartford: n.p., 1844), 172; Catharine Esther Beecher, *Miss Beecher's Domestic Receipt Book* (New York: Harper, 1846), 292; Mrs. Bliss, *The Practical Cook Book* (Philadelphia: Lippincott, Grambo, 1850), 249.

23. [Sarah Rutledge], *The Carolina Housewife* (Charleston: W. R. Babcock, 1847), 45, 117, 219; [Sarah Rutledge], *The Carolina Housewife,* 2d ed. (Charleston: W. R. Babcock, 1851), 195.

24. Porcher, "Report of the Indigenous Medicinal Plants," 743.

25. Eliza Leslie, *Miss Leslie's New Receipts for Cooking* (Philadelphia: T. B. Peterson, 1854), 209.

26. *Country Gentleman* 9 (June 11, 1857): 382–83; *Country Gentleman* 10 (July 2, 1857): 16; S. B. Buckle, *Country Gentleman* 13 (May 19, 1859): 318 (quote); Jos. M. Foy, "Culture of the Pea Nut," *Country Gentleman* 16 (August 30, 1860): 143; *New England Farmer* 13 (May 1861): 245; Letter from N. N. Nixon, Wilmington, North Carolina, February 7, 1868, *Carolina Farmer* 1 (January 1869): 73–75; *People's Press of Wilmington,* July 10, 1833, September 4, 1835, as quoted in F. Roy Johnson, *The Peanut Story* (Murfreesboro, N.C.: Johnson Publishing Co., 1964), 49–50, 57, 59; "Pea-Nut Culture in North Carolina," *North Carolina Advertiser,* as quoted in *The Country Gentleman* 26 (October 26, 1865): 270; H. E. Colton, "Peanuts and Peanut Oil," *Scientific American* 24 (March 4, 1871): 149.

CHAPTER 3: SOLDIERS AND VENDORS

1. Francis Peyre Porcher, *Resources of the Southern Fields and Forests, Medical, Economical, and Agricultural* (Charleston: Evans and Cogswell, 1863), 194–95; Brian W. Jones, *The Peanut Plant: Its Cultivation and Uses* (New York: Orange Judd, 1885), 56; "Pea-Nut Culture in North Carolina," 270; R. B. Handy, *Peanuts: Culture and Uses,* Farmer's Bulletin No. 25 (Washington, D.C.: USDA, 1895), 21; Tomlinson, "Peanut as a Food Constituent," 111.

2. "An Ohio Soldier in the 73rd Infantry," ms., Tennessee Archives, Nashville, located by Janet Gray, who forwarded it to the author in an e-mail dated October 15, 1999 (first quote); Virginia Clay-Clopton, *A Belle of the Fifties: Memoirs of Mrs. Clay of Alabama, Covering Social and Political Life in Washington and the South, 1853–66, Gathered and Edited by Ada Sterling* (New York: Doubleday, Page, 1904), 224–25 (second quote); Elizabeth Lyle Saxon, *A Southern Woman's War Time Reminiscences* (Memphis, Tenn.: Press of The Pilcher Printing Co., 1905), 38; Jones, *The Peanut Plant,* 58–59 (third quote); *Guide for Nut Cookery,* 382; George Washington Carver, *How to Grow the Peanut and 105 Ways of Preparing It for Human Consumption,* Bulletin No. 31 (Tuskegee, Ala.: Tuskegee Institute Experiment Station, 1916), 30.

3. Luther Frank, *Songs of the South in the War between the States, 1861–1865,* Decca, 1940s?; A. Pender, in Henry Steele Commager, *The Blue and Gray* (New York: Bobbs-Merrill, 1950), 584–85 (lyrics).

4. Colton, "Peanuts and Peanut Oil," 149.

5. John Chandler Gregg, *Life in the Army: In the Departments of Virginia, and the Gulf, Including Observations in New Orleans, with an Account of the Author's Life and Experience in the Ministry* (Philadelphia: Perkinpine and Higgins, 1868), 139; Thomas F. Devoe, *The Market Assistant* (New York: Hurd and Houghton, 1867), 399–400 (quotes). A similar statement appears in Todd Goodhouse, ed., *A Domestic Cyclopedia of Practical Information* (New York: Henry Holt, 1877), 386; "Foreign Trade of the United States, Annual, 1790–1929, Nuts, Domestic Exports, Imports, Reexports and Nut Balance, Quantity and Value," *Report FS 51* (Washington, D.C.: Statistical and Historical Research of the Bureau of Agricultural Economics of the USDA, July 1930), 18.

6. Woolley, "Tom Rowland—Peanuts," 184; Thomas Rowland, *Note Book,* as cited in Johnson, *Peanut Story,* 13; "Thomas B. Rowland," 110–11 (quote).

7. "Pea-Nuts," 449; Woolley, "Tom Rowland—Peanuts," 190 (quote).

8. "Pea-Nuts," 449; Gil Robinson, *Old Wagon Show Days* (Cincinnati: Brockwell Co., 1925), 57 (quote).

9. Colton, "Peanuts and Peanut Oil," 149; *Cultivator and Country Gentleman* 36 (July 21, 1871): 468 (quotes).

10. "Pea-Nuts," 449.

11. Ibid. (first quote); *Harper's Magazine* 17 (November 1888): 938 (other quotes).

12. "Pea-Nuts," 449 (first quote); Colton, "Peanuts and Peanut Oil," 149 (second quote). It was unusual that 300,000 bushels were headed for the United States. In 1870–71 the Franco-Prussian War disrupted the French peanut trade with Africa, and the ships carrying these peanuts were diverted to America for the duration of the war. As the war was relatively short, many ships later continued on to Europe.

13. See, for example, in chronological order: Fearing Burr, *Field and Garden of America*, 2d ed. (Boston: J. E. Tilton and Co., 1865), 544–46; *Maryland Farmer* 4 (February 1867): 54, (July 1867): 202, (September 1867): 268; "The Culture of Peanuts," *Cultivator and Country Gentleman* 31 (April 9, 1868): 262; Charles W. Dickerman [assisted by Charles Flint], *The Farmer's Book* (Philadelphia: Zeigler McCurdy, 1868), 667; United States Department of Agriculture, *Report of the Commissioner of Agriculture for the Year 1868* (Washington, D.C.: USDA, 1869), 220–24; William N. White, *Gardening for the South, or How to Grow Vegetables and Fruits* (New York: Orange Judd, 1868), 234–35; N. N. Nixon, February 7, 1868, *Carolina Farmer* 1 (January 1869): 73–75; "The Culture of Peanuts," *Cultivator and Country Gentleman* 33 (May 13, 1836): 371–72; "The Culture of Peanuts," *Cultivator and Country Gentleman* 35 (February 17, 1870): 100; "Culture of Peanuts," *Cultivator and Country Gentleman* 35 (March 24, 1870): 180; *Rural Carolinian* 1 (May 1870): 476–77, (July 1870): 609; *Cultivator and Country Gentleman* 36 (February 23, 1871): 116; *Rural Carolinian* 3 (April 1872): 428–29; *Country Gentleman* 39 (November 26, 1874): 757; *Cultivator and Country Gentleman* 35 (April 21, 1870): 246; O. L. Barber, "Method of Growing Peanuts," *Country Gentleman* 35 (May 26, 1870): 325; *Rural Carolinian* 4 (October 1872): 55; *Country Gentleman* 39 (November 26, 1874): 757; *Rural Carolinian* 6 (December 1875): 836; *Country Gentleman* 41 (November 30, 1876): 760, (December 14, 1876): 792, (December 28, 1876): 822; Jones, *The Peanut Plant*, 9.

14. W. B. Jester, "Story of the American Peanut Corporation," *Peanut Journal and Nut World* 18 (March 1939): 9.

15. Gwaltney-Bunkley Peanut Co., *The Land of the Peanut: Louisiana Purchase Exposition Edition, June 14, 1904* (Smithfield, Va.: Gwaltney-Bunkley Peanut Co., 1904), cover (quote), 31–32; Jester, "Story of the American Peanut Corporation," 9; Marion G. Everett and Patsy D. Barham, *A History of the Smithfield Ham Industry* (Smithfield, Va.: Wight County Museum, 1993), 3, 5, 8, 16.

16. W. B. Jester, "Story of the Pretlow Peanut Company," *Peanut Journal and Nut World* 19 (November 1939): 13; Edward F. Gilliam, "Pretlow Peanut Company Has Interesting History Dating Back to Turn of Century," *Peanut Journal and Nut World* 35 (November 1955): 17, 19, 45.

17. W. B. Jester, "Story of the Franklin Peanut Company," *Peanut Journal and Nut World* 19 (December 1939): 7–8; undated Franklin Peanut Co. advertising card (quotes).

18. George Odell, *Annals of the New York Stage*, 15 vols. (New York: Columbia University Press, 1927–49), 6:231 (quote); Stuart Thayer, "Here We Go Again," *Bandwagon* 47 (September–October 1993): 29; *Evening Journal* (Lewiston, Me.), July 11, 1882, as cited in Robert Loeffler, "Soda Pop, Lemonade, among Beverages Served in Circuses since Early 1800s," *White Tops* 56 (September–October 1983): 38–40; *Peanut Journal and Nut World* 10 (March 1931): 19; John B. Pinner, "Why Peanuts?" *Peanut Journal and Nut World* 17 (June 1938): 11–12; Edward G. Maxwell, "A Virginia-Born Industry Grows Up," *Baltimore Morning Sunday Sun* August 25, 1940, reprinted in *Peanut Journal and Nut World* 20 (November 1940): 9–10; Alice M. Geffen and Carole Bergile, "A Most Flavored Food: Peanut Butter Is All Things to All People—Even Calorie-Counters," *Americana* (June 1989): 41; Woolley, "Tom Rowland—Peanuts," 198; "Thomas B. Rowland," 113.

19. Robinson, *Old Wagon Show Days*, 57; *Syracuse Courier*, June 26, 1876, as quoted in Loeffler, "Soda Pop, Lemonade," 37, 40 (first quote); Ernest Schlee Millette and Robert Wyndham, *The Circus That Was: The Autobiography of a Star Performer* (Philadelphia: Dorrance, 1971), 76 (second quote); *Lansing Republican*, June 26, 1874, as quoted in Thayer, "Here We Go Again," 29 (third quote).

20. L. G. Loup, "The Story of One of America's Finest Confections," *Peanut Journal* 2 (January 1923): 11, 36–37 (first quote); *Detroit Free Press*, May 1879, and *Pantagraph* (Bloomington, Ill.), September 13, [1879?] (second quote), and *Evening Dispatch* (York, Pa.), August 9, 1881 (third quote), as quoted in Thayer, "Here We Go Again," 29; *Daily Citizen* (Jackson, Miss.), September 29, 1877 (fourth quote), and *Post* (Rochester, Minnesota), May 21, 1880 (fifth quote), as cited in Loeffler, "Soda Pop, Lemonade," 38–40.

21. Charles Fenno Hoffman, *A Winter in the West*, 2 vols. (New York: Harper, 1835), 1:206; Harriet Beecher Stowe, *Dred: A Tale of the Great Dismal Swamp*, 2 vols. (Boston: Phillips, Sampson, 1856), 1:9, 50–51 (first quote); Samuel L. Clemens, *The Gilded Age: A Tale of To-day, by Mark Twain and Charles Dudley Warner* (Hartford: American Publishing Co., 1873), 333; Mary Akins, *The Little Pea-nut Merchant: or, Harvard's Aspiration* (Boston: For the author, 1869), 164, 165, 167 (other quotes).

22. Lyman Hotchkiss Bagg, *Four Years at Yale: By a Graduate of '69* (New Haven: C. C. Chatfield, 1871), 70–71 (quote); Waldron Kintzing Post, *Harvard Stories: Sketches of the Undergraduate* (New York: Putnam, 1893), 108.

23. Jones, *The Peanut Plant*, 56–57.

24. "Thomas B. Rowland," 110–11; *Grocer's Bulletin* 1 (April 21, 1881): 15; New England Grocer Office, *Grocer's Companion and Merchant's Hand-book* (Boston: New England Grocer Office, 1883), 108–9; *Grocer's Vindicator* 1 (January 28, 1888): 23; C. Jevne Co., *Importing Grocers* (Chicago: C. Jevne, 1892), 40.

25. United States Patent Office, Patent No. 604,994, issued to C. O. Luce, May 31, 1898; Woolley, "Tom Rowland—Peanuts," 202–3; "Thomas B. Rowland," 113; Allen Chaffee, "Theses on Origin and History of the Peanut," *Peanut Journal and Nut World* 14 (April 1935): 9–11; "Peanut Vending Machines Take in Big Money," *Peanut Journal* 5 (June 1926): 26; Jasper Guy Woodroof, *Peanuts: Production, Processing, Products* (Westport, Conn.: AVI, 1966), 193.

26. Woolley, "Tom Rowland—Peanuts," 201; "Thomas B. Rowland," 113.

27. "Social Rise of the Peanut," *Richmond Dispatch*, as quoted in *Good Housekeeping*,

December 1902, 468 (first quote); Etta Morse Hudders, "The Rise of the Peanut," *Table Talk* 18 (March 1903): 114 (second quote); Bosman and Lohman Co., *The Story of Nut-Let Peanut Butter: From the Vine to the Table* (Norfolk, Va.: Bosman and Lohman, c. 1914), 3 (third quote).

CHAPTER 4: DOCTORS AND VEGETARIANS

1. Peter G. Rose, *Foods of the Hudson: A Seasonal Sampling of the Region's Bounty* (Woodstock, N.Y.: Overlook Press, 1993), 21–22; W. B. Nash, "Peanut Butter Is a Splendid Food of Rare Merit," *Peanut Journal* 2 (November 1922): 9–10 (quote), 35; "George A. Bayle Dies Suddenly of Apoplexy," December 19, 1921, clipping in the archives of the Missouri Historical Society, Saint Louis; A. P. Grohens, "Peanut Butter History and Development of the Peanut Butter Industry," *Peanut Promoter* 3 (July 1920): 65, 67, 69, 71, 78.

2. John Harvey Kellogg, "Statement Concerning Invention of Peanut Butter, Transcript from: Michigan State Supreme Court Record; Case of John Harvey Kellogg, the Kellogg Food Co., and Sanitarium Equipment Co. v. Kellogg Toasted Corn Flake Co., et al.," 3 vols., typescript (1920), 2:369.

3. Sylvester Graham, *Treatise on Bread and Bread-Making* (Boston: Light and Stearns, 1837); William A. Alcott, *Vegetable Diet* (New York: Fowlers and Wells, 1850).

4. "A Long Lifetime of Service to Humanity," *Good Health* 79 (January 1944): 4–8.

5. Ibid., 4.

6. United States Patent Office, Patent No. 567,901, issued to John H. Kellogg, dated September 15, 1896, filed November 4, 1895 (first quote); John H. Kellogg, "Good and Bad Foods," S[eventh] D[ay] A[dventist] General Conference's *Daily Bulletin* 8 (March 5, 1899): 152 (second quote).

7. Kellogg, "Good and Bad Foods," 152.

8. Richard W. Schwarz, *John Harvey Kellogg, M.D.* (Nashville, Tenn.: Southern Publishing Association, [1970]), 85.

9. The Sanitas Nut Butters are advertised in the 1897–98 J. F. Conrad catalog, clipping file, Missouri Historical Society.

10. Anna Colcord, *A Friend in the Kitchen or, What to Cook and How to Cook It* (Oakland, Calif.: Pacific Press Publishing Co., 1899), 107–8.

11. Vegetarian Supply Co., *I've Come Out of My Burrow to Borrow* (Providence, R.I.: Vegetarian Supply Co., 1899), n.p., in "American Poetry, 1871–1900," Harris Collection, Brown University Library, Providence, Rhode Island.

12. Lambert, *Guide for Nut Cookery*, 152; Colcord, *Friend in the Kitchen*, 107; E. G. Fulton, *Vegetarian Cook Book: Substitutes for Flesh Foods* (Mountain View, Calif.: Pacific Press Publishing Association, 1904), 241–43; E. E. Kellogg, *Science in the Kitchen*, rev. ed. (Battle Creek, Mich.: Modern Medicine Publishing Co., [1904]), 398–421.

13. Lambert, *Guide for Nut Cookery*, 103–4, 107–11; Sarah Tyson Rorer, *Mrs. Rorer's New Cook Book* (Philadelphia: Arnold, 1902), 534; *Use Peanut Flour to Save Wheat, 1918*, Circular No. 110 (Washington, D.C.: USDA, 1918), n.p.; [John H. Kellogg], "Peanut Milk," *Good Health* 55 (October 1920): 589; "Statement of Mr. George Washington Carver, United Pea-

nut Association of America, Tuskegee, Ala.," *Tariff Information, 1921 Hearings Before the Committee on Ways and Means. House of Representatives on Schedule G. Agricultural Products and Provisions. January 21, 1921,* No. 14 (Washington, D.C.: Government Printing Office, 1921), 1551; Carver, *How to Grow the Peanut,* 16; Helen Watkeys Moore, *Camouflage Cookery: A Book of Mock Dishes* (New York: Duffield, 1918), 37, 44; George W. Carver, "Creative Thought and Action Two of the Greatest Needs of the South," *Peanut Journal and Nut World* 12 (November 1932): 9; National Peanut Council, *Peanuts: Their Food Value, and Over One Hundred Sure-fire Peanut Recipes to Add Zest to Your Menus* (Suffolk, Va.: National Peanut Council, c. 1941), 29.

14. "Peanut Cream," *Table Talk* 18 (January 1903): 34.

15. E. F. Haskell, *The Housekeeper's Encyclopedia* (New York: D. Appleton, 1861), 81–82; T. J. Crowen, *The American Lady's System of Cookery* (New York: Dick and Fitzgerald, 1866), 329, 405; Richard J. Hooker, *A History Food and Drink in America* (Indianapolis: Bobbs-Merrill, 1981), 242.

16. Anna Churchill Carey, "Some New Sandwiches," *Good Housekeeping,* May 1896, 205; *Table Talk* 11 (July 1896): 244; Marion Harland [pseud. for Mary Virginia Terhune] and Christine Terhune Herrick, *The National Cookbook* (New York: Scribner, 1896), 6; Women's Guild of Saint Mark's Church, *Clever Cooking* (Seattle: Metropolitan Printing and Binding Co., 1896), 218 (quote); "Peanuts. Palatable Peanuts. Since Physicians Have Declared the Nut Nutritious, It Is Popular," *Philadelphia Press,* as quoted in John R. Parry, *Nuts for Profit: A Treatise on the Propagation and Cultivation of Nut-Bearing Trees* (Parry, N.J.: By the author, 1897), 151; Elle W. Eliel, *Poetry in Cookery: A German American Cook Book* (Peoria, Ill.: J. W. Franks, 1897), 352; *Ransom's Family Receipt Book* (Buffalo, N.Y.: D. Ransom, 1898), 20; *Southern Housekeeper: A Book of Tested Recipes Collected by the Home Department of the Ladies' Missionary Society of the Central Presbyterian Church* (Atlanta: Franklin Printing and Publishing Co., 1898), 89; Oswego West Baptist Church, *A Friend in the House: Common Sense Rules for Healthful Every-Day Living* (Oswego, N.Y.: Times Book and Job Print, 1898), 172; Young Lady Workers of the Methodist Episcopal Church, *The Carbondale Cook Book of Tried and Tested Recipes* (Carbondale, Pa.: Methodist Episcopal Church, 1898), 54; *The First M. E. Church Cook Book* (Marysville, Ohio: Shearer and Shearer, 1899), 101. I have examined several earlier sources for peanut butter. For instance, the *Oxford English Dictionary Supplement* quotes a June 24, 1889, reference in the *Kansas Times and Star,* "The latest fad on restaurant and boarding house tables here is 'peanut butter.'" The *Times* and *Star* were two different newspapers. I have searched both papers for this date but located no source reference. Likewise, S. T. Rorer's *Sandwiches* (Philadelphia: Arnold, 1894) has been quoted with a "Nut Butter" recipe dated 1894. However, this does not appear in the 1894 edition; it does appear in a revised version of the book published in 1912, but with a copyright date of 1894.

17. Julia Davis Chandler, "Peanuts and Pralines," *Boston Cooking-School Magazine* 6 (November 1901): 188–89; Beech-Nut Packing Co., *Beech-Nut Peanut Butter: The Great Tea and Luncheon Delicacy as Served in New York Tea-Rooms* (Canajoharie, N.Y.: Beech-Nut Packing Co., 1914), 7–10.

18. Lambert, *Guide for Nut Cookery,* 71 (quote), 79, 103; Rorer, *Mrs. Rorer's New Cook*

Book, 75, 535; Hudders, "Rise of the Peanut," 114; *Boston Cooking-School Magazine* 14 (May 1910): x, 15 (November 1910): 204, 16 (November 1911): 192; Elma Iona Locke, "The Peanut as Food," *Table Talk* 26 (October 1911): 576; Gertrude R. Lombard, "The Food Value of the Peanut," *Good Housekeeping,* December 1912, 842–43; "Peanut Butter Pinwheels," *Good Housekeeping,* July 1913, 126–27.

19. Beech-Nut Packing Co., *Beech-Nut Peanut Butter,* 10–21.

20. Edward Halsey diary entry for May 29, 1899, as quoted in R. Parr and G. Litster, *What Hath God Wrought: The Sanatarium Health Food Co.* (Berkeley Vale, N.S.W., Australia: The Sanatarium Health Food Co., 1996), 19; *Journal of Agriculture* (Natal) 2 (1899): 437. Raw peanut paste continued to be manufactured in South Africa as originally made by Kellogg. See Woodroof, *Peanuts,* 127.

21. Linda Campbell Franklin, *Three Hundred Years of Kitchen Collectibles,* 4th ed. (Iola, Wisc.: Krause, 1997), 44–45.

22. A. P. Grohens, "Peanut Butter," *Spice Mill* 38 (December 1915): 1451–52; United States Patent Office, Patent No. 625,400, by Joseph Lambert, issued May 23, 1899; United States Patent Office, Patent No. 625,394, by Charles Hook, assigned to Joseph Lambert, issued May 23, 1899; Grohens, "Peanut Butter History," 65, 67, 69, 71, 78.

23. Lambert, *Guide for Nut Cookery,* back page.

24. Grohens, "Peanut Butter," 1451–52; idem, "Peanut Butter History," 65, 67, 69, 71, 78.

25. United States Patent Office, Patent No. 721,651, by A. W. Straub, issued February 24, 1903; Geffen and Bergile, "A Most Flavored Food," 40–43; David R. Francis, *The Universal Exposition of 1904* (St. Louis: Louisiana Purchase Exposition Co., 1913), 587; Grohens, "Peanut Butter," 1451–52; Albert P. Grohens, "Thirty Years Ago Peanut Butter Was Practically Unknown," *Peanut Journal* 8 (January 1929): 25.

26. Grohens, "Thirty Years Ago," 25; William Renwick Beattie, *Making and Using Peanut Butter,* Circular No. 384 (Washington, D.C.: USDA, 1936), 1; United States Patent Office, Trademark No. 32,254, for "Peanut Butter," Atlantic Peanut Refinery, issued December 20, 1898; United States Patent Office, Trademark No. 32,589, for "Peanolia" Peanut-Butter, issued March 14, 1899, filed February 17, 1899, in use since September 1, 1898; A. L. Winton, "Peanut Butter and Peanolia," *Connecticut Experiment Station Report* 23, part 2 (New Haven: Tuttle, Morehouse and Taylor, 1899), 138 (quote).

27. *American Grocer* 63 (May 16, 1900): 10–11.

28. Hudders, "Rise of the Peanut," 113–14.

29. Albert P. Grohens, "Peanut Butter," *Spice Mill* 40 (September 1917): 1094; "When Peanuts Were a Fad," *Peanut Promoter* 6 (March 1923): 9–10; "The Beginning of the Buffalo Brand," *Peanut Journal* 3 (November 1923): 35; *Peanut Journal* 5 (August 1926): 10.

30. United States Patent Office, Trademark No. 40,102, for "Old Dominion" peanut butter, issued April 14, 1903; *Monthly Exponent of Good Living,* clipping in the archives of the Missouri Historical Society; "George A. Bayle Dies Suddenly of Apoplexy"; *Table Talk* 20 (September 1905): vii.

31. *American Grocer* 79 (June 24, 1908): 11 (first quote); "Peanut Butter," *American Grocer* 88 (November 20, 1912): 7 (second quote); *Good Housekeeping,* June 1913, 25; H. J. Heinz Co., *The Story of Peanutville: A Tale for Little Children* (Pittsburgh, Pa.: H. J. Heinz Co.,

1915), n.p.; Bosman and Lohman Co., *Story of Nut-Let Peanut Butter;* C. A. A. Utt, "Some Data on Peanut Butter," *Journal of Industrial and Engineering Chemistry* 6 (September 1914): 746–47.

32. "Peanuts in the Americas," 28–39.

33. Homer Columbus Thompson, *The Manufacture and Use of Peanut Butter,* Circular No. 128 (Washington, D.C.: USDA, 1920), 5 (quote); Grohens, "Thirty Years Ago," 25; Nash, "Peanut Butter Is a Splendid Food," 9–10, 35.

34. *Table Talk* 20 (September 1905): vii; "Beech-Nut Packing Company Products," a typewritten list of products produced by the company, Canajoharie Library and Art Gallery, Canajoharie, N.Y.; "Beech-Nut," *Fortune,* November 1936, 85–93, 206, 208, 210, 212; "Bit of History about the Growth and Progress of a Great Industry," *Peanut Journal* 9 (January 1930): 17–20 (quote, p. 18).

35. *American Grocer* 79 (June 24, 1908): 11.

36. *Spice Mill* 36 (May 1913): 472.

37. Beech-Nut Packing Co., *Beech-Nut Peanut Butter;* idem, *A Hundred and One Recipes with Beech-Nut Peanut Butter,* 3d ed. (Canajoharie, N.Y.: Beech-Nut Packing Co., 1920); Ida Bailey Allen, *The Beech-Nut Book of Menus and Recipes* (Canajoharie, N.Y.: Beech-Nut Packing Co., 1924); Beech-Nut Packing Co., *The Chefs' Book: The Beech-Nut Recipes of Famous Chefs* (Canajoharie, N.Y.: Beech-Nut Packing Co., [1925]); Grohens, "Peanut Butter" (December 1915), 1451.

38. Victor Ayer, "A Splendid Banquet Surprise," *National Food Magazine* 28 (February 1910): 115–18; Charles Robson, ed., *The Manufactories and Manufacturers of Pennsylvania of the Nineteenth Century* (Philadelphia: Galaxy Publishing Co., 1875), 385–87; "H. J. Heinz of Heinz Noble and Co.," 167 and 169 Second Ave., Pittsburgh, "Book of 1875 and 1876," n.p., and "H. J. Heinz with F. and J. Heinz, July 1, [18]76," n.p., manuscripts in the Heinz Family archive, Pittsburgh.

39. *Good Housekeeping,* June 1913, 25 (first quote); H. J. Heinz Co., *The Heinz Book of Salads* (Pittsburgh, Pa.: H. J. Heinz Co., 1925), 82 (other quotes).

40. *Peanut Journal* 1 (August 1922): 17–18, 20; Nash, "Peanut Butter Is a Splendid Food," 9–10, 35; *Peanut Journal* 1 (July 1922): 7–8, 34.

41. Al Silverman, "Everybody's Nuts about Peanut Butter," *Coronet* 48 (September 1960): 147.

42. "Patented Process of Making Peanut Butter," *Spice Mill,* reprinted in *Peanut Journal* 4 (September 1925): 8–9; United States Patent Office, Patent 1,445,174, issued February 13, 1923; United States Patent Office, Patent 1,528,077, issued March 3, 1925; United States Patent Office, Patent 1,756,702, to Joseph L. Rosefield, Alameda, California; A. F. Freeman and W. Sidney Singleton, "Prevention of Oil Separation in Peanut Butter—A Review," *Peanut Journal and Nut World* 31 (February 1952): 23; *Peanut Journal* 10 (November 1930): 18.

43. Information from <http://brands.bestfoods.com/skippy/history.asp> and <http://www.bestfoods.com/skippy_history_tibbetts.html>, both accessed May 7, 2000.

44. Rick Plummer, "Peter Pan Peanut Butter and the Sky King Show," at <http://home.kscable.com/fcr/peterpan.html> accessed May 29, 2000; <http://ca.destru.com/MidYear/brands.html>, accessed May 29, 2000; *Peanut Journal* 5 (July 1926): 21; John

Crook, *Peter Pan, or The Boy Who Wouldn't Grow Up* (London: Prince and Reynolds, c. 1905); E. K. Pond, *Here's Something New—Peter Pan* (Chicago: E. K. Pond, c. 1928), n.p.
    45. Plummer, "Peter Pan Peanut Butter and the Sky King Show."

CHAPTER 5: UNSHELLED AND SHELLED

    1. *Peanut Journal* 2 (November 1922): 35; Johnson, *Peanut Story,* 53.
    2. National Peanut Council, *Peanuts: Their Food Value,* 24; Chaffee, "Theses," 9–11; "Thomas B. Rowland," 110–11; *Peanut Journal and Nut World* 19 (November 1939): 17, 32.
    3. *Peanut Promoter* 5 (January 1922): 6; *Peanut Journal and Nut World* 22 (April 1943): 15; "Thomas B. Rowland," 110; *Baltimore Sun* article, reprinted in *Peanut Journal* 1 (January 1922): 27.
    4. C. Cretors and Co., *C. Cretors and Co., The First Hundred Years: 1885–1985* (Chicago: C. Cretors, 1985), 7, 133.
    5. Ibid., 1–2.
    6. *Scientific American* 71 (December 29, 1894): 405 (quote); C. Cretors and Co., *C. Cretors and Co.,* 13, 17; "Canadians Report on Third Annual IPA Regional Popcorn-Concession Conference," *Popcorn Merchandiser* 9 (May 1954): 2; H. S. Bailey and J. A. LeClerc, "The Peanut, A Great American Food," in *Yearbook of the USDA, 1917* (Washington, D.C.: USDA, 1918), 290–91.
    7. "Peanut Vendor Left Estate of $100,000," *Spice Mill* 45 (June 1922): 1076.
    8. *Peanut Journal* 8 (December 1928): 18.
    9. H. H. Thompson, "Food Value of the Peanut," *Peanut Journal* 1 (November 1921): 22; C. W. Murphy, "Brooklyn National League Clubs Roasts Peanuts for Patrons, " *Peanut Journal* 2 (September 1923): 13–14 (quote); Jack Norworth, "Take Me Out to the Ball Game," 1908.
    10. "Thomas B. Rowland," 113 (quote); *Peanut Journal* 7 (May 1928): 23.
    11. "Gooda Peanuta," *Spice Mill* 49 (April 1916): 452; "Indianapolis Man Claims Originating Salted Peanuts," *Peanut Promoter* 3 (December 1919): 21; Chaffee, "Theses," 9–11; Hudders, "Rise of the Peanut," 114 (quote).
    12. *Spice Mill* 44 (January 1921): 165–66.
    13. "Prolific Peanuts: Mr. Peanut Grows Up and Becomes Symbol of Huge Industry," *Literary Digest* 123 (March 6, 1937): 40–42; "$10,000,000 Worth of Peanuts Were Sold Last Year by Messrs. Obici and Peruzzi, Who Own Planters Nut and Chocolate Co.," *Fortune,* April 1938, 80; Daisy Nurney, "Peanut King in America Fifty Years," *Peanut Journal and Nut World* 18 (April 1939): 13; "Amedeo Obici, Founder of a Great Industry and Pioneer in Commercializing Peanuts, Dies at 69," *Peanut Journal and Nut World* 26 (June 1947): 24.
    14. "How Advertising Put Mr. Peanut on the Map," *Peanut Promoter* 7 (December 1924): 13–14; "Prolific Peanuts," 40–42; Nurney, "Peanut King in America Fifty Years," 13; "The Story of Peanuts," mimeographed paper produced by the Public Relations Department of the Planters LifeSavers Co., Winston-Salem, N.C., January 29, 1990, 1; United States Trademark No. 38,883, issued to Amedeo Obici on September 8, 1902.
    15. *Peanut Journal and Nut World* 35 (January 1956): 13; "Prolific Peanuts," 42.

16. *Peanut Journal and Nut World* 12 (February 1933): 11; "How Advertising Put Mr. Peanut on the Map," 13–14; *Peanut Journal and Nut World* 35 (January 1956): 13; "Planters Celebrates 25th Anniversary in Place of Its Birth," *Peanut Journal* 10 (January 1931): 22; Jan Lindenberger with Joyce Spontak, *Planters Peanut Collectibles, 1906–1961* (Atglen, Pa.: Schiffer, 1995), 5.

17. "How Advertising Put Mr. Peanut on the Map," 13–14; *Peanut Journal and Nut World* 35 (January 1956): 13; "$10,000,000 Worth of Peanuts," 83; "Amedeo Obici, Founder of a Great Industry," 24.

18. "Planters Annual Convention Held in Suffolk," *Peanut Promoter* 7 (February 1924): 15; "Amedeo Obici, Founder of a Great Industry," 24.

19. "How Advertising Put Mr. Peanut on the Map," 13–14; W. C. Johnson, "Building an Industry on Peanuts," *Commonwealth* 2 (November 1935): 12.

20. W. C. Johnson, "Building an Industry on Peanuts," 30; *Peanut Promoter* 4 (December 1921): 58; "How Advertising Put Mr. Peanut on the Map," 33; *Norfolk Virginian-Pilot* article, reprinted in *Peanut Journal* 1 (January 1922): 17; "Planters Acquire King Peanut Company," *Peanut Promoter* 9 (March 1926): 9; "$10,000,000 Worth of Peanuts," 84; *Peanut Journal and Nut World* 12 (February 1933): 11.

21. "Amedeo Obici, Founder of a Great Industry," 24; "Mrs. Louise Musante Obici Dies after Long Illness," *Peanut Journal and Nut World* 17 (October 1938): 13; *Peanut Journal* 9 (September 1930): 35.

22. "Peanut Packer Starts to Advertise," *Printer's Ink* 99 (June 21, 1917): 67–68.

23. Ibid.; "$10,000,000 Worth of Peanuts," 80; "Interesting Booklet on Virginia Peanut Industry," *Spice Mill* 40 (January 1917): 109.

24. "$10,000,000 Worth of Peanuts," 144; Judith Wathall, "Interview of Christine Gentile and Delcy Ann Gentile," as in *Peanut Papers for Peanut Pals* 1 (January–February 1979): 6–7; Lindenberger with Spontak, *Planters Peanut Collectibles, 1906–1961*, 6; "How Advertising Put Mr. Peanut on the Map," 33; e-mail from Jim Meyers, grandson of Andrew Wallach, to Joyce Spontak, May 18, 2000; "The Story of Peanuts," 2; *Richmond Dispatch* article, reprinted in *Good Housekeeping*, December 1902, 468; United States Patent Office, Trademark No. 38,883, issued to Amedeo Obici, September 8, 1902. Other anthropomorphized peanuts appeared in Charles J. Wilson, *Peanut Dance* (New York: Howley, Haviland, 1894), sheet music, cover, and Elizabeth Gordon's *Mother Earth's Children: The Frolics of Fruits and Vegetables* (Chicago: P. F. Volland, 1913), 74.

25. "Peanut Meal in Bread Making," *Spice Mill* 41 (March 1918): 372.

26. United State Patent Office, Trademark No. 121,818, issued to Planters Nut and Chocolate Co., May 28, 1918; "Peanut Packer Starts to Advertise," 67–68 (quotes); "How Advertising Put Mr. Peanut on the Map," 33.

27. John Allen Murphy, "War-Time Advertising Puts a Brand of Peanuts on National Map," *Spice Mill* 41 (November 1918): 1436 (quote); *Saturday Evening Post*, February 23, 1918, 34; *Peanut Journal* 1 (January 1922): 16; *Peanut Promoter* 6 (December 1922): insert; *Peanut Journal* 9 (March 1930): 11, 25.

28. John Allen Murphy, "War-Time Advertising Puts a Brand of Peanuts on National Map," *Printer's Ink* 104 (October 10, 1918): 65–66, 69.

29. *Peanut Journal* 1 (January 1922): 16 (first quote); *Peanut Journal and Nut World* 16 (November 1936): 15–16 (other quotes); "$10,000,000 Worth of Peanuts," 78.

30. *Peanut Journal* 1 (January 1922): 16; Vicki Gold Levi and Lee Eisenberg, *Atlantic City, 125 Years of Ocean Madness: Starring Miss America, Mr. Peanut, Lucy the Elephant, the High Diving Horse, and Four Generations of Americans Cutting Loose* (New York: C. N. Potter, 1979), 113; *Peanut Journal* 6 (July 1927): 19; "Nut Industry Must Make Advertising Basis of Sales Production," *Peanut Journal and Nut World* 15 (October 1936): 5; W. C. Johnson, "Suffolk's Unique Peanut Float Wins Second Prize," *Peanut Journal and Nut World* 15 (October 1936): 11.

31. *Peanut Journal* 8 (June 1929): 17; *Peanut Journal* 9 (March 1930): 11 (quote).

32. *Peanut Journal* 9 (March 1930): 11, 25; "$10,000,000 Worth of Peanuts," 80, 148.

33. W. C. Johnson, "Building an Industry on Peanuts," 12, 30; "Prolific Peanuts," 40–42.

34. "$10,000,000 Worth of Peanuts," 78; Nurney, "Peanut King in America Fifty Years," 13; "Amedeo Obici, Founder of a Great Industry," 24.

CHAPTER 6: SOUP TO OIL NUTS

1. Lambert, *Guide for Nut Cookery;* E. Kellogg, *Science in the Kitchen;* Fulton, *Vegetarian Cook Book.*

2. Carver, *How to Grow the Peanut.*

3. Hudders, "Rise of the Peanut," 113–14.

4. Bessie R. Murphy, *Peanuts for Breakfast, Dinner, Supper* (Chicago: Rand McNally, 1920).

5. [Rutledge], *Carolina Housewife,* 1st ed., 45; Women's Centennial Committees, *National Cookery Book,* 26; *Table Talk* 14 (February 1899): 64; Celestine Eustis, *Cooking in Old Creole Days* (New York: R. H. Russell, 1904), 9; E. Kellogg, *Science in the Kitchen,* 398; *Table Talk* 9 (March 1894): 117; Eliel, *Poetry in Cookery,* 62.

6. "Peanuts. Palatable Peanuts," 151; Lambert, *Guide for Nut Cookery,* 71, 179, 303–4.

7. *American Grocer* 63 (May 16, 1900): 10. Peanut soup recipes appeared in the following: Ladies' Aid Society, *Universalist Ladies' Recipe Book* (Galesburg, Ill.: Evening Mail Press, 1900), 16; Rufus Estes, *Good Things to Eat as Suggested by Rufus* (Chicago: By the author, 1911), 13–14; Mary Minerva Lawrence, *Six Texas Food Products: Recipes and Food Values,* Bulletin No. 1823 (Austin: University of Texas, 1918), 19; Women's Central Committee of Food Conservation, *Patriotic Food Show. Official Recipe Book. Containing All Demonstrations Given during Patriotic Food Show. St Louis, February 2–10, 1918* (St. Louis: Women's Central Committee of Food Conservation, 1918), as in *Fifty Years of Prairie Cooking: Introduction and Suggested Recipes by Louis Szathmáry* (New York: Arno Press, 1973), 15; Frances Lowe Smith, *More Recipes for Fifty* (Boston: Whitcomb and Barrows, 1918), 79; *Use Peanut Flour to Save Wheat, 1918;* Murphy, *Peanuts for Breakfast, Dinner, Supper,* 4; *Peanut Promoter* 6 (December 1922): 36; Seattle Fruit and Flower Mission, *Fruit and Flower Mission Cook Book* (Seattle: Seattle Fruit and Flower Mission, 1924), 40; Women's Club of Hackensack, *Women's Club Cook Book* (Hackensack, N.J.: Home Economics Department of the Women's Club of Hackensack, 1924), 11; J. H. Tilden, *Practical Cook*

Book (Denver, Colo.: Frank J. Wolf, 1926), 194; Pond, *Here's Something New,* n.p.; Nancy Carey, *Soup to Nuts* (Philadelphia: Macrae Smith, 1929), 19; Beatrice Cole Wagner, "Peanut Butter Makes Host of Tasty Dishes," *Peanut Journal and Nut World* 10 (July 1931): 9–10; *Peanut Journal and Nut World* 10 (October 1931): 24; *Pictorial Review Standard Cook Book* (New York: Pictorial Review Co., 1934), 69; "Mississippi Whites Use Carver Recipes for Peanut Soup," *Pittsburgh Courier,* December 3, 1932; *Peanut Journal and Nut World* 17 (July 1938): 9; W. R. Beattie, *Making and Using Peanut Butter,* Circular No. 394, rev. ed. (Washington, D.C.: USDA, 1941), 14; Lillie Mae Daughtrey, *Favorite Recipes of Colfax Country Club Women* (Colfax County, N.M.: Colfax County Home Demonstration Clubs, 1946), reprinted in *Southwestern Cookery: Indian and Spanish Influences, Introduction and Suggested Recipes by Louis Szathmáry* (New York: Arno Press, 1973), 111; Marion Brown, *The Southern Cook Book* (Chapel Hill: University of North Carolina Press, 1951), 31; Rorer, *Mrs. Rorer's New Cook Book,* 75; Sarah Tyson Rorer, *Mrs. Rorer's Vegetable Cookery and Meat Substitutes* (Philadelphia: Arnold and Co., 1909), 33; *Boston Cooking-School Magazine* 15 (November 1910): 204; Locke, "Peanut as Food," 574; Bosman and Lohman Co., *Story of Nut-Let Peanut Butter,* 34; Larkin Co., *Larkin Housewives' Cook Book: Good Things to Eat and How to Prepare Them* (Buffalo: Larkin Co., 1915), 11; Carver, *How to Grow the Peanut,* 8–9; National Peanut Council, *Peanuts: Their Food Value,* 28.

8. Homer Thompson, *Manufacture and Use of Peanut Butter,* 15; G. W. Carver, "Peanut Butter—A One Hundred Per Cent Food Product," *Peanut Journal and Nut World* 10 (March 1931): 7, 15. Recipes appeared in the following: Beech-Nut Packing Co., *A Hundred and One Recipes,* 4–5; Cornelia Fox, "Peanut Recipes," *Peanut Journal and Nut World* 10 (April 1931): 17–18; *Y.M.C.A. Cook Book,* 4th ed. (Grand Forks, N.D.: n.p., 1924), reprinted in *Along the Northern Border: Cookery in Idaho, Minnesota and North Dakota, Introduction and Suggested Recipes by Louis Szathmáry* (New York: Arno Press, 1973) 6; [Ebell Society of the Santa Ana Valley], *Cook Book* (Santa Ana, Calif.: A. G. Flagg, 1926), 20.

9. *Berliner klinische Wochenschrift,* as cited in *Scientific American* 70 (January 6, 1894): 8.

10. H. Graham Yearwood, comp., *West Indian and Other Recipes* ([Barbados]: [Advocate], 1932), 6; *The Congressional Cook Book: Favorite National and International Recipes,* rev. ed. (Washington, D.C.: The Congressional Club, 1933), 499; Diana and Paul von Welanetz, *The Von Welanetz Guide to Ethnic Ingredients* (Los Angeles: J. P. Tarcher, 1982), 675; Theodore Francis Garrett, ed., *The Encyclopaedia of Practical Cookery: A Complete Dictionary of All Pertaining to the Art of Cookery and Table Service,* 8 vols. (London: L. Upcott Gill, Bazaar Buildings, W.C., [1890]), 5:131 (quote).

11. Hooker, *History Food and Drink in America,* 242.

12. *Good Housekeeping,* July 1900, 41 (quote); *Good Housekeeping,* October 1900, 204; *Good Housekeeping,* March 1913, 412.

13. Marion Harland [pseud. for Mary Virginia Terhune], *Marion Harland's Complete Cook Book* (Indianapolis: Bobbs-Merrill Co., 1903), 236; Lombard, "Food Value of the Peanut," 843; *Good Housekeeping,* February 1913, 261; Carver, *How to Grow the Peanut,* 20–21; Smith, *More Recipes for Fifty,* 169–70, 172; T. A. Gagnon, *Tried and Tested Recipes: Mrs. T. A. Gagnon's Cook Book for Practical Housekeeping* (Grafton, N.D.: Grafton News and Times Print, 1919), 74.

14. Beech-Nut Packing Co., *Beech-Nut Peanut Butter*, 5, 9–13 (quote, p. 12); idem, *A Hundred and One Recipes*, 14–16; *Peanut Journal* 6 (November 1926): 20.

15. Bosman and Lohman Co., *Story of Nut-Let Peanut Butter*, 32 (quote), 34; Agnes Carroll Hayward, *Yacht Club: Manual of Salads* (Chicago: Tildesley, 1914), 23.

16. Larkin Co., *Larkin Housewives' Cook Book*, 48.

17. Recipes appeared in the following: Ladies of the Parish Aid Society, comp., *A Cook Book of Tested Recipes* (Brooklyn, N.Y.: Saint John's Church, 1914), 59; Murphy, *Peanuts for Breakfast, Dinner, Supper*, 8; Homer Thompson, *Manufacture and Use of Peanut Butter*, 14, 16; Good Housekeeping, *Good Housekeeping's Book of Menus, Recipes and Household Discoveries*, 10th ed. (New York: Good Housekeeping, 1922), 242; *Peanut Promoter* 6 (January 1923): 36, 38; Butterick Publishing Co., *The New Butterick Cook Book Revised and Enlarged by Flora Rose* (New York: Butterick Publishing Co., 1924), 449; H. J. Heinz Co., *Heinz Book of Salads*, 31; *Peanut Journal* 4 (March 1925): 20; *Peanut Journal* 4 (August 1925): 20; [Ebell Society of the Santa Ana Valley], *Cook Book*, 53; Pond, *Here's Something New*, n.p.; *Peanut Journal* 10 (November 1930): 9, 17–18; "Tried and Approved Peanut Butter Recipes," *Peanut Journal* 9 (October 1930): 9–10; *Peanut Journal and Nut World* 10 (October 1931): 24; *Peanut Journal and Nut World* 11 (November 1931): 20; *American Cookery* 38 (November 1934): 228; *Peanut Journal and Nut World* 17 (July 1938): 9; Beattie, *Making and Using Peanut Butter*, rev. ed., 13; National Peanut Council, *Peanuts: Their Food Value*, 38–39; Seattle Fruit and Flower Mission, *Fruit and Flower Mission Cook Book* (Seattle: Seattle Fruit and Flower Mission, 1924), 154; Women's Club of Hackensack, *Women's Club Cook Book*, 34; "Peanut Jumble Salad," *Peanut Journal* 4 (August 1925): 20; Pond, *Here's Something New*, n.p.

18. Handy, "Peanuts: Culture and Uses," 21; Tomlinson, "Peanut as a Food Constituent," 111.

19. *Cultivator and Country Gentleman* 31 (April 9, 1868): 262; Jones, *The Peanut Plant*, 59–60; E. Kellogg, *Science in the Kitchen* (Battle Creek, Mich.: Health Publishing Co., 1892), 110 (first quote); "Domestic Peanut Oil Factory," Philadelphia *Times* article, reprinted in the *American Grocer* 58 (September 22, 1897): 6 (second quote); C. L. Newman, *Peanuts*, Bulletin No. 84 (Fayetteville: Arkansas Agricultural Experiment Station, 1904), 129.

20. Carver, *How to Grow the Peanut*, 9–12.

21. Bailey and LeClerc, "The Peanut, A Great American Food," 296, 301.

22. *Use Peanut Flour to Save Wheat*, 1918.

23. "Peanut Milk a Substitute," *Peanut World* 1 (December 1919): 25; *Peanut Promoter* 4 (September 1921): 21; Murphy, *Peanuts for Breakfast, Dinner, Supper*, 2; Homer Thompson, *Manufacture and Use of Peanut Butter*, 16; *American Miller* article, reprinted in *Peanut Promoter* 4 (February 1921): 22; *Peanut Journal* 8 (June 1929): 9.

24. John H. Kellogg, *The New Dietetics: What to Eat and How: A Guide to Scientific Feeding in Health and Disease* (Battle Creek, Mich.: Modern Medicine Publishing Co., 1921), 358; "Statement of Mr. George Washington Carver," 154. Recipes appeared in the following: Good Housekeeping, *Good Housekeeping's Book of Menus*, 64; Metropolitan Life Insurance Co., *Metropolitan Life Cook Book* ([New York]: Metropolitan Life Insurance Co., 1922), 17; *Peanut Journal* 2 (January 1923): 38; Seattle Fruit and Flower Mission, *Fruit and*

Flower Mission Cook Book, 175; Women's Club of Hackensack, *Women's Club Cook Book,* 44; *American Cookery* 29 (March 1925): 593–94; *American Cookery* 30 (October 1925): 117; *Peanut Journal* 4 (March 1925): 20; *Peanut Journal* 7 (February 1928): 27; Lenna Francis Cooper and Margaret Allen Hall, *The New Cookery,* 11th ed. (Battle Creek, Mich.: Modern Medicine Publishing Co., 1929), 83; "Tried and Approved Peanut Butter Recipes," 9; *Peanut Journal* 10 (November 1930): 9; *Peanut Journal and Nut World* 10 (October 1931): 24; *Pictorial Review Standard Cook Book* (New York: The Pictorial Review Co., 1934), 38; *American Cookery* 39 (April 1935): 546; *American Cookery* 36 (November 1931): 275–76; *American Cookery* 41 (October 1936): 167; National Peanut Council, *Peanuts: Their Food Value,* 18–19, 37; *Peanut Journal and Nut World* 20 (January 1941): 17.

25. Leslie, *Directions for Cookery,* 352; idem, *Miss Leslie's New Receipts,* 209 (quote); John D. Hounihan, *Bakers' and Confectioners' Guide and Treasure* (Staunton, Va.: Printed for the author, 1877), 89; *Good Housekeeping,* December 1903, 587; Simon Kander and Henry Schoenfeld, comps., *The "Settlement Cookbook": The Way to a Man's Heart* (1903; New York: New American Library, 1985), 155; *Boston Cooking-School Magazine* 9 (August/September 1904): 112–13; Locke, "Peanut as Food," 576; Mary M. Wright, *Candy-Making at Home: Two Hundred Ways to Make Candy with Home Flavor and Professional Finish* (Philadelphia: Penn Publishing Co., 1915), 137–38; Murphy, *Peanuts for Breakfast, Dinner, Supper,* 11–12; *Peanut Journal* 1 (December 1921): 27; *Peanut Journal* 4 (March 1925): 20; Alice Bradley, *The Candy Cook Book* (Boston: Little, Brown, 1929), 184; Janet M. Hill, *Cooking for Two* (Boston: Little, Brown, 1928), 334; National Peanut Council, *Peanuts: Their Food Value,* 46; Bosman and Lohman Co., *Story of Nut-Let Peanut Butter,* 32; H. J. Heinz Co., *Story of Peanutville,* n.p.

26. Recipes appeared in the following: Fannie Merritt Farmer, *Boston Cooking-School Cook Book* (New York: Little, Brown, 1896), 408–9; *Boston Cooking-School Magazine* 1 (Autumn 1896): 124; *Table Talk* 8 (February 1898): 61; West Baptist Church, *Friend in the House,* 157; *Ransom's Family Receipt Book,* 16; Mary Harris Frazer, *Kentucky Receipt Book* (Louisville: Bradley and Gilbert, 1903), 232, 248; Harland, *Marion Harland's Complete Cook Book,* 287; Kander and Schoenfeld, *The "Settlement Cookbook,"* 148; *Boston Cooking-School Magazine* 10 (March 1906): 403; Woman's Society of the Winnetka Congregational Church of Winnetka, Ill., *Good Recipes* (Chicago: Lakeside Press, R. R. Donnelley, 1906), 38; *The P.E.O. Cook Book,* souvenir ed. (Knoxville, Iowa: Curtis and Gilson, 1908), 102; *Table Talk* 23 (April 1908): 158; *Boston Cooking-School Magazine* 14 (June–July 1909): 53; Locke, "Peanut as Food," 576; *Celebrated Actor Folks' Cookeries: A Collection of the Favorite Foods of Famous Players* (New York: Mabel Rowland, 1916), 134; Carver, *How to Grow the Peanut,* 11–14; Beech-Nut Packing Co., *Beech-Nut Peanut Butter,* 18, 20; H. J. Heinz Co., *Story of Peanutville,* n.p.; Larkin Co., *Larkin Housewives' Cook Book,* 87; *American Cookery* 21 (March 1917): 636, 22 (November 1917): 281; Janet M. Hill, "Seasonable and Tested Recipes," *American Cookery* 22 (November 1917): 281; Lawrence, *Six Texas Food Products,* 19; Smith, *More Recipes for Fifty,* 64; *Use Peanut Flour to Save Wheat,* 1918; Murphy, *Peanuts for Breakfast, Dinner, Supper,* 12; Homer Thompson, *Manufacture and Use of Peanut Butter,* 16; Isabelle Clark Swezy, comp., *My One Hundred Best Recipes with Cooking Helps* (Seattle: Rogers Co., 1923), 28–30; Gagnon, *Tried and Tested Recipes,* 158, 161; Beech-Nut Pack-

ing Co., *A Hundred and One Recipes,* 22; Eugene Smith and Lane Bishop, comps. and eds., for the League of Saint James Women, *The Village Cook Book* (Birmingham, Mich.: Birmingham Eccentric, n.d.), 100; *Peanut Journal* 1 (December 1921): 27; Metropolitan Life Insurance Co., *Metropolitan Life Cook Book,* 60; *American Cookery* 28 (March 1924): 601; Allen, *Beech-Nut Book of Menus,* 20; *Peanut Journal* 4 (March 1925): 20; *The Butterick Book of Recipes and Household Helps* (Chicago: Butterick Publishing Co., 1927), 135; *Liberty Magazine* article, reprinted in Ethel Somers, "Peanut Recipes Give Variety to Meals," *Peanut Journal* 7 (March 1928): 23; Cooper and Hall, *New Cookery,* 450; *Peanut Journal* 10 (November 1930): 9; "Tried and Approved Peanut Butter Recipes," 9; *Choice Recipes by Moscow Women* (Moscow, Idaho: Hospitality Committee of the Presbyterian Ladies' Aid, 1931), 44; *American Cookery* 37 (October 1932): 200; Allen Prescott, *The Wifesaver's Candy Recipes* (New York: Blue Ribbon Books, 1934), 104; Beattie, *Making and Using Peanut Butter,* rev. ed., 15; *American Cookery* 42 (October 1937): 169; Dorcas Society of Saint John Lutheran Church, *Dorcas Cook Book* (Sioux City, Iowa: Leeds Press Print, 1939), 37, 40.

27. Peter Rose, *The Sensible Cook: Dutch Foodways in the Old and the New World* (Syracuse, N.Y.: Syracuse University Press, 1989), 18, 29; Kellogg, "Good and Bad Foods," 152; John Ayto, *Food and Drink from A to Z: A Gourmet's Guide,* rev. ed. (Oxford: Oxford University Press, 1993), 115; Carver, *How to Grow the Peanut,* 13; Murphy, *Peanuts for Breakfast, Dinner, Supper,* 16; *Peanut Journal* 1 (May 1922): 24; National Peanut Council, *Peanuts: Their Food Value,* 46.

28. Recipes appeared in the following: Women's Centennial Committees, *National Cookery Book,* 269; [Rutledge], *Carolina Housewife,* 1st ed., 117, 219; Mrs. Bliss, *Practical Cook Book,* 179; [Rutledge], *Carolina Housewife,* 2d ed., 34, 98; *Cultivator and Country Gentleman* 31 (April 9, 1868): 262; *Good Housekeeping,* July 21, 1888, 134; Ladies of the First Baptist Church, *Exeter Cook Book,* rev. ed. (Exeter, N.H.: Ladies of the First Baptist Church, 1889), 101; Harriet S. McMurphy, *The Ideal Receipt Book* (Southington, Conn.: Peck, Stow, and Wilcox, 1898), 53; Lambert, *Guide for Nut Cookery,* 352, 367; Ladies' Aid Society, *Universalist Ladies' Recipe Book,* 114; Beech-Nut Packing Co., *A Hundred and One Recipes,* 17–18, 20, 21; E. E. Kellogg, comp., *Healthful Cookery: A Collection of Choice Recipes for Preparing Foods, with Special Reference to Health* (Battle Creek, Mich.: Modern Medicine Publishing Co., 1904), 230–31; Paul Richards, *Paul Richards' Pastry Book,* 2d ed. (Chicago: Hotel Monthly Press, 1907), 32; Helen Cramp, *The Winston Cook Book* (Philadelphia: John C. Winston, 1913), 307; Lombard, "Food Value of the Peanut," 843; H. J. Heinz Co., *Story of Peanutville,* n.p.; Larkin Co., *Larkin Housewives' Cook Book,* 67; Carver, *How to Grow the Peanut,* 14, 18, 23; *Use Peanut Flour to Save Wheat, 1918; Peanut Journal* 4 (July 1925): 26; Ladies of the First Congregational Church, *Victory Cook Book* (Jersey City, N.J.: Ladies of the First Congregational Church, 1919), 92; Murphy, *Peanuts for Breakfast, Dinner, Supper,* 14; Homer Thompson, *Manufacture and Use of Peanut Butter,* 16; *Peanut Journal* 4 (March 1925): 20.

29. Sloane, *Voyage to the Islands,* 2:369; Watson, "Some Account of an Oil," 380; Long, *History of Jamaica,* 3:789; Barham, *Hortus Americanus,* 185; Loskiel, *History of Missions,* 67; Lunan, *Hortus Jamaicensis,* 2:348; *Cultivator and Country Gentleman* 31 (April 9, 1868):

262; "Ground-nuts," 293–94; Johnson, *Peanut Story,* 24; Hammons, "Early History and Origin of the Peanut," 33; Davidson, *Oxford Companion to Food,* 357; Lambert, *Guide for Nut Cookery,* 71–73, 251–52; Locke, "Peanut as Food," 574; *Peanut Promoter* 3 (May 1920): 66; *Peanut Journal* 1 (May 1922): 24; I. H. Burkhill, "Groundnut or Pea-Nut (*Arachis hypogaea* Linn.)," *Bulletin of Miscellaneous Information/Royal Botanic Gardens, Kew,* Nos. 178–80 (October–December 1901): 180; Davidson, *Oxford Companion to Food,* 357.

30. "Boiled Peanuts Much Esteemed by Folk in South Carolina," *Peanut Promoter* 8 (September 1925): 39 (quotes); Woodroof, *Peanuts,* 237–38; John P. McDermott, "Charleston, S.C., Salesman Distributes Canned Boiled Peanuts," *Post and Courier* (Charleston, S.C.), October 6, 1999, at <http://www.charleston.net>, accessed June 10, 2000; *Peanut Journal* 7 (May 1928): 23; Jim Auchmutey and Lea Donosky, eds. *True South: Travels through a Land of White Columns, Black-Eyed Peas and Redneck Bars* (Atlanta: Longstreet, 1994), 44–46.

31. Mr. Fooshe, "Eat Peanuts Raw or Roast Them Yourself," *Peanut Promoter* 3 (June 1920): 37–38 (quote); G. W. Carver, "The Peanut's Place in Everyday Life," *Peanut Journal* 4 (December 1924): 9; *Peanut Journal and Nut World* 17 (February 1938): 11; Georgia Peanut Co., *Book of Recipes for Uncle Remus Brand Peanuts* ([Moultrie, Ga.]: Georgia Peanut Co., n.d.); W. B. Jester, "What You Can Do with a Pound of Peanuts," *Peanut Journal and Nut World* 21 (April 1942): 13; idem, "The Versatile Peanut Is Helping Win the War," *Peanut Journal and Nut World* 21 (June 1942): 19.

32. Sloane, *Voyage to the Islands,* 1:184; Watson, "Some Account of an Oil," 381 (quotes). Brownrigg's experiment to produce oil from peanuts was also discussed in Long, *History of Jamaica,* 3:789, and Lunan, *Hortus Jamaicensis,* 2:348.

33. Hooker, *History Food and Drink in America,* 28–29.

34. Watson, "Some Account of an Oil," 381, 383 (first and second quotes, respectively); *Annual Report of the Commissioner of Patents for the Year 1847,* Part 2: Agriculture, 190–91 (third and fourth quotes); Allen, *American Farm Book,* 168; Burke, *Reminiscence of Georgia,* 126 (fifth quote).

35. Woodroof, *Peanuts,* 4–5; *Pigs and Peanuts: Virginia Traditions* (Glen Allen, Va.: Prism Publishing, 1997).

36. A. M. Thoun, *Cours complet d'agriculture* (Paris: Marchant, Drevet, Crapart, Calle et Ravier, 1805), 159–60; Burkhill, "Groundnut or Pea-Nut," 184–85; Brooks, "Peanuts and Colonisation," 37.

37. Flückiger and Hanbury, *Pharmacographia,* 186; Bella Southorn, *The Gambia: The Story of the Groundnut Colony* (London: George Allen and Unwin, 1952), 183–85; A. A. O. Jeng, "An Economic History of the Gambian Industry 1830–1924: The Evolution of an Export Economy" (Ph.D. diss., Centre of African Studies, University of Birmingham, Eng., 1978); Brooks, "Peanuts and Colonisation," 29, 34; Thoun, *Cours complet d'agriculture,* 159–60; Artemas Ward, *The Grocers' Hand-Book and Directory for 1883* (Philadelphia: Philadelphia Grocer Publishing Co., 1882), 157; "Peanut Oil," *Table Talk* 11 (June 1896): vi, viii; Burkhill, "Groundnut or Pea-Nut," 184–85; Frank Cussans, "Origin of the Bordeaux Peanut Oil Industry," *Peanut Journal And Nut World* 14 (June 1935): 24.

38. "Peanut Oil," *Scientific American* 71 (October 6, 1894): 216; "Domestic Peanut Oil

Factory," 6; "The Peanut-Oil Industry," *American Grocer* 63 (May 16, 1900): 10; *Scientific American Supplement* 52 (August 10, 1901): 21,409.

39. "Domestic Peanut Oil Factory," 6; Parry, *Nuts for Profit*, 143; Handy, "Peanuts: Culture and Uses," 21; Newman, *Peanuts*, 129; Tomlinson, "Peanut as a Food Constituent," 109–11; *Peanut Journal and Nut World* 21 (December 1941): 12–13, 33.

40. "Ground-nuts," 293–94; "Peanut Oil," *Table Talk* 11 (June 1896): vi, viii; A. H. Church, *Food-grains for India* (London: Chapman and Hall, 1886), 127; George Everhard Rumpf, *Herbarium amboinense*, 5 vols. (Amsterdam: Francisum Chaguion, Hermannum Uytwere, 1747), 5:426–28; Willich, *Domestic Encyclopedia*, 2:438; Flückiger and Hanbury, *Pharmacographia*, 186–88; Handy, "Peanuts: Culture and Uses," 4; Burkhill, "Groundnut or Pea-Nut," 183; Ralph Augustus Waldron, "The Peanut (Arachis hypogaea)—Its History, Histology, Physiology, and Utility" (Ph.D. diss., University of Pennsylvania, 1918), 308–9; Goodrich, "Early Notices of the Peanut in China," 405–9; Glenn C. W. Ames, "Peanuts: Domestic, World Production and Trade," *Research Report* 215 (Athens, Ga.: Department of Agricultural Economics, College Station, 1975).

41. Davidson, *Oxford Companion to Food*, 551; Trinchinetti, "Observations and Experiments," 396; P. H. Felker, *The Grocers' Manual: A Guide Book for the Information and Use of Grocers*, 2d ed. (New York: American Grocer Publishing Association, 1878), 181 (quote).

42. Ramsay, *History of South Carolina*, 2:349; Long, *History of Jamaica*, 3:789 (first quote); Lunan, *Hortus Jamaicensis*, 2:348; *Annual Report of the Commissioner of Patents for the Year 1847*, Part 2: Agriculture, 190–91 (other quotes).

43. New England Grocer Office, *Grocer's Companion*, 108–9 (quotes); Ward, *Grocers' Hand-Book and Directory for 1883*, 158.

44. B. W. Jones, *The Peanut Plant* (New York: Orange Judd, 1902), 56 (quote); "Peanut Oil," *Scientific American* 71 (October 6, 1894): 216; "Domestic Peanut Oil Factory," 6; "Peanut-Oil Industry," 10; *Scientific American Supplement* 52 (August 10, 1901): 21, 409.

45. Woodroof, *Peanuts*, 11.

46. "Peanuts Aid in Winning War," *Cleveland Press*, August 10, 1918, reprinted in *Spice Mill* 41 (September 1918): 1158; *New York Times* article, reprinted in the *American Grocer* 100 (September 25, 1918): 6 (quote).

47. W. Clayton, "Modern Margarin Technology—An Outline of Its History and Manufacture," *Peanut Promoter* 3 (September 1920): 43, 45, 47, 49; S. F. Riepma, "Peanut Oil in Margarine," *Peanut Journal and Nut World* 33 (September 1954): 13; J. van Alphen, "Hippolyte Mège Mouriès," in *Margarine: An Economic Social and Scientific History, 1869–1969*, ed. J. H. Van Stuyvenberg (Liverpool, Eng.: Liverpool University Press, 1969), 5–7.

48. J. H. van Stuyvenberg, "Aspects of Government Intervention," in *Margarine: An Economic Social and Scientific History, 1869–1969*, ed. J. H. Van Stuyvenberg (Liverpool, Eng.: Liverpool University Press, 1969), 283–90.

49. *Table Talk* 11 (June 1896): vi, viii; *Scientific American* 71 (October 6, 1894): 216; Bailey and LeClerc, "The Peanut, A Great American Food," 300; "Margarine and Peanuts," *Peanut Promoter* 7 (February 1924): 7–9; J. S. Abbott, "Nut Margarin and Peanut Industry," *Peanut Journal* 6 (November 1926): 23; van Stuyvenberg, "Aspects of Government Intervention," 287.

50. "Margarine and Peanuts," 7–9; "Housewives Broke Oleomargarine Boycott," *Peanut Promoter* 7 (April 1924): 14.

51. "Margarine and Peanuts," 7–9 (quotes); "Holds Lobby Responsible for Anti-Margarine Laws," *Peanut Journal and Nut World* 15 (March 1936): 9; Riepma, "Peanut Oil in Margarine," 13; van Stuyvenberg, "Aspects of Government Intervention," 284.

CHAPTER 7: SWEET AND NUTTY

1. Sidney W. Mintz, *Sweetness and Power: The Place of Sugar in Modern History* (New York: Elisabeth Sifton, Viking, 1985), 21–22.

2. Beecher, *Miss Beecher's Domestic Receipt Book*, 292 (first quote); Stowe, *Dred*, 1:51 (second quote).

3. MacClenny, *History of the Peanut*, 5. For more information about popcorn's history, see Andrew F. Smith, *Popped Culture: A Social History of Popcorn in America* (Columbia: University of South Carolina Press, 1999).

4. San Grael Society of the First Presbyterian Church, *The Web-Foot Cook Book* (Portland, Ore.: W. B. Ayer, 1885), 191.

5. Cracker Jack Co., *Fifty Years* (Chicago: Cracker Jack Co., 1922), n.p.; "The More You Eat," *Fortune*, June 1947, 144; Alex Jaramillo, *Cracker Jack Prizes* (New York: Abbeville, 1989), 8.

6. Cracker Jack Co., *Fifty Years*, n.p.; "The More You Eat," 144; Jaramillo, *Cracker Jack Prizes*, 8.

7. *The "Home Queen" World's Fair Souvenir Cook Book* (Chicago: Geo. F. Cram, 1893), 551; Jaramillo, *Cracker Jack Prizes*, 8.

8. *"Home Queen,"* 551; Henry G. Abbott [pseud. for George H. A. Hazlitt], *Historical Sketch of the Confectionery Trade of Chicago* (Chicago: Jobbing Confectioners Association, 1905), 51; Jaramillo, *Cracker Jack Prizes*, 8.

9. "The More You Eat," 144; Cracker Jack Co., *Fifty Years*, n.p.; "How 'Cracker Jack' Was Given Its Name" (Chicago: Cracker Jack Co., c. 1950), broadside (quotes); "Information from the Cracker Jack History Book #1—to 1954," dated 1982, collection of Harriet Joyce; *Official Gazette*, United States Trademark No. 28,016, registered March 24, 1896.

10. *Grocery World* 22 (July 13, 1896): 8, 23, 25; H. Abbott, *Historical Sketch of the Confectionery Trade*, 51.

11. Henry Eckstein diary, collection of Ronald Toth Jr.

12. *Billboard* 14 (August 9, 1902): 28.

13. Emma Garman Krape, comp., *The Globe Cook Book* (Freeport, Ill.: Journal Printing Co., 1901), 232–33.

14. *Confectioner's Gazette* 34 (October 12, 1912): 12 (first quote); *Confectioner's Gazette* 35 (February 10, 1914): 10 (other quotes).

15. *Confectioner's Gazette* 34 (June 10, 1913): 11; *Saturday Evening Post*, June 7, 1919, 102; Jaramillo, *Cracker Jack Prizes*, 11–12; *Confectioner's Gazette* 35 (February 10, 1914): 10; Cracker Jack Co., *Fifty Years*, n.p.; *Grocer's Criterion* 31 (July 4, 1904): 52; *Confectioner's Gazette* 34 (October 12, 1912): 12; Ravi Piña, *Cracker Jack Collectibles with Price Guide* (Atglen, Pa.:

Schiffer, 1995); undated photocopied material on Cracker Jack, supplied by Forest Wanberg Jr., former vice president for operations, Borden's Cracker Jack division.

16. "Information from the Cracker Jack History Book #1—to 1954"; Jerry L. Hess, *Snack Food: A Bicentennial History* (New York: Harcourt Brace Jovanovich, [1976]), 204.

17. *Billboard* 49 (April 16, 1937): 94; "The More You Eat," 144.

18. Sophie D. Coe and Michael D. Coe, *The True History of Chocolate* (New York: Thames and Hudson, 1996), 241–45.

19. Ibid., 250–51.

20. George Augustus Sala, *America Revisited: From the Bay of New York to the Gulf of Mexico, and from Lake Michigan to the Pacific,* 2 vols. (London: Vizetelly, 1882), 1:107.

21. [Hannah Mary Peterson], *The National Cook Book* (Philadelphia: Robert E. Peterson, 1850), 278; *The Art of Confectionery* (Boston: J. E. Tilton and Co., 1866), 55.

22. Recipes appeared in the following: Mrs. A. P. Hill, *Housekeeping Made Easy: Mrs. Hill's New Family Receipt Book for the Kitchen* (New York: James O'Kane, 1867), 330; M. L. Tyson, *The Queen of the Kitchen: A Collection of Old Maryland Receipts for Cooking from a Receipt Book Used for Many Years. All Tried and Approved* (Baltimore: Lucas Brothers, 1870), 234; Marion Harland [pseud. for Mary Virginia Terhune], *Breakfast, Luncheon and Tea* (New York: Scribner, 1875), 383–84; Ladies of the Westminster Presbyterian Church, *Cook Book of the Northwest,* 2d ed. (Keokuk, Iowa: R. B. Ogden, 1875), 147; Hounihan, *Bakers' and Confectioners' Guide and Treasure,* 283–84; May Perrin Goff, ed., *The Household: A Cyclopaedia of Practical Hints for Modern Homes with a Full and Complete Treatise on Cookery* (Detroit: Detroit Free Press, 1881), 447; *Ransom's Family Receipt Book,* 17; *The First Texas Cookbook: A Thorough Treatise on the Art of Cookery, with Forewords by David Wade and May Faulk Koock* (Austin, Tex.: Eakins Press, 1986; first published by Ladies Association of the First Presbyterian Church, Houston, Tex., 1883), 164; *The Successful Housekeeper: A Manual of Universal Application* (Harrisburg, Pa.: Pennsylvania Publishing Co., 1883), 96–97; Lucy W. Bostwick, *Margery Daw in the Kitchen and What She Learned There,* 6th ed. (Auburn, N.Y.: By the author, 1885), 76.

23. Women's Centennial Committees, *National Cookery Book,* 269.

24. *The Candy-Maker: A Practical Guide to the Manufacture of the Various Kinds of Plain and Fancy Candy* (New York: Jesse Haney, 1878), vii.

25. Saint Francis Street Methodist Episcopal Church, South, *Gulf City Cook Book* (Mobile, Ala.: Ladies of the Saint Francis Street Methodist Episcopal Church, South, 1878, reprint, Tuscaloosa: University of Alabama Press, 1990), Introduction by George H. Daniels, 185–86.

26. Garrett, *Encyclopaedia of Practical Cookery,* 5:131.

27. Woolley, "Tom Rowland—Peanuts," 201; "Peanuts and Their Various Treatments," *Spice Mill* 33 (June 1910): 454 (quote).

28. *Candy Factory* article, reprinted in *Peanut Journal* 1 (June 1922): 15, 19; *Western Confectioner* article, reprinted in *Peanut Journal* 5 (March 1926): 9–10; Ray Broekel, *The Great American Candy Bar Book* (Boston: Houghton Mifflin, 1982), 101.

29. Jones, *The Peanut Plant* (1885 ed.), 58; *Good Housekeeping,* December 1897, 246; Parry,

Nuts for Profit, 152; Ladies Aid Society, Methodist Episcopal Church, Monroe, N.Y., *The Cook's Counsellor* (Newburgh, N.Y.: Newburgh Journal Print., 1900), 91; Young Woman's Auxiliary, *Tested Recipes* (Chicago: 41st Street Presbyterian Church, n.d. c. 1910), 77; Sherwood Snyder, *The Art of Candy Making Fully Explained* (Dayton, Ohio: Health Publishing Co., 1915), 76–77; Carver, *How to Grow the Peanut*, 11; Murphy, *Peanuts for Breakfast, Dinner, Supper*, 14; *Peanut Journal* 1 (January 1922): 25; *The Esculent for Advancement of the Best Eating* (January 1906): 35; Bosman and Lohman Co., *Story of Nut-Let Peanut Butter*, 38 (quotes).

30. <http://www.squirrelbrand.com/history.html>, accessed June 10, 2000.

31. Broekel, *Great America Candy Bar Book*, 20–21; <http://www.googoo.com/history.cfm>, accessed June 6, 2000.

32. "Otto Schnering Curtiss Candy Founder Dies," *Chicago Tribune*, January 12, 1953, sec. F, 5; James Trager, *The Food Chronology: A Food Lover's Compendium of Events and Anecdotes, From Prehistory to the Present* (New York: Henry Holt, 1995), 429; <http://www.urbanlegends.com/products/baby.ruth/baby_ruth_candy_bar.html>, accessed May 29, 2000; Sharon Kapnick, "Sweet Beginnings: How Some Famous Chocolate Treats Evolved to Stand the Taste of Time," *Arizona Republic*, February 13, 1993 (quote).

33. *Collier's* 78 (July 31, 1926): 21; *Peanut Journal and Nut World* 21 (August 1942): 7; Broekel, *Great America Candy Bar Book*, 22–25.

34. *Peanut Journal and Nut World* 21 (August 1942): 7; Joël Glenn Brenner, *The Emperors of Chocolate: Inside the Secret World of Hershey and Mars* (New York: Broadway Books, 2000), 170.

35. *Peanut Journal* 6 (January 1927): 22–23; *Peanut Journal* 8 (March 1929): 46.

36. O. Henry [William Sydney Porter], "The Gold That Glittered," *New York World Magazine*, May 22, 1904, 4; Williamson Candy Co., *Sixty New Ways to Serve a Famous Candy* (Chicago: Williamson Candy Co., 1926), 3–4; Broekel, *Great America Candy Bar Book*, 99–100.

37. *Peanut Journal and Nut World* 31 (June 1952): 18; *Peanut Journal* 2 (February 1923): 11–12; "Candy as a Food Item in the Nation's Diet," *Peanut Journal and Nut World* 21 (July 1942): 7.

38. *Peanut Journal* 4 (February 1925): 20; Williamson Candy Co., *Sixty New Ways to Serve a Famous Candy*; "The Story of Oh Henry!," *Peanut Journal* 6 (February 1927): 13–14.

39. Broekel, *Great America Candy Bar Book*, 17–18, 66–67; *Peanut Journal and Nut World* 29 (July 1950): 25; *Peanut Journal and Nut World* 52 (July 1973): 17; <http://www.hersheys.com/products/reese/index.html>, accessed May 7, 2000; Pamela C. Whitenack, archivist, Hershey Community Archives, Hershey, Pennsylvania, telephone interview with author, July 5, 2000 (quote).

40. *Peanut Journal and Nut World* 43 (March 1964): 12; Trager, *Food Chronology*, 441, 464.

41. <http://www.snickers.com/info/>, accessed June 18, 2000.

42. Trager, *Food Chronology*, 441, 547; Brenner, *Emperors of Chocolate*, 46, 57–59.

43. Broekel, *Great America Candy Bar Book*, 44–45, 87, 88, 91–92; Whitenack interview; Louis Untermeyer, *A Century of Candymaking, 1847–1947: The Story of the Origin and Growth of New England Confectionery Company* (Boston: Barta, 1947), 44, 47, 83.

44. Broekel, *Great America Candy Bar Book,* 105–6, 119–20.

45. *Peanut Journal and Nut World* 21 (November 1941): 17.

CHAPTER 8: SCIENTISTS AND PROMOTERS

1. "Carver of Tuskegee," *Peanut Promoter* 3 (April 1920): 43, 45, 47; Linda O. McMurry, *George Washington Carver: Scientist and Symbol* (New York: Oxford University Press, 1982), 8–11.

2. Maxine Block, ed., *Current Biography* (New York: H. W. Wilson, 1968), 148–49; McMurry, *George Washington Carver,* 18–41; "Prof. Carver to Tell White Virginians about the Peanut," *New York Age,* October 7, 1922; John W. Kitchens and Lynne B. Kitchens, *Guide to the Microfilm Edition of the George Washington Carver Papers at Tuskegee Institute* (Tuskegee Institute, Ala.: Division of Behavioral Science Research, Carver Research Foundation, 1975), 2.

3. Kitchens and Kitchens, *Guide to the Microfilm Edition of the George Washington Carver Papers,* 3.

4. Jessie Rich, *The Uses of the Peanut on the Home Table,* Bulletin No. 13 (Austin: University of Texas, 1915); "Numerous Wholesome Food Uses of the Peanut," *Spice Mill* 38 (June 1915): 670–71.

5. "Possibilities of the Peanut," *American Missionary,* June 1921, Reel 60, George Washington Carver Archive, Library of Congress.

6. George Washington Carver to Chief, Bureau of Plant Industry, February 24, 1916, Reel 5, George Washington Carver Archive; Carver, *How to Grow the Peanut,* 7–8.

7. [J. Kellogg], "Peanut Milk," 589–90 (first quote); Lester Walton, "George W. Carver, Scientist, Has Made 165 By-Products from Peanuts," *New York World,* May 18, 1923, p. 1, Reel 60, George Washington Carver Archive (second quote); Harry J. Albus, *The Peanut Man: The Life of George Washington Carver in Story Form* (Grand Rapids, Mich.: Wm. B. Eerdmans, 1948), 72 (third quote).

8. Carver's peanut bulletin was reprinted or revised at least nine times. It was last published in 1994. Bessie C. Moore to Carver, January 17, 1917, and Alice Davis to Carver, June 30, 1917, Reel 5, George Washington Carver Archive; *Tuskegee Student,* April 28, 1917, Reel 60, George Washington Carver Archive; "Carver of Tuskegee," 43, 45, 47.

9. Gertrude Blodgett, "Wonders of the Peanut Food," *Spice Mill* 40 (June 1917): 714; *New York Times* article, reprinted in the *American Grocer* 100 (September 25, 1918): 6.

10. *Historical Statistics of the United States: Colonial Times to 1970,* 2 vols. (Washington, D.C.: U.S. Department of Commerce, Bureau of the Census, 1975), 1:516; *New York Times* article, reprinted in the *American Grocer* 100 (September 25, 1918): 6.

11. "National Bodies Advocating the Peanut," *Spice Mill* 41 (January 1918): 118; *Spice Mill* 41 (May 1918): 620 (quotes).

12. "Peanut Meal in Bread Making," 372; Carver, "Peanut's Place in Everyday Life," 9; *New York Times* article, reprinted in *American Grocer* 100 (September 25, 1918): 6; Women's Central Committee of Food Conservation, *Patriotic Food Show,* 22; Ladies of the First Congregational Church, *Victory Cook Book,* 40; *American Miller* article, reprinted in *Pea-*

nut Promoter 4 (February 1921): 22; H. H. Thompson, "Food Value of the Peanut," 22 (quote).

13. *Peanut Promoter* 3 (December 1919): 43; Brinkley, "The Peanut," 23–24; "The Lowly Peanut Signs a New Declaration of Independence," *Montgomery Advertiser,* January 31, 1935 (quote).

14. "More than Forty Uses for Peanuts," *Spice Mill* 41 (April 1918): 496–97; Judson D. Stuart, "Peanuts and Patriotism," *Forum* 58 (September 1917): 375–80.

15. *Table Talk* article, reprinted in *Spice Mill* 41 (August 1918): 1036.

16. "Foreign Trade of the United States, Annual, 1790–1929," 18–22 (quote); "Wants Four-cent Duty on Peanuts," *New York Journal of Commerce,* January 22, 1921, 1.

17. "Statement of Mr. George Washington Carver," 1543; *Spice Mill* 46 (December 1923): 2563–64; "Wants Four-cent Duty on Peanuts"; *Southern Nut Growers' Journal,* April 1921, Reel 60, George Washington Carver Archive.

18. *Peanut Promoter,* February 1921, and the *Southern Nut Growers' Journal,* April 1921, Reel 60, George Washington Carver Archive; *Spice Mill* 45 (November 1922): 2051; *Spice Mill* 46 (December 1923): 2563–64; "Lowly Peanut Yields Milk, Ink. Stain and Food to Negro," *New York World,* January 22, 1921, Reel 60, George Washington Carver Archive; "Statement of Mr. George Washington Carver," 1543–51 (quotes).

19. *Spice Mill* 45 (November 1922): 2051; *Spice Mill* 46 (December 1923): 2563–64; "Lowly Peanut Yields Milk, Ink, Stain and Food to Negro" (first quote); "President P. D. Bain's Annual Address Covering Many Important Peanut Matters," *Spice Mill* 44 (July 1921): 1268 (second quote); "Do We Appreciate the True Value of the Peanut?" *Peanut Promoter* 4 (November 1921): 20 (third quote).

20. "Wants Four-cent Duty on Peanuts."

21. *Peanut Promoter* 4 (May 1921): 20; *Washington Colored American,* January 27, 1921, Reel 60, George Washington Carver Archive; "Newspapers Talking about the Peanut Exhibit of Prof. Carver," *Peanut Promoter* 4 (April 1921): 54, Reel 60, George Washington Carver Archive; "Do We Appreciate the True Value of the Peanut?" 20 (first quote); "Prof. Carver to Tell White Virginians about the Peanut"; *Spice Mill* 45 (November 1922): 2051 (remaining quotes); *Manufacturer's Record* 88 (May 7, 1925): 1; *Peanut Journal* 4 (July 1925): 9; *Peanut Journal* 4 (January 1925): 22.

22. "How Scientist's 145 Varieties Helped Lowly Goober Rise," *Popular Science Monthly* 102 (May 1923): 68.

23. *Spice Mill* 45 (November 1922): 2051; *Current Opinion* 75 (July 1923): 92–93; George Washington Carver, "What Is a Peanut?" *Peanut Journal* 3 (November 1923): 33–35, 54–55; "How Scientist's 145 Varieties Helped Lowly Goober Rise"; "Negroes to Press Claims for Rights," *Christian Science Monitor,* September 5, 1923, 4; "Peanut Milk a Substitute," 25; George Washington Carver, *The American Food Journal,* August 1920, reprinted in *Good Health* 55 (October 1920): 589–91 (first quote); article from *Popular Mechanics,* May 1920, Reel 60, George Washington Carver Archive; "Possibilities of the Peanut" and *Yazoo Daily Sentinel,* April 12, 1920, Reel 60, George Washington Carver Archive; Walton, "George W. Carver, Scientist, Has Made 165 By-Products," 1; *Southwestern Christian Advocate,* June 17, 1920, Reel 60, George Washington Carver Archive (second quote).

24. Cobo, *Historia del Nuevo Mundo*, 1:359–60; Lambert, *Guide for Nut Cookery*, 72–73, 304; McMurry, *George Washington Carver*, 180.

25. Carver, "Peanut's Place in Everyday Life," 9–10; "A Combined Use for Oranges and Peanuts," *Manufacturer's Record* 88 (August 13, 1925), Reel 60, George Washington Carver Archive; *Peanut Journal* 6 (February 1927): 10; G. W. Carver, "The Peanut and Its Essential Place on the Daily Menu," *Peanut Journal* 8 (February 1929): 13; *East Nashville News*, October 20, 1932; <http://peanutsusa.com/what/history.html>, accessed February 6, 2000; McMurry, *George Washington Carver*, 234.

26. *The American* (Baltimore), June 15, 1923; *Peanut Journal* 4 (September 1925): 7.

27. *The American* (Baltimore), June 15, 1923 (first quote); *Peanut Journal* 4 (July 1925): 10 (second quote).

28. *The American* (Baltimore), June 15, 1923; *Atlanta Constitution*, August 26, 1923; *Peanut Journal* 4 (July 1925): 10; *Afro-American* (Baltimore), July 13, 1925, Reel 60, George Washington Carver Archive; Kitchens and Kitchens, *Guide to the Microfilm Edition of the George Washington Carver Papers*, 4.

29. *Peanut Journal* 5 (November 1925): 24 (quotes); *Afro-American* (Baltimore), July 13, 1925.

30. Kitchens and Kitchens, *Guide to the Microfilm Edition of the George Washington Carver Papers*, 4; *Peanut Journal* 5 (October 1926): 28 (quotes); *Montgomery News*, March 7, 1927; *Peanut Journal* 7 (December 1927): 15.

31. *Peanut Journal and Nut World* 20 (August 1941): 15 (quote); Kitchens and Kitchens, *Guide to the Microfilm Edition of the George Washington Carver Papers*, 6.

32. "Do We Appreciate the True Value of the Peanut?" 20 (first quote); *Peanut Journal and Nut World* 10 (November 1931): 19 (other quotes).

33. Carver, "Peanut's Place in Everyday Life," 9–10; *Birmingham (Alabama) Age-Herald*, January 1, 1934, as in George Washington Carver Archive (quotes); McMurry, *George Washington Carver*, 242.

34. "Peanut Oil to Cure Paralysis," *Millen (Georgia) News*, November 9, 1933 (first quote); McMurry, *George Washington Carver*, 243 (second quote).

35. McMurry, *George Washington Carver*, 244.

36. *Atlanta Journal*, April 9, 1934 (quotes); "Peanut Oil in the Treatment of Infantile Paralysis," unidentified clipping dated 1934, as in George Washington Carver Archive.

37. McMurry, *George Washington Carver*, 246.

38. Kitchens and Kitchens, *Guide to the Microfilm Edition of the George Washington Carver Papers*, 6; McMurry, *George Washington Carver*, 246 (quotes).

39. McMurry, *George Washington Carver*, 253.

40. Kitchens and Kitchens, *Guide to the Microfilm Edition of the George Washington Carver Papers*, 6.

41. *Peanut Journal and Nut World* 35 (December 1955): 13; *Peanut Journal and Nut World* 35 (February 1956): 13; George B. Freeman, "Kiwanis Kid's Day Peanut Sale Exceed Million Dollar Net Return," *Peanut Journal and Nut World* 39 (October 1960): 11.

42. *Chicago Defender*, June 23, 1923.

43. Bob Barry to Carver, August 23, 1920, Reel 5, George Washington Carver Archive; *Peanut Journal* 8 (August 1929): 23; *Peanut Journal and Nut World* 10 (June 1931): 6 (quote).

44. Albus, *Peanut Man;* Barbara Mitchell, *A Pocketful of Goobers: A Story about George Washington Carver* (Minneapolis: Carolrhoda Books, 1986); Patricia McKissack and Fredrick McKissack, *George Washington Carver: The Peanut Scientist* (Hillside, N.J.: Enslow, 1991).

45. June Jordan, "Notes on the Peanut," *Passion: New Poems, 1977–1980* (Boston: Beacon, 1980), 44.

46. John Walter, "105 Ways to Prepare Peanuts," *Successful Farming* 92 (May 1994): 50–51.

CHAPTER 9: WAR AND PEACE

1. D. O. Segrest, "War Creates Demand for Peanut Oil," *Peanut Journal and Nut World* 22 (November 1942): 19.

2. "$10,000,000 Worth of Peanuts," 142, 148; *Peanut Journal and Nut World* 12 (February 1933): 5; "Prolific Peanuts," 42.

3. *Peanut Journal and Nut World* 21 (August 1942): 7; "Fats and Oils: There's Time to Do a Job," *Fortune,* April 1942, 178; Jester, "The Versatile Peanut," 18–19; Cedric Adams, *Cedric Adams Cook Book on Fish and Sea-Food Cookery* (Winona, Minn.: Universal F. G. H. Creations, 1942).

4. Jester, "What You Can Do with a Pound of Peanuts," 13–14; "War Raises Peanut to New Heights Due to Oil Shortages," *Peanut Journal and Nut World* 21 (April 1942): 15.

5. "Shortage of Containers and Labor Restricting Potential Excellent Demand for Peanut Products," *Peanut Journal and Nut World* 23 (December 1943): 19; Harold Clay, "Movement of 1944 Crop Peanuts Retarded by Labor Shortage and Late Southeastern Season," *Peanut Journal and Nut World* 24 (December 1944): 21–22; *Peanut Journal and Nut World* 24 (February 1945): 22 (quote).

6. *Peanut Journal and Nut World* 23 (April 1944): 21.

7. *Historical Statistics of the United States: Colonial Times to 1970,* 1:331.

8. W. B. Jester, "Peanut Butter, the Cinderella Food, a Good Alternate to Meat," *Peanut Journal and Nut World* 22 (April 1943): 13–14; "United States Armed Forces Provide Huge Outlet for Peanuts in 1943," *Peanut Journal and Nut World* 23 (October 1944): 24.

9. Jester, "What You Can Do with a Pound of Peanuts," 13–14; "War Raises Peanut to New Heights Due to Oil Shortages," 15; Ray, "Peanuts and the Peanut Industry," 24–26; Harold Clay, "Peanut Butter, Salted Peanuts and 1942 Peanuts Removed from Price Ceiling Regulations," *Peanut Journal and Nut World* 21 (July 1942): 8; Segrest, "War Creates Demand for Peanut Oil," 19; *Historical Statistics of the United States: Colonial Times to 1970,* 1:486, 516.

10. "Peanuts Important in 1943 War Effort," *Peanut Journal and Nut World* 22 (February 8, 1943): 9 (quote); "OPA Restates Price Control Over Peanuts and Peanut Products," *Peanut Journal and Nut World* 22 (June 1943): 13–14; "Peanuts Also Served," *Peanut Journal and Nut World* 25 (November 1945): 46; Brown R. Rawlings, "Peanuts in Transition," *Peanut Journal and Nut World* 29 (February 1950): 24, 33, 48–52.

11. "Agricultural Department Order Fixing Price Support Prices and Loans on Peanuts," *Peanut Journal and Nut World* 25 (September 1946): 29; Rawlings, "Peanuts in Transition," 24, 33, 48–52.

12. Planters Edible Oil Co., *Cooking the Modern Way: 129 Ways to Better Meals* (Suffolk, Va.: Planters Edible Oil Co., 1948); idem, *Planters Passover Recipe Book* (Suffolk, Va.: Planters Edible Oil Co., n.d.); idem, *They Taste So-o-o Good* (Suffolk, Va.: Planters Edible Oil Co., 1955).

13. K. Blunt, "Vegetable Oils and Their Use in Cooking," *Journal of Home Economics* 10 (1918): 23.

14. <http://www.pg.com/cgi-bin/cgiAbout/history.cgi?about>, accessed May 7, 2000; <http://www.peanutbutterlovers.com/History/index.html>, accessed May 29, 2000.

15. <http://www.washington.edu/newsroom/news/1997archive/03–97archive/k031897.html>, accessed May 7, 2000; Procter and Gamble Co., *Jif Choosy Mothers' Peanut Butter Cookbook* (Cincinnati: Procter and Gamble, 1979).

16. <http://www.pe.net/checker/peanut.htm>, accessed May 7, 2000; <http://www.pg.com/schldays/fnb/nutshell.htm>, accessed May 7, 2000.

17. <http://www.hersheys.com/products/reese/index.html>, accessed May 7, 2000; Brenner, *Emperors of Chocolate,* 204–5, 224–25, 273–78, 311–12, 321; Whitenack interview.

18. Brenner, *Emperors of Chocolate,* 321.

19. James D. Russo, *Cracker Jack Collecting for Fun and Profit* (n.p.: By the author, 1976), 17; Hess, *Snack Food,* 204.

20. *The Popcorn Market* (New York: Packaged Facts, 1989), 61–62.

21. Ibid., 62; S. K. Hargis, "New Markets for the Peanut Industry to Develop," *Peanut Journal* 4 (February 1926): 11–12.

22. Jester, "Peanut Butter, the Cinderella Food," 13–14; Woodroof, *Peanuts,* 157, 159–60 (quote).

23. "Peanut Consumption in Schools Soars in Fiscal 1976," *Peanut Journal and Nut World* 55 (September 1976): 8; "Great Goober Fun and Fact Folder Ready for Teachers," *Peanut Journal and Nut World* 56 (March 1977): 10.

24. "Costly Peanut Industry: Carter Peanut Family and Price Supports," *Time,* July 19, 1976, 48; Jimmy Carter, *An Hour before Daylight: Memories of a Rural Boyhood* (New York: Simon and Schuster, 2001), 25, 27, 51, 56–57 (quote), 146–47.

25. Harold Isaacs, *Jimmy Carter's Peanut Brigade* (Dallas: Taylor, 1977); "Carter Inauguration Publicity Bonanza for Peanut Industry," *Peanut Journal and Nut World* 56 (March 1977): 6; Sandra Fenichel Asher, *The Great American Peanut Book* (New York: Grosset and Dunlap, 1977), 40–41; Roxanne Roberts, "The Elements of a Well-Rounded, Inaugural Ball," *Washington Post,* January 20, 1997, E28.

26. "Peanuts in the News," *Peanut Journal and Nut World* 56 (November 1976): 7.

27. <http://www.swcp.com/hughes/peanut.htm>, accessed May 29, 2000.

28. "Carter Inauguration Publicity Bonanza for Peanut Industry," 6.

29. "Georgia Peanut Commission Gives Carter Distinguished Service Award," *Peanut Journal and Nut World* 56 (May 1977): 12.

30. "Peanut Promoters Capitalize on Carter-Peanuts Connection," *Peanut Journal and Nut World* 56 (January 1977): 12.

31. "Up from Peanuts," *Peanut Journal and Nut World* 56 (January 1977): 7.

32. Cynthia Rubin and Jerome Rubin, *Peanut One Goes to Washington: The Peanut Cook*

Book, Including Jimmy and Rosalynn's Favorite Recipes (Charlestown, Mass.: Emporium Publications, 1976); John Williams, comp., *The Peanut Cookbook of Plains, Georgia* ([Plains, Ga.]: John and Cindy Williams, 1976); Leila B. Holmes, *Plain Georgia Cookin': One Hundred Peanut Recipes* (Thomasville, Ga.: Barnes, 1977); Ginnie Bedell, *Plains, Georgia, Home of Jimmy Carter: Peanut Recipes* ([Plains, Ga.]: Plains Investors Publications, 1980); *Hugh Carter's Peanut Cook-book: Over 125 Recipes Using the Very Nutritious Peanut* (Decatur, Ga.: Ken-Dor, 1977).

CHAPTER 10: REVOLUTION AND TRANSFORMATION

1. W. E. McClenny, "The Growth of Peanut Industry," *Peanut World* 1 (August 1919): 3.

2. Sue Eaton Pretlow, "Old-Time Peanut Picking in Southampton County, Va.," *Peanut World* 1 (May 1931): 8.

3. McClenny, "Growth of Peanut Industry," 3.

4. Edward H. Knight, *Knight's American Mechanical Dictionary,* 3 vols. (New York: Hurd and Houghton, 1876), 2:1644; McClenny, "Growth of Peanut Industry," 3–4.

5. McClenny, "Growth of Peanut Industry," 3–4; Charlie S. Wilkins, "History of the Peanut Crop," *Peanut Journal and Nut World* 27 (September 1948): 25–26.

6. <http://www.peanutbutterlovers.com/History/index>, accessed May 7, 2000.

7. A. L. Steere, "The Development of the Sheller," *Peanut World* 1 (August 1919): 5; Wilkins, "History of the Peanut Crop," 25–26; Brinkley, "The Peanut," 23–24 (quote).

8. "The Story of Peanuts," 4.

9. "Negro Migrations Affect Peanut Industry," *Peanut Promoter* 4 (August 1923): 19, 38.

10. Walter J. Hirsh, "Arachis-Hypogaea," *Peanut Journal and Nut World* 22 (December 1942): 22

11. David Traxel, *1898: The Tumultuous Year of Victory, Invention, Internal Strife, and Industrial Expansion that Saw the Birth of the American Century* (New York: Knopf, 1998), 294.

12. United States Patent Office, Trademark No. 25,942, issued to Williams and Sons, January 29, 1895; United States Patent Office, Trademark No. 27,214, issued to Williams and Sons, November 12, 1895.

13. William I. Walsh, *The Rise and Decline of the Great Atlantic and Pacific Tea Company* (Secaucus, N.J.: Lyle Stuart, 1986), 15–25.

14. *Grocer's Bulletin,* 15.

15. Hirsh, "Arachis-Hypogaea," 22.

16. Ibid.

17. For samples of these studies, see the "Research and Agricultural Bulletins/Experiment Station Reports" section in the bibliography of this book.

18. *Tariff Information, 1921 Hearings Before the Committee on Ways and Means; House of Representatives on Schedule G; Agricultural Products and Provisions; January 21, 1921,* No. 14 (Washington, D.C.: Government Printing Office, 1921); "Peanut Farmer and Vegetable Oil Tariff," *Peanut Promoter* 7 (January 1924): 7–8; MacClenny, *History of the Peanut,* 15; "$10,000,000 Worth of Peanuts," 148.

19. <http://www.peanutsusa.com/what/history.html>, accessed May 7, 2000.

20. "How Scientist's 145 Varieties Helped Lowly Goober Rise."

21. *Peanut Journal* 3 (March 1924): 13.

22. Brenner, *Emperors of Chocolate,* 254–56.

23. "Koogle: Does It Pass the Peanut Butter Test?" *Consumer Report,* June 1975, 338–39; "Peanut's Flavor Source Revealed," *Agricultural Research* 41 (September 1993): 22; "Much Ado about Peanuts: Tom's Low Calorie, Salted Peanuts," *Consumer Report,* September 1966, 4–5; "Peanut Butter: It's Just Not for Kids Anymore," *Consumer Report,* September 1995, 576–79.

24. Urban L. Diener, Robert E. Pettit, and Richard J. Cole, "Aflatoxins and Other Mycotoxins in Peanuts," in Pattee and Young, *Peanut Science and Technology,* 486.

25. *Peanut Journal and Nut World* 55 (January 1976): 14; Joe W. Dorner, Richard J. Cole, and Paul Blankenship, "Effect of Biological Control Inoculum Rate on Preharvest Aflatoxin Contamination of Peanuts," USDA Agricultural Research Service Web site, <http://www.nalusda.gov/ttic/tektran/data/000007/91/0000079147.html>, accessed July 23, 2001; "Press Briefed on Aflatoxin," *Peanut Journal and Nut World* (February 1974): 13; "Aflatoxin Cited in Peanut Butter Recall," *Consumer Report,* September 1976, 493–94.

26. <http://www.peanutbutterlovers.com/>, accessed May 7, 2000.

27. Carrie L. Masia, Kimberly B. Mullen, and Joseph R. Scotti, "Peanut Allergy in Children: Psychological Issues and Clinical Considerations," *Education and Treatment of Children* 21 (November 1998): 514–31; Hugh Sampson, as cited in "Researchers Close in on Source of Peanut Allergy," Johns Hopkins University press release, November 23, 1996.

28. Michelle Crouch, "Bans on Peanuts Spark School Debates," *Charlotte Observer,* October 19, 1999, <http://www.charlotte.com/>, distributed by Knight Ridder/Tribune Information Services, accessed July 23, 2001; Stephanie Salkin, "Peanut Bans in Schools?" *FoodService Director* 11 (December 15, 1998): 42.

29. "Airline Snack Foods: The Peanut Potential," *Pediatric Alert* 24 (August 12, 1999): 86; Vickie Rogers, "The Puzzle of the Peanut," *Food Manufacture* 74 (June 1999): 22; "Peanut Allergy Update," *Current Health* 2 25 (March 1999): 2.

30. Rogers, "Puzzle of the Peanut," 22.

CHAPTER 11: AN AMERICAN ICON AND A GLOBAL FUTURE

1. <http://www.peanutsusa.com/what/manuf.html>, accessed June 6, 2000.

2. William Kaufman, *The "I Love Peanut Butter" Cookbook* (Garden City, N.Y.: Doubleday, 1965); Annabelle Simon, *The Gourmet Peanut Butter Cookbook* (Boston: Little, Brown, 1975).

3. Dorothy Frank, *The Peanut Cookbook* (New York: Clarkson N. Potter, 1976), 2, 9; idem, *Cooking with Nuts* (New York: Clarkson N. Potter, 1979).

4. Asher, *Great American Peanut Book;* Larry Zisman and Honey Zisman, *The Great American Peanut Butter Book* (New York: St. Martin's, 1985).

5. Norman Kolpas, *The Big Little Peanut Butter Cookbook* (Chicago: CB Contemporary Books, 1990).

6. Linda Romanelli Leahy with Jack Maguire, *The World's Greatest Peanut Butter Cookbook* (New York: Villard, 1994).

7. Joe S. Sugg, "Peanut Promotion Succeeds," *Peanut Journal and Nut World* 55 (August 1976): 12; "Popular, Plentiful Peanut Butter," *Good Housekeeping*, April 1966, 244; "Work Wonders with Peanut Butter," *Ladies Home Journal*, September 1968, 112–13; *Gourmet*, February 1984, 168, June 1987, 198, April 1988, 162, July 1988, 117, October 1988, 256.

8. <http://members.xoom.com/chockie/babruthturn.html>, accessed May 29, 2000; Jim Papanikolaw, "Domestic Peanut Oil Prices Slide Due to Pressure from Supplies," *Chemical Market Reporter* 255 (April 26, 1999): 7.

9. Monica Bayley, *Black Africa Cook Book* (San Francisco: Determined Productions, 1977), 40; Carolyn Quick Tillery, *The African-American Heritage Cookbook* (Secacus, N.J.: Carol Publishing Group, 1996), 38, 131, 148, 160, 188, 199, 299.

10. Lina Beard, "Menagerie Made of Peanuts," *Ladies' Home Journal*, October 1908, 42; Natalie Donna, *Peanut Craft* (New York: Lothrop, Lee, and Shepard, 1974).

11. Joe Bowers, *The Peanut Stand* (New York: H. De Marsan, 1860, 1878), sheet music; James Unsworth, *The Peanut Gal: Comic Song Banjo Song* (New York: J. Wrigley, 1860, 1867), sheet music; [Ballads and Songs] (San Francisco: Theodore C. Boyd, 1860, 1869); Tony Pastor, *Pastor's "444" Combination Songster. Embracing All the New Comic and Irish Lyrics, as Sung by That Celebrated Vocalist and Comedian* (New York: Dick and Fitzgerald [1864]), 66 (first quote); Wilson, *Peanut Dance*, cover (second quote).

12. George Weinberg, *Peanuts! 5 a Bag* (New York: Richmond-Robbins, 1923), sheet music; Don Azpiazu, *The Peanut Vendor (El Manisero)* (New York: Edward B. Marks, 1930), sheet music (first quote); National Peanut Council, *Peanuts: Their Food Value*, 56; June Christy, the Four Freshmen, Stan Kenton Orchestra, "The Peanut Vendor," *Highlights from "Road Show,"* Capitol Records; Duke Ellington, *Duke Ellington His Piano and His Orchestra at the Bal Masque*, Columbia Special Products; Herbie Mann, "Peanut Vendor," *Sound of Mann*, n.p.; Richard Maltby, "Peanut Vendor," *Maltby Swings for Dancers*, Roulette; Stan Kenton Orchestra, "Peanut Vendor," *Salute to Stan Kenton Orchestra*, Crown; "Peanut Vendor," *Starlite Orchestra;* "The Peanut Vendor," *A Selection of Standards from the Catalog of Fred Fisher Music Company* ([New York: Fred Fisher Music, 1998]); Paquito D'rivera, "A Mi Que / el Manisero (The Peanut Vendor)," *Tropicana Nights*, Chesky Records; Frankie Yankovic and His Yanks, "Peanuts," *Polkas and Waltzes: Just for Fun*, Columbia Records; Whoopee John, "Peanut Polka," *Whoopee John's Forty Greatest Hits* Part 1, Polka City 1004; "The Peanut Song," *College Songs*, Vol. 1: For the Piano and Organ (n.p.: Academic Ed., n.d.); Chubby Checker, "Peanut Butter," *Let's Twist Again*, Parkway Records; Herb Alpert, "Peanuts," *Whipped Cream and Other Delights*, A and M Records; Peanut Butter Conspiracy, *Nuggets*, Rhino Records; Jim Schattauer, *Mister Jim*, audiocassette, J. Schattauer.

13. <http://www.roadsideamerica.com/attract/GAASHpeanut.html>, accessed May 29, 2000.

14. Ibid.

15. Roberta Bowen, ed., *The Prize Insider*, Cracker Jack Collector's Association, phone interview with author, December 6, 1997; Russo, *Cracker Jack Collecting for Fun and Profit;*

Jaramillo, *Cracker Jack Prizes;* Piña, *Cracker Jack Collectibles with Price Guide;* Larry White, *Cracker Jack Toys: The Complete, Unofficial Guide for Collectors* (Atglen, Pa.: Schiffer, 1997).

16. Lindenberger with Spontak, *Planters Peanut Collectibles, 1906–1961,* 6–7; Richard D. Reddock, *Planters Peanuts Advertising and Collectibles* (Des Moines: Wallace-Homestead, 1978); Jan Lindenberger with Joyce Spontak, *Planters Peanut Collectibles since 1961* (Atglen, Pa.: Schiffer, 1995); Jan Lindenberger with Joyce Spontak, *Planters Peanut Collectibles, 1906–1961,* 2d ed. (Atglen, Pa.: Schiffer, 1999).

17. Barbara E. Mauzy, *Peanut Butter Glasses with Values* (Atglen, Pa.: Schiffer, 1997); <http://www.peanutbutterlovers.com/Fan/index.html>, accessed June 6, 2000.

18. White, *Gardening for the South,* 234–35; *Good Housekeeping,* December 1903, 587.

19. "Peanut Cream," 34.

20. Gordon, *Mother Earth's Children,* 74.

21. Swezy, *My One Hundred Best Recipes; Peanut Journal and Nut World* 20 (January 1941): 17; *Good Housekeeping,* June 1913, 25 (first quote); H. J. Heinz Co., *Story of Peanutville,* n.p.; *Peanut Journal* 8 (August 1929): 24 (second quote).

22. Bosman and Lohman Co., *Story of Nut-Let Peanut Butter,* 23 (first quote), 25; H. H. Thompson, "Food Value of the Peanut," 22; "What an Appeal to Children Did for Peanut Butter," *Spice Mill* 45 (November 1922): 2052 (other quotes); "$10,000,000 Worth of Peanuts," 83; Judith Wathall, "Advertising Planters Peanuts," *Peanut Papers for Peanut Pals* 1 (July–August 1979): 3.

23. George W. Hoke, *Peanuts* (Rochester, N.Y.: Eastman Teaching Films, Encyclopaedia Britannica Films, 1928, 1945); *Peanuts for the Good and Healthly Life,* film strip (Chicago: The Council, 1979); W. B. Jester, "Kernel Peanut, the Hero of the Movies," *Peanut Journal and Nut World* 18 (December 1938): 12; "Peanut Butter Goes to School in Growers," *Peanut Journal and Nut World* 40 (November 1960): 15; *The Story of Peanut Butter,* 4 min., color, super 8 mm, 1972; *Food: The Story of a Peanut Butter Sandwich,* 15 min., color, 16 mm, 1975; *Peanut Butter in School-lunch Program. Hearing before the Subcommittee on Departmental Administration and Crop Insurance, on the Use of Peanut Butter, July 13, 1956* (Washington, D.C.: U.S. Government Printing Office, 1956); *Peanut Journal and Nut World* 40 (November 1960): 15.

24. Brenner, *Emperors of Chocolate,* 273–78.

25. <http://www.ticktock.simplenet.com/arch06.html>, accessed May 29, 2000; <http://members.aol.com/mrbernard/RescuersArchivesOld/Section10.html>, accessed May 29, 2000; *Peanut Journal and Nut World* 39 (March 1960): 17.

26. *Peanut Journal and Nut World* 51 (September 1972): 6.

27. Peanut-related children's books and recordings include: Arlene Erlbach, *Peanut Butter* (Minneapolis: Lerner Publications, 1994); Claire Llewellyn, *Peanuts* (New York: Children's Press, 1998); Raffi, *Singable Songs for the Very Young: Great with a Peanut-Butter Sandwich,* MCA Records; Robin Oz, *Peanut Butter: A Traditional Song* (Glenview, Ill.: Scottforesman, 1993); *Sixteen Songs Kids Love to Sing* (Greenfield, Mass.: Northeast Foundation for Children, 1998); *Tom Paxton's Fun Food Songs,* LaserLight Audio CD; Jerry Pallotta, *Reese's Pieces Peanut Butter: Candy in a Crunchy Shell: Counting Board Book*

(Wellesley, Mass.: Corporate Board Books, 1998); Charles Micucci, *The Life and Times of the Peanut* (Boston: Houghton Mifflin, 1997); Oliver S. Owen, *Seed to Peanut* (Edina, Minn.: Abdo and Daughters, 1996); Jane Sholinsky, *Peanut Parade* (New York: J. Messner, 1979); Franklin Watts, *Peanuts* (Chicago: Children's Press, 1978); Rose Wyler, *Science Fun with Peanuts and Popcorn* (New York: J. Messner, 1986); Solveig Paulson Russell, *Peanuts, Popcorn, Ice Cream, Candy and Soda Pop and How They Began* (Nashville: Abingdon Press, 1970); Remy Charlip, *Peanut Butter Party, Including the History, Uses, and Future of Peanut Butter* (Berkeley, Calif.: Tricycle Press, 1999); Hugh Maddox, *Billy Boll Weevil: A Pest Becomes a Hero* (Huntsville, Ala.: Strode, 1976); Mitchell, *Pocketful of Goobers;* McKissack and McKissack, *George Washington Carver;* Beatrice S. Smith, *From Peanuts to President* (Milwaukee: Raintree Editions, 1977); Catherine Siracusa, *The Peanut Butter Gang* (New York: Hyperion Books for Children, 1996); Gertrude Stonesifer, *The Peanut Butter Kid* (Mahomet, Ill.: Wild Rose Pub., 1995); Jane Norman and Frank Beazley, *The Adventures of Tick-i-ty Ted: The Search for the Peanut Butter King* (Gladwyne, Pa.: Pixanne Enterprises, 1993); Charles Keller, *The Nutty Joke Book* (Englewood Cliffs, N.J.: Prentice-Hall, 1978); Judy Ralph, *Peanut Butter Cookbook for Kids* (New York: Hyperion Books for Children, 1995); Natalie Donna, *The Peanut Cookbook* (New York: Lothrop, Lee, and Shepard, 1976).

28. Stuart Berg Flexner, *Listening to America: An Illustrated History of Words and Phrases from Our Lively and Splendid Past* (New York: Simon and Schuster, 1982), 437; Stephen Davis, *Say, Kids! What Time Is It? Notes from the Peanut Gallery* (Boston: Little, Brown, 1987); Charles M. Schulz and June Dutton, *Peanuts Cook Book* (San Francisco: Determined Productions, 1969); "Congress Honors 'Peanuts' Creator," June 6, 2000, AP Online via COMTEX; U.S. Senate, 106th Congress, 2d Session, S. 2060, February 10, 2000, at <http://jsgovinfo.about.com>, accessed June 19, 2001.

29. Broekel, *Great America Candy Bar Book,* 119; Brenner, *Emperors of Chocolate,* 204–5; <http://www.hersheys.com/products/reese/index.html>, accessed May 7, 2000.

30. Brenner, *Emperors of Chocolate,* 204–5; <http://www.hersheys.com/products/reese/index.html>, accessed May 7, 2000; Whitenack interview.

31. <http://www.clarkbar.com/>, accessed June 10, 2000; <http://wb56.com/news/05129902.htm>, accessed June 10, 2000.

32. <http://home.kscable.com/fcr/peterpan.html>, accessed May 29, 2000; <http://www.conagra.com/peterpan.html>, accessed May 7, 2000; <http://ca.destru.com/MidYear/brands.html>, accessed May 29, 2000; "BestFoods History," <http://www.bestfoods.com/profile_timeline.shtml>, accessed June 10, 2000.

33. <http://www.peanutsusa.com/what/export.html>, accessed June 6, 2000

34. Brenner, *Emperors of Chocolate,* 14–15, 35, 282, 290.

35. National Agricultural Statistics Service, USDA, as at <http://www.fas.usda.gov/wap/circular/1998/98%2D02/feb98wap2.htm>, accessed February 6, 2000.

36. John F. Mariani, *The Dictionary of American Food and Drink* (New York: Hearst Books, 1994), 228; <http://www.stern.nyu.edu/cperlich/stories/story176>, accessed May 7, 2000; <http://www.peanutsusa.com/what/manuf.html>, accessed June 6, 2000.

Selected Bibliography and Resources

The selected bibliography below lists general works, particularly those emphasizing the culinary and social aspects of peanuts. These are among more than thirty-five thousand works on peanuts, including over a thousand master's theses and doctoral dissertations, that have been entered into a database maintained by the University of Georgia College of Agriculture and Environmental Sciences, Tifton, Georgia. The additional resources given below also represent a selection of those available.

PEANUT HISTORY

Blake, A. "The Most Travelled Food in the World, the Peanut." In *Food on the Move: Proceedings of the Oxford Symposium on Food and Cookery, 1996,* edited by Harlan Walker, 34–37. Devon, Eng.: Prospect Books, 1997.

Born, Thomas Elliott. "Goobers, Ground Pease, Pindars, and Peanuts: The Transformation of the Texas Peanut Culture, 1890–1990." Master's thesis, Texas A&M University, 1992.

Goodrich, L. Carrington. "Early Notices of the Peanut in China." *Monumenta Serica: Journal of Oriental Studies of the Catholic University of Peking* 2 (1936–37): 405–9.

Hammons, Ray O. "Early History and Origin of the Peanut." In American Peanut Research and Education Association, *Peanuts—Culture and Uses: A Symposium,* 17–45. Roanoke, Va.: Stone Printing Co., for the American Peanut Research and Education Association, [1973].

———. "Origin and Early History of the Peanut." In *Peanut Science and Technology,* edited by Harold K. Pattee and Clyde T. Young, 1–20. Yoakum, Tex.: American Peanut Research and Education Society, 1982.

———. "The Origin and History of the Groundnut." In *The Groundnut Crop: A Scientific Basis for Improvement,* edited by J. Smartt, 24–39. London: Chapman and Hall, 1994.

Higgins, B. B. "Origin and Early History of the Peanut." In *The Peanut, the Unpredictable Legume,* edited by Frank Arant et al., 18–27. Washington, D.C.: National Fertilizer Association, 1951.

Johnson, F. Roy. *The Peanut Story.* Murfreesboro, N.C.: Johnson Publishing Co., 1964.

Krapovickas, A. "The Origin, Variability and Spread of the Groundnut (*Arachis hypogaea*)." Translated by J. Smartt. In *The Domestication and Exploitation of Animals and Plants,* edited by Peter J. Ucko and G. W. Dimbleby, 427–41. Chicago: Aldine-Atherton, 1969.

MacClenny, Wilbur E. *History of the Peanut.* Suffolk, Va.: The Commercial Press, 1935.

Smith, Andrew F. "Peanut Butter: A Vegetarian Food That Went Awry." *Petits Propos Culinaires* 65 (September 2000): 60–72.

Woolley, Edward Mott. "Tom Rowland—Peanuts." *McClure's Magazine,* December 1913, 183–202.

BOOKS AND COOKBOOKS FOR CHILDREN

Charlip, Remy. *Peanut Butter Party, Including the History, Uses, and Future of Peanut Butter.* Berkeley, Calif.: Tricycle Press, 1999.

Donna, Natalie. *The Peanut Cookbook.* New York: Lothrop, Lee, and Shepard, 1976.

Eames-Sheavly, Marcia. *The Great American Peanut.* Ithaca, N.Y.: Cornell University Extension, 1994.

Erlbach, Arlene. *Peanut Butter.* Minneapolis: Lerner Publications, 1994.

Llewellyn, Claire. *Peanuts.* New York: Children's Press, 1998.

Micucci, Charles. *The Life and Times of the Peanut.* Boston: Houghton Mifflin, 1997.

Oliver S. Owen. *Seed to Peanut.* Edina, Minn.: Abdo and Daughters, 1996.

Ralph, Judy. *Peanut Butter Cookbook for Kids.* New York: Hyperion Books for Children, 1995.

Russell, Solveig Paulson. *Peanuts, Popcorn, Ice Cream, Candy and Soda Pop and How They Began.* Nashville: Abingdon Press, 1970.

Sholinsky, Jane. *Peanut Parade.* New York: J. Messner, 1979.

Watts, Franklin. *Peanuts.* Chicago: Children's Press, 1978.

Wyler, Rose. *Science Fun with Peanuts and Popcorn.* New York: J. Messner, 1986.

PEANUT COLLECTIBLES

Jaramillo, Alex. *Cracker Jack Prizes.* New York: Abbeville, 1989.

Lindenberger, Jan, with Joyce Spontak. *Planters Peanut Collectibles, 1906–1961.* Atglen, Pa.: Schiffer, 1995; 2d ed., 1999.

———. *Planters Peanut Collectibles since 1961.* Atglen, Pa.: Schiffer, 1995.

Mauzy, Barbara E. *Peanut Butter Glasses with Values.* Atglen, Pa.: Schiffer, 1997.

Piña, Ravi. *Cracker Jack Collectibles with Price Guide.* Atglen, Pa.: Schiffer, 1995.

Reddock, Richard D. *Planters Peanuts Advertising and Collectibles.* Des Moines: Wallace-Homestead, 1978.

Russo, James D. *Cracker Jack Collecting for Fun and Profit*. N.p.: By the author, 1976.

White, Larry. *Cracker Jack Toys: The Complete, Unofficial Guide for Collectors*. Atglen, Pa.: Schiffer, 1997.

COOKBOOKS AND PAMPHLETS

Asher, Sandra Fenichel. *The Great American Peanut Book*. New York: Grosset and Dunlap, 1977.

Carter, Hugh. *Hugh Carter's Peanut Cook-book: Over 125 Recipes Using the Very Nutritious Peanut*. Decatur, Ga.: Ken-Dor, 1977.

Dandar, Helen O. *The 3-in-1 Cook Book: Featuring Unique Yogurt, Zucchini, and Peanut Butter Recipes*. Penndel, Pa.: Sterling Specialties Cookbooks, 1980.

Foster, Frank. *Gourmet Goobers*. San Angelo, Tex.: D. J. Designs, 1977.

Frank, Dorothy. *The Peanut Cookbook*. New York: Clarkson N. Potter, 1976.

Hoffman, Mable. *The Peanut Butter Cookbook*. New York: HP Books, 1996.

Holmes, Leila B. *Plain Georgia Cookin': One Hundred Peanut Recipes*. Thomasville, Ga.: Barnes, 1977.

Kaufman, William. *The "I Love Peanut Butter" Cookbook*. Garden City, N.Y.: Doubleday, 1965.

Kolpas, Norman. *The Big Little Peanut Butter Cookbook*. Chicago: CB Contemporary Books, 1990.

Leahy, Linda Romanelli, with Jack Maguire. *The World's Greatest Peanut Butter Cookbook*. New York: Villard, 1994.

Meisel, Judi. *The Peanut Butter Cookbook: From Soup to Nuts with America's Favorite Spread*. New York: Smithmark, 1993.

Peanutty Food: Over 125 Recipes Using the Very Nutritious Peanut: Meats, Vegetables, Salads, Soups, Sandwiches, Cookies, Cakes, Pies, Candies, Breads, Snacks: Practical Food Ideas for Kids, Teens, and Adults. Decatur, Ga: Ken-Dor, 1976.

Rogers, Ford. *Nuts—A Cookbook*. New York: Simon and Schuster, 1993.

Rubin, Cynthia, and Jerome Rubin. *Peanut One Goes to Washington: the Peanut Cook Book: Including Jimmy and Rosalynn's Favorite Recipes*. Charlestown, Mass.: Emporium Publications, 1976.

Simon, Annabelle. *The Gourmet Peanut Butter Cookbook*. Boston: Little, Brown, 1975.

Williams, John, comp. *The Peanut Cookbook of Plains, Georgia*. [Plains, Ga.]: John and Cindy Williams, 1976.

Zisman, Larry, and Honey Zisman. *The Great American Peanut Butter Book*. New York: St. Martin's, 1985.

GENERAL NUT AND PEANUT BOOKS

Asher, Sandra Fenichel. *The Great American Peanut Book*. New York: Grosset and Dunlap, 1977.

Carder, Shirl. *The Nut Lovers' Cookbook*. Berkeley, Calif.: Celestial Arts, 1984.

Feinman, Jeffrey. *From Carver to Carter: The Complete Guide to Peanuts—In a Nutshell.* New York: Kensington, 1977.

Frank, Dorothy C. *Cooking with Nuts.* New York: Clarkson N. Potter, 1979.

Jones, Brian W. *The Peanut Plant: Its Cultivation and Uses.* New York: Orange Judd, 1885.

MacPherson, Mary. *Completely Nuts: A Cookbook and Cultural History of the World's Most Popular Nuts.* Ontario: Doubleday Canada, 1995.

Mandry, Kathy. *The First American Peanut Growing Book.* New York: Subsistence Press Book/Random House, 1975.

Parry, John R. *Nuts for Profit: A Treatise on the Propagation and Cultivation of Nut-Bearing Trees.* Parry, N.J.: By the author, 1897.

Pigs and Peanuts: Virginia Traditions. Glen Allen, Va.: Prism Publishing, 1997.

Roper, William, ed. *The Peanut and Its Culture.* Petersburg, Va.: American Nut Journal, [1905].

Rosengarten, Frederic, Jr. *The Book of Edible Nuts.* New York: Walker, 1984.

Selsam, Millicent E. *Complete Story and Photos of the Start of the Peanut.* New York: Morrow, 1969.

Weatherly, Jo. *Jo Weatherly's Fancy Peanut Recipes: Fun to Make, Delicious, Tested.* [Oakland, Neb.]: J. Weatherly, 1978.

Woodroof, Jasper Guy. *Peanuts: Production, Processing, Products.* Westport, Conn.: AVI, 1966; 2d ed., 1973.

———, ed. *Peanuts: Production, Processing, Products.* 3d ed. Westport, Conn.: AVI, 1984.

ADVERTISING AND PROMOTIONAL BOOKLETS

Alabama Peanut Producers Association. *Around the Clock Recipes with Alabama Peanuts.* Dothan, Ala.: Alabama Peanut Producers Association, 1985.

———. *Fun Food Cooking with Peanuts.* Dothan, Ala.: Alabama Peanut Producers Association, n.d.

———. *A Treasury of Best Loved Alabama Peanut Recipes.* Dothan, Ala.: Alabama Peanut Producers Association, n.d.

Baxley, Joan M. *People Pleasin' Peanut Treats.* Madill, Okla.: Oklahoma Peanut Commission, 1983.

Baxter Lane Co. *How to Enjoy Virginia Peanuts in the Old Dominion Tradition.* Richmond: Baxter Lane Co., 1977.

Beard, James. *How to Cook Better with Planters French-Process Peanut Oil.* N.p.: Planters Peanuts, 1961.

Bedell, Ginnie. *Plains, Georgia, Home of Jimmy Carter: Peanut Recipes.* [Plains, Ga.]: Plains Investors Publications, 1980.

Beech-Nut Packing Co. *Beech-Nut Peanut Butter: The Great Tea and Luncheon Delicacy as Served in New York Tea-Rooms.* Canajoharie, N.Y.: Beech-Nut Packing Co., 1914.

———. *Beech-Nut Peanut Butter with Some Views of the Home of Beech-Nut Products and the Fine Class of People Who Put Them Up.* Canajoharie, N.Y.: Beech-Nut Packing Company, n.d.

————. *A Hundred and One Recipes with Beech-Nut Peanut Butter.* 3d ed. Canajoharie, N.Y.: Beech-Nut Packing Co., 1920.

Bosman and Lohman Co. *The Story of Nut-Let Peanut Butter; From the Vine to the Table.* Norfolk, Va.: Bosman and Lohman, c. 1914.

Derby Foods, Inc. *Peter Pan Peanut Butter in Your Daily Diet: A Book of Choice Recipes and Important Nutritional Information.* Chicago: Derby Foods, n.d.

E. K. Pond Co. *Here's Something New—Peter Pan.* Chicago: E. K. Pond, c. 1928.

Fisher, William. *Peanuts in the Fifth Federal Reserve District.* Richmond: Federal Reserve Bank of Richmond, 1946.

Fisher Roasting Co. *Fisher's Salted in the Shell Peanuts and Almonds: Best Seller and Repeater of the Day.* Saint Paul, Minn.: Fisher Roasting Co., 1930.

Florida Peanut Producers Association. *Florida Peanut Cookbook.* N.p.: Florida Peanut Producers Association, n.d.

Georgia Agricultural Commodity Commission for Peanuts. *Historic Georgia Rich in Tradition Peanut Cook Book: Cherished "Family Recipes" from the Deep South.* Tifton, Ga.: Georgia Agricultural Commodity Commission for Peanuts, n.d.

Georgia Peanut Commission. *Peanuts, a Southern Tradition: A Collection of Peanut Recipes.* Tifton, Ga.: Georgia Peanut Commission, 1984.

Georgia Peanut Co. *Book of Recipes for Uncle Remus Brand Peanuts.* [Moultrie, Ga.]: Georgia Peanut Co., n.d.

Gwaltney-Bunkley Peanut Co. *The Land of the Peanut: Louisiana Purchase Exposition Edition, June 14, 1904.* Smithfield, Va.: Gwaltney-Bunkley Peanut Co., 1904.

Huntley Manufacturing Co. *Peanut Cleaning, Shelling, Grading and Roasting Machinery for Whole and Shelled Nuts.* Catalog No. 69. Silver Creek, N.Y.: Huntley Manufacturing Co., n.d.

Huston Co. *Peanuts: Culture and Marketing of the White Spanish Variety in the Southeastern States.* 3d ed. Columbus, Ga.: Tom Huston Peanut Co., 1932.

Koinonia Partners. *Koinonia Cookbook: Recipes for Pecans, Peanuts, Soy.* Americus, Ga.: Koinonia Partners, 1980.

Nashville-Chattanooga and Saint Louis Railroad. *Peanut and Soya Bean Oil Manufacture.* Nashville, Tenn.: Nashville-Chattanooga and Saint Louis Railroad, c. 1918.

National Peanut Council. *Peanuts: Some Ideas for Use in Quantity Cookery.* Atlanta, Georgia: National Peanut Council, n.d.

————. *Peanuts: Their Food Value, and Over One Hundred Sure-fire Peanut Recipes to Add Zest to Your Menus.* Suffolk, Va.: National Peanut Council, c. 1941.

New Mexico Department of Agriculture. *New Mexico Valencias: "The Ballpark Peanut."* Las Cruces, N.M.: New Mexico Department of Agriculture in Cooperation with New Mexico Peanut Commission, 1995.

Oklahoma Peanut Commission. *How to Cook-a-peanut: Blanching, French Frying, Oil Roasting, Dry Roasting, Sugar Coating, Candies, Appetizers, Cookies, Pies, Storing.* Madill, Okla.: Oklahoma Peanut Commission, 1985.

————. *It's Easy to be a "Gourmet" with Peanuts and Other Fine "Oklahoma" Peanut Products.* Madill, Oklahoma: Oklahoma Peanut Commission, n.d.

————. *It's Easy to Be a Gourmet . . . with Saucy Peanuts . . . and Other Fine Oklahoma Recipes!* Madill, Okla.: Oklahoma Peanut Commission, 1963.

————. *Microwave Magic: Recipes from Your Oklahoma Peanut Commission.* Madill, Okla.: Oklahoma Peanut Commission, 1984.

Owens, Betsy. *Peanuts.* Raleigh: North Carolina Agricultural Extension Service, 1980.

Owens, Betsy, and Marilyn Hubert. *Peanuts Add Pizzazz to Meals and Snacks.* Tifton, Ga: Georgia Peanut Commission, n.d.

Peanut Advisory Board. *Harvest a Gold Mine of Nutrition—Healthy Eating with Peanuts.* Atlanta: Peanut Advisory Board, n.d.

Planters Edible Oil Co. *Cooking the Modern Way: 129 Ways to Better Meals.* Suffolk, Va.: Planters Edible Oil Co., 1948.

————. *Planters Passover Recipe Book.* Suffolk, Va.: Planters Edible Oil Co., n.d.

————. *They Taste So-o-o Good.* Suffolk, Va.: Planters Edible Oil Company, 1955.

Procter and Gamble Co. *Jif Choosy Mothers' Peanut Butter Cookbook.* Cincinnati: Procter and Gamble, 1979.

South Carolina Peanut Board. *Peanut Recipes.* Columbia: South Carolina Peanut Board, 1999.

Standard Brands, Inc. *Mr. Peanut's Guide to Nutrition.* New York: Standard Brands, Inc., 1970.

Sunny Jim Peanut Butter. *Gourmet Cooking with Sunny Jim Peanut Butter.* Seattle: A Catholic Northwest Progress Publication, n.d.

Texas Department of Agriculture. *Cooking with Texas Peanuts.* Austin, Tex.: Texas Department of Agriculture, 1980.

————. *Texas Peanuts.* Austin, Texas: Texas Department of Agriculture, 1980.

Texas Peanut Producers Board. *Peanuts: Nature's Masterpiece of Food Values.* Gorman, Tex.: Texas Peanut Producers Board, 1999.

U.S. Department of Agriculture, Agricultural Research Service, Human Nutrition Research Division. *Peanut and Peanut Butter Recipes.* Washington, D.C.: USDA, 1954; rev. 1964.

Vegetarian Supply Co. *I've Come Out of My Burrow to Borrow.* Providence, R.I.: Vegetarian Supply Co., 1899.

Virginia-Carolina Seed Peanut Co. *Improved Seed Peanuts Catalogue.* Petersburg, Va.: Virginia-Carolina Seed Peanut Co., 1905.

Wilkes-Barre Can Co. "Black Diamond Trade Mark. Peanut and Peanut Butter Containers." Advertisement. Wilkes-Barre, Pa.: Wilkes-Barre Can Co., n.d.

RESEARCH AND AGRICULTURAL BULLETINS/
EXPERIMENT STATION REPORTS

American Peanut Research and Education Association. *Peanuts—Culture and Uses: A Symposium.* Roanoke, Va.: Stone Printing Co., [1973].

American Peanut Research and Education Society. *Proceedings* 13 (November 1981).

Arant, Frank, et al. *The Peanut, the Unpredictable Legume.* Washington, D.C.: National Fertilizer Association, 1951.

Batten, E. T. *Peanut Culture.* Bulletin No. 218. Blacksburg, Va.: Virginia Polytechnic Institute, 1918.

Beattie, J. H. *Growing Peanuts.* Farmer's Bulletin No. 2063. Washington, D.C.: USDA, 1954.

Beattie, W. R. *Peanuts.* Farmer's Bulletin No. 356. Washington, D.C.: USDA, 1909.

———. *The Peanut.* Farmer's Bulletin No. 431. Washington: USDA, 1917.

Campbell, Clara Mae. "The Use of Peanuts as an Important Food." Master's thesis, University of Georgia, 1944.

Carver, George Washington. *How to Grow the Peanut and 105 Ways of Preparing It for Human Consumption.* Bulletin No. 31. Tuskegee, Ala.: Tuskegee Institute Experiment Station, 1916. Ninth Edition, 1994.

Diener, Urban L., Robert E. Pettit, and Richard J. Cole. "Aflatoxins and Other Mycotoxins in Peanuts." In *Peanut Science and Technology,* edited by Harold K. Pattee and Clyde T. Young, 486–519. Yoakum, Tex.: American Peanut Research and Education Society, 1982.

Duggar, J. F., E. F. Cauthen, J. T. Williamson, and O. H. Sellers. *Growing Peanuts in Alabama.* Bulletin No. 194. Opelika, Ala.: Alabama Experiment Station of the Alabama Polytechnic Institute, Auburn, 1917.

Jaffa, M. E. *Nuts and Their Use as Food.* Farmer's Bulletin No. 332. Washington: USDA, 1910.

Pattee, Harold K., and Clyde T. Young, eds. *Peanut Science and Technology.* Yoakum, Tex.: American Peanut Research and Education Society, 1982.

Peanut and Peanut Butter Recipes. Home and Garden Bulletin No. 36. Washington, D.C.: USDA, 1954.

Rich, Jessie. *The Uses of the Peanut on the Home Table.* Bulletin No. 13. Austin: University of Texas, 1915.

Ruston, Ismail. "Development of a Process for Production of a Beverage Based on Peanuts." Ph.D. diss., Lund University, Sweden, 1995.

Spencer, A. P., and E. W. Jenkins. *Peanuts for Oil Production.* Bulletin No. 12. Gainesville: University of Florida Division of Agricultural Extension and USDA, 1918.

Thompson, H. C., and H. S. Bailey. *Peanut Oil.* Farmer's Bulletin No. 751. Washington, D.C.: USDA, 1916.

Waldron, Ralph Augustus. "The Peanut (Arachis hypogaea)—Its History, Histology, Physiology, and Utility." Ph.D. diss., University of Pennsylvania, 1918.

PEANUT ORGANIZATIONS

Adult Peanut Butter Lovers' Fan Club
500 Sugar Mill Road, Suite 105A
Atlanta, GA 30350
Telephone: (404) 933-0796
Fax: (404) 933-0796
Web: <http://www.peanutbutterlovers.com>

Alabama Peanut Producers Association
1810 Reeves Street
Dothan, AL 36304
Telephone: (334) 792-6482

American Peanut Council
1500 King Street, Suite 301
Alexandria, VA 22314-2737
Telephone: (703) 838-9500
Fax: (703) 838-9508/9089
E-mail: peanutsusa@aol.com
Web: <http://www.peanutsusa.com>

American Peanut Research and Education Society (APRES)
376 Agriculture Hall
Oklahoma State University
Stillwater, OK 74078
Telephone: (405) 744-9634
E-mail: jrs@mail.pss.okstate.edu
Web: <http://www.clay.agr.okstate.edu/apres/welcome.htm>

American Peanut Shellers Association
P.O. Box 70157
Albany, GA 31708-0157
Telephone: (229) 888-2508
Fax: (229) 888-5150

Cracker Jack Collection
The Center of Science and Industry
280 East Broad Street
Columbus, OH 43215
Telephone: (614) 228-COSI; (toll free) 1–888–819–COSI
Web: <http://www.cosi.org>

Cracker Jack Collector's Association
c/o Roberta Bowen, editor, *The Prize Insider*
305 East Minton Drive
Tempe, AZ 85282
Telephone: (602) 831-1402

Florida Peanut Producers Association
2741 Penn Avenue, Suite 1
Marianna, FL 32448
Telephone: (850) 526-2590

Georgia Peanut Commission
110 East Fourth Street
Tifton, GA 31793
Telephone: (229) 386-3470

Georgia Peanut Producers Association
1408 Third Avenue
Albany, GA 31707
Telephone: (229) 432-9001; (toll free) 1-800-99-PNUTS
Fax: (912) 432-7447
E-mail: gappa@georgiapeanuts.org
Web: <http://www.georgiapeanuts.org>

National Peanut Board
50 Hurt Plaza, Suite 1220
Atlanta, GA 30303
Telephone: (404) 222-9100
E-mail: peanutboardmh@aol.com

North Carolina Peanut Growers Association
P.O. Box 8
103 Triangle Court
Nashville, NC 27856-0008
Telephone: (252) 459-5060
Fax: (252) 459-7396
E-mail: bob@aboutpeanuts.com

Peanut Advisory Board
500 Sugar Mill Road
Suite 105A
Atlanta, GA 30350
Telephone: (770) 998-7311
E-mail: pabnuts@aol.com
Web: <http://www.peanutbutterlovers.com>

Peanut Butter and Nut Processors Association
9005 Congressional Court
Potomac, MD 20854
Telephone: (301) 365-2521
Fax: (301) 365-7705

Peanut Educational Service
P.O. Box 845
Nashville, NC 27856
Telephone: (252) 459-9977
Fax: (252) 459-7396
E-mail: betsy@aboutpeanuts.com
Web: <http://www.aboutpeanuts.com/educ.html>

The Peanut Institute
P.O. Box 70157
Albany, GA 31708-0157
Telephone: (229) 888-0216; (toll free) 1-888-speanut
Fax: (229) 888-5150
Web: <http://www.Peanut-Institute.org>

Peanut Pals
804 Hickory Grade Road
Bridgeville, PA 15017
Telephone: (412) 221-7599
E-mail: Peanuts999@AOL.COM

Virginia-Carolina Peanut Promotions
103 Triangle Court
Nashville, NC 27856
Telephone: (252) 459-9977
Fax: (252) 459-7396
E-mail: info@aboutpeanuts.com
Web: <http://www.aboutpeanuts.com/index.html>

Virginia Peanut Growers Association, Inc.
P.O. Box 356
23020 Main Street
Capron, VA 23829-0356
Telephone: (804) 658-4573
Fax: (804) 658-4531
E-mail: vapeanut@f-a-s-t.net

Index

Acosta, José de, 6

Adult Peanut Butter Lovers Fan Club, 126

Africa: Bambara ground nuts and peanuts in, 8–10; Cape Verde, peanuts in, 67; and cookbooks, 123; early exploration of, 3; Gambia, peanuts in, 16, 67; and ground peanuts, 18; Guinea Bissau, peanuts in, 9; Liberia, peanuts imported into U.S. from, 16; MacCarthy Island and Portuguese Guinea, peanut cultivation in, 67; Mali, Ibn Batuta notes groundnuts in, 8; Mozambique, peanuts in, 8; Nigeria, groundnuts in 9; peanut butter in, 36; peanut exports from, 22, 24; and peanut oil, 67–68; peanut soup, 14, 58–59; and raw and boiled peanuts, 64; Sao Thomé, peanuts in, 13; Senegal, peanuts in, 9, 67; Sierra Leone, peanut trade, 67; and slave trade as conduit of peanuts to New World, 12, 13, 16–18; South Africa, peanuts in, 8, 36

African Americans: as consumers and preparers of peanuts, 13–14; and cookbooks, 123; as growers/pickers of peanuts, 87, 91, 99, 111, 113; and peanut folklore, 13–14; and peanut song, 124; and peanut superstitions, 13; as vendors of peanuts, 19, 23, 26. *See also* Carver, George Washington; Tuskegee Institute/University

Akins, Mary, 27

Alabama: Barbour County, early peanut cultivation in, 17; Carver in, 93, 95; Dothan, as "Peanut Capital," 125; Enterprise Coffee County, peanut cultivation in, 90; growing peanuts in, 24, 87–90; peanut beverages in, 21; and peanut production today, 132. *See also* Tuskegee Institute/University

Alcott, Louisa May, 31

Alcott, William, 31

Alvares de Almada, André, 9

Alpert, Herb, 125

Alva, Walter, 6

American Academy of Allergy, Asthma and Immunology, 119

American Peanut Corporation, 25

Anderson, R. L., 17

Apios tuberosa (American groundnut), 11

Arkansas, 89; Fayette, 86

Arkell, Bartlett, 40

Asher, Sandra Fenichel, 122

Asia: arrival of peanut in China, Malaysia, Vietnam, 8; China, as site of extensive peanut growing, 15; China, peanut oil in, 68, 91; China and India, low cost of peanuts in, 91; China's exports of peanuts, 131; and cookbooks, 131; early European exploration of, 2–3; India, and peanuts, 8, 18, 68; Indonesia, peanut introduced into, 8; Japan, and peanuts, 8, 77, 91, 101, 132; peanut oil in, 68; peanuts in, historically, 8, 10; peanuts in,

ANDREW F. SMITH is president of the American Forum for Global Education in New York City. He teaches culinary history at the New School University and is the author of numerous books, including *The Tomato in America, Popped Culture, Pure Ketchup, Souper Tomatoes,* and *The Saintly Scoundrel: The Life and Times of Dr. John Cook Bennett.*

The University of Illinois Press
is a founding member of the
Association of American University Presses.

Composed in 10.5/13 Minion
with Polonaise display
by Jim Proefrock
at the University of Illinois Press
Designed by Paula Newcomb
Manufactured by Thomson-Shore, Inc.

University of Illinois Press
1325 South Oak Street
Champaign, IL 61820-6903
www.press.uillinois.edu